THE AMERICAN FOOTBALL BOOK

THE AMERICAN FOOTBALL BOOK

KEN THOMAS

WITH A FOREWORD BY NICKY HORNE

ORBIS PUBLISHING · LONDON

In association with Channel Four Television Company Limited

ACKNOWLEDGEMENTS

I am most grateful to the National Football League for permission to reproduce the 1983 Playing Schedule and for their promptness in responding to my many requests for material and information.

The bulk of photographs were supplied by NFL Properties Inc and here I express my thanks to David Boss, Valeria Watson and Louise Payne for their tolerance and efficiency. The Pro Football Hall Of Fame chipped in with a few and the balance came from the Clubs listed below:- Atlanta Falcons; Baltimore Colts; Buffalo Bills; Chicago Bears; Cleveland Browns; Dallas Cowboys; Detroit Lions; Houston Oilers; Kansas City Chiefs; Los Angeles Raiders; New England Patriots; New York Giants; New York Jets; Philadelphia Eagles; Pittsburgh Steelers; St. Louis Cardinals; San Diego Chargers; Seattle Seahawks; Tampa Bay Buccaneers. To them all I express my gratitude.

I am no less grateful to the following Clubs who supplied photographic material and information:- Cincinnati Bengals; Denver Broncos; Green Bay Packers; Los Angeles Rams; Miami Dolphins; Minnesota Vikings; New Orleans Saints; San Francisco 49ers; Washington Redskins.

Two good friends have helped considerably: Nick Wridgway, who throughout the 1982 season painstakingly compiled the statistical information which is reproduced with his kind permission, and my technical mentor, Jack Hodges of Los Angeles, California – thanks Nick and Jack.

I express my thanks to Peter Arnold, whose editorial expertise has, hopefully, transformed my clumsy prose into something worth reading, and to Paul Welti and Mick Hodson, who stage-managed the design.

Finally and in anticipation of another season of Football enjoyment, I thank Mrs Elaine Rose, producer, and that intrepid duo, Nicky Horne and Miles Aiken, of Cheerleader Productions.

First published in Great Britain by Orbis Publishing Limited, London 1983
© 1983 by Ken Thomas
© illustrations by Orbis Publishing Limited

ISBN 0-85613-584-4

The American Football Book is associated with Channel Four Television's coverage of the sport produced by Cheerleader Productions Limited.

Typeset in Great Britain by Cylinder Typesetting Ltd.
Printed in Great Britain by Eyre & Spottiswoode Ltd.

PHOTOGRAPHS
Allsport F/C, B/C; Mansell Collection 8; National Football League Properties 12, 14/5, 20, 21t, 22, 23, 24, 25t, 26t, 30, 32t, 34/5t, 39b, 40b, 41c, 44c, 48tl, 49t, 50, 72, 75; NFLP/Bill Amatucci 64/5b; NFLP/Associated Press 70/1; NFLP/Fred Anderson 138/9, 146/7; NFLP/Vernon Biever 43, 44t, 46t, NFLP/David Boss 48tr, 58c, 130/1; NFLP/George Brace 68/9; NFLP/Dick Burnell 108/9; NFLP/Tom Croke 94/5; NFLP/George Gellatty 61; NFLP/Hall of Fame 25b, 28, 33t, 36/7t, 36c, 36b, 38; NFLP/Robert Harmeyer Jnr. 101; NFLP/Don Lansu 136/7; NFLP/John McDonough 144/5; NFLP/Al Messerschmitt 48/9b, 62/3; NFLP/Russ Reid 77; NFLP/Frank Rippon 149; NFLP/Vic Stein 73; NFLP/Tampa Bay Buccaneers 56, 140/1; NFLP/Teamphoto 26b, 28/9, 40/1t, 46b; NFLP/U.P.I. 27, 32/3b, 34/5b, 44/5b; NFLP/Herb Weitman 42; NFLP/Len Witt 45b; Atlanta Falcons 142/3; Baltimore Colts 91; Buffalo Bills 93; Chicago Bears 132/3; Cleveland Browns 74, 103; Dallas Cowboys 122/3; Detroit Lions 134/5; Houston Oilers 66c, 66b, 67, 104/5; Kansas City Chiefs 41b, 110/1; Los Angeles Raiders 112/3; New England Patriots 97; New York Giants 124/5; New York Jets 99; Philadelphia Eagles 39t, 126/7; Pittsburgh Steelers 66t, 106/7; St. Louis Cardinals 128/9; San Diego Chargers 112/3, 114/5; Seattle Seahawks 116/7; Tampa Bay Buccaneers 140/1;

CONTENTS

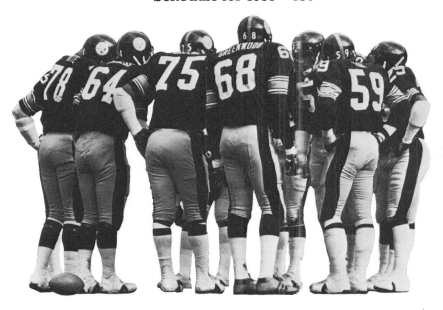

FOREWORD

So there I was in my tiny cupboard they call an office at Capital Radio in London, when the 'phone went.

'Hallo, this is Derek Brandon. I am a TV producer and I'm going to be producing one of the most exciting sports programmes ever to hit British television screens.'

'That's nice,' I said. 'Now how can I help?'

'Well,' continued the effervescent Mr Brandon, 'I like the way you talk on the radio and I know that you have been to America many times to do interviews; I also know that you have been to see a few American Football games.'

'Ahh, I thought. The plot purees. American Football on British telly. What a great idea.

Brandon continued: 'Tell me, Nicky, do you know anything about American Football?'

'Well I know it's a game of territory and they have a thing called "downs" but I really don't know too much more about it except it's truly incredible to watch.'

'So you don't know too much about it?'

'Not really'.

'Well,' continued Brandon to my utmost surprise. 'you're the man for me. I would like you to present the programme on Channel 4.'

Since that most bizarre conversation I have learnt a great deal about this game of games and my enjoyment of it increases with every week of the season. I am absolutely delighted that the programme has been so successful for all of us at Cheerleader Productions and the people at Channel 4 who had the foresight to see its potential on British television.

This book is a perfect companion to our programme and I hope that you will enjoy it and continue to enjoy American Football on Channel 4.

Thank you for supporting us.

Nicky Horne

CHAPTER 1
THE EARLY DAYS

American Football owes a great deal to the game of rugby, popularised by the schools and universities of nineteenth century England. But it would be quite wrong to suggest that rugby football had simply been packaged and transported across the Atlantic to be vulgarised (as some might feel) by the young men of the New World. The two games, together with soccer, should be seen as having evolved from the traditional diversion, the Shrove Tuesday brawl, in which a mob from one town 'played' that from another, using a ball which was not indispensible. First banned by Edward II in 1314, then by James I, the 'game' was given Royal approval by Charles II (a monarch remembered not least for his commitment to freedom of expression) and took root as 'Football'.

Above Football was a character-building diversion for the fun-loving students at Princeton in 1860.

Left Mob football in England was more than once banned by law – not surprising considering this scene in London during the reign of Edward II.

In 1823, William Webb Ellis did the unthinkable by catching the ball in his hands and then running with it for the first-ever touchdown. This would lead to the separation of Football (English style), as represented by the Football Association (formed 1863) and Rugby, as represented by the Rugby Football Union (formed 1871).

Before then, however, early colonists had carried the tradition for the primeval bun fight to America, where the annual lapse into irresponsibility continued.

As early as 1657, the city fathers of Boston felt the need to make the practice unlawful, and for the next two centuries it erupted only occasionally, before resurfacing in grand style in the great universities of the north-east. It was the natural expression of inter-class rivalry when at Harvard, the freshmen would take on the sophomore class (second year students) in a yearly thrash which rapidly became known as 'Bloody Monday'. At Yale, too, and with that spontaneity aroused by particular times of the year, young men would peel off their coats and go at it. The game spread to Princeton, where it would continue, but at both Harvard and Yale, the authorities had seen enough and it was banned.

The year was 1860 and these same young men would shortly respond to the call of distant cannon. However during this period of Civil War (1861-1865), there appeared the rubber ball which, with its predictable bounce, encouraged the application of dribbling skills and the development of inter-passing. Now in the high schools, the game later known as soccer was evolving along lines parallel to and yet quite independent of the movement in England.

The trend to soccer gained momentum in 1869 when Princeton and Rutgers, substituted for what had been a maniacal feud over an antiquated artillery piece the first recorded intercollegiate game, won 6-4 by Rutgers. But it is to Harvard, who had independently evolved a variation which allowed a player to carry the ball (the Boston Game), that American Football is indebted. By their stubborn commitment to ball-handling, they were obliged to travel far afield in the search for opponents. In a game against McGill University (Canada) in 1874 they acquired a taste for the fifteen-man rugby which had found favour north of the border. When they converted Yale in 1875, Princeton and Rutgers, now joined by Columbia and others, fell into line. For the time being, soccer in America was dead.

It is appropriate to consider the rules of rugby at that time. There were fifteen men in a team and possession of the ball was

Above The Harvard-McGill game in 1875. The first match between the sides took place the year before. *Above right* The Yale team in 1880. Walter Camp has the ball under his arm.

Right Walter Camp, the Father Of American Football, in 1890.

contested by using the scrummage as it is known today. There were goal posts but the crossbar was more likely to be a length of rope some eleven feet above the ground. In tackling, a player could make contact only above the waist and below the shoulder of an opponent – obstruction (blocking) and running in front of the ball-carrier (offside) were strictly illegal. There was no substitution, even in the case of injury. Strangest of all was the status of the touchdown which, rather than earning numerical points, merely entitled the scorers to 'try' a kick at goal. (It is clear how the modern use of the word 'try' arose). Games were decided by the number of successful kicks.

Watching the second Harvard-Yale game in 1875 was a fresh-faced lad, 6 feet tall and weighing barely 11 stone. He was to make his mark as a fanatically fit and highly effective Yale halfback, but more than this, he became known as the Father of American Football. Walter C. Camp spent six playing years with the Elis (Yale), firstly as the acolyte of the captain, Gene Baker, and then as leader of the team.

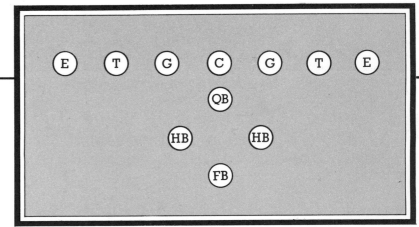

Camp's original formation, the forerunner of the modern T formation. The names of the player positions followed naturally: those at the extremities of the line became the 'ends' (E); those next to the 'ends', who did most of the tackling, became the 'tackles' (T); those who guarded the center became 'guards' (G) (in the modern game they are also considered to guard the running backs); the man in the middle of the front line became the 'center' (C); the man one quarter of the way back from the line became the 'quarterback' (QB); the two who were half the way back became the 'halfbacks' (HB); and the last man in line became the 'fullback' (FB).

Camp had heard of the game between Yale and a team of visiting English gentlemen, the Eton Players, played in 1873. At the request of the visitors, the teams fielded only eleven men each rather than the customary hordes, in what was a soccer game. This had led to a far more open and attractive style of play. 'Why couldn't this work in the new rugby?' he questioned.

In 1880 his proposal was tried. More significantly, and again at his suggestion, the scrummage was discarded in favour of a scrimmage. To Camps way of thinking, it had always been madness that a team in possession should be obliged to compete for the ball (using the scrummage), every time forward progress came to a halt, as in Rugby Union. Under his new system, the team would retain possession and each new play would be initiated when one member of the team heeled the ball to a colleague, supported by the remaining players arranged in some formation or other. The most common formation is illustrated, the T formation which is used to this day.

The only problem with this new scrimmage principle was that it became possible for a team to retain possession indefinitely, often for half the game at a time. To remedy this inherent weakness, Walter Camp in 1882 hit upon a system which related rights of possession to yards gained – a system of downs. In this, the team which did not gain five yards using three or fewer scrimmage plays (downs) would be obliged to transfer possession to the opposition. This made it necessary for the pitch to be marked out with a series of crossfield lines at five yard intervals, giving the appearance of a gridiron, which naturally led to American Football's alternative name: Gridiron Football.

A year later Camp introduced a system of numerical points in which a touchdown was worth two points, a conversion four, a field goal five and a safety one point. With this final act of phase one, the stage was set for five unbroken years of spectacular open-field running which regularly attracted crowds of up to 30,000. Camp sat back and watched, and found time to indulge in that schoolboy diversion of picking the best squad drawn from all the college players then playing, the All-American team. Selection was equivalent to becoming an international player, though in the case of American Football there is no international competition. Camp's selections, made in collaboration with Caspar Whitney, a journalist, went unchallenged from 1889 until his death in 1925. Since then several media bodies have independently felt qualified to maintain the tradition.

The University of Chicago practise the T formation in 1904.

The University of Chicago playing
Northwestern in 1904.

Things had been happening elsewhere in the game, notably
at Princeton, where they had discreetly introduced the tactic of
using a man on each side of the runner, the object being to
obstruct would-be tacklers. This was of course illegal but since it
went unpenalised it was a matter of only a short time before the
emergence of leading obstructors, clearing the way for the

ball-carrier. In 1885 this 'blocking', which had become an accepted but unwritten part of the game, received formal approval. By now, little more than the goal posts and the ball remained of what ten years before had been rugby.

Ironically it was another Camp innovation in 1888 which led to a period of the most brutal and violent play in the game's

history, yet which by reaction obliged the rules makers to complete the design which has since remained essentially unchanged. His introduction of tackling below the waist but still above the knees was considered at the time to be of minor significance, but now with the ball-carrier presenting a bigger target, open-field running and passing (still not forward) became far less profitable. Several massed formations, notably those with names like the turtleback, the wedge and probably the mobile blockhouse, were developed. Somewhere in the middle of the formation would be the ball-carrier. As this juggernaut of a student body crashed its way down the field, it scattered lone tacklers, many of whom would not regain consciousness. In the quest for impregnability, the players would have leather handles sewn into the waistbands of their pants, enabling teamates to grab hold and keep the formation intact. In the event that forward progress came to a halt, the ball-carrier, again by use of the handles, might even be flung bodily screaming through the air to gain extra yards.

The wedge formation. Dangerous in itself, when it became the 'flying wedge' it was lunacy, and in 1894 all forms of wedge formation were banned.

The most savage tactic, which led to a temporary pause in this lunacy, was Harvard's 'flying wedge'. In a normal wedge play, the eleven men lined up in a V-shaped formation with the sharp end pointing towards the enemy. The man at the point would very gently kick the ball before picking it up and withdrawing into the wedge for the assault. In the Harvard variation, ten men would stand some twenty yards behind the lone man who was about to initiate the play. They would surge forward, converging to form the wedge and timing their arrival to coincide with his gentle tap. This gave the howling mob a vastly increased momentum – it was already flying.

In 1894 all forms of the wedge were banned, but a variety of alternative mass momentum plays (interlocking interference formations) persisted. More than this, gratuitous fist fighting and kicking became the norm.

The furore generated by this uncontrolled violence, by now a standard tactic, came to head in 1905 when eighteen young men were killed and countless others seriously injured. It was too much even for President Roosevelt, that patron of all pursuits physical, who threatened to ban the game completely unless something was done. Something, of course, was done. Under the Chairmanship of Camp, the 1906 Rules Committee outlawed interlocking interference formations (derivatives of the wedge), the ground gaining system was modified to ten yards in four

downs and the forward pass was legalised. The latter was at the instigation of John W. Heisman, a brilliant coach whose name is etched in the Trophy now awarded annually to the best college player. For years he had been campaigning and the involvement of President Roosevelt added just the muscle he needed.

At this 1906 meeting, the scoring system too came under scrutiny and the suggestions made led to the adoption in 1912 of the values which have remained to this day: a touchdown six points, conversion one, field goal three and safety two. It is interesting to note that in rugby, too, a numerical points system has evolved and that the modern philosophy is to give the greatest reward for scoring a touchdown.

The players had not yet adopted the kind of protective gear we now take for granted. Back in 1877, the Princeton team took to the field sporting tightly-laced canvas jackets, corsets by any other name, but they never caught on. However, it was during the dark days of extreme violence that protective headwear first came into fashion. Edgar Poe, the quarterback of Princeton and one of six footballing brothers, adopted a form of face mask to protect his broken nose and shortly afterwards in 1906, his team

The six footballing Poe brothers of Princeton. Edgar Allan holds the ball. Johnny is far right.

went the whole hog by wearing leather helmets. For lower body protection, the players wore padded trousers made of densely-woven cotton (moleskins), but for the upper body there was still nothing more than a woollen sweater – they had not yet taken on the appearance of swamp men.

The story so far has centred on the universities of the east, in particular the big three (Harvard, Princeton and Yale), which is quite proper since it was there that the game first became established. Their students graduated, often as theologians and always Football crazy, and each spread his chosen gospel throughout the United States. In the case of Football, the Pacific shores of California had been reached by 1890. Yet even in the early 1870s, merely borne by the winds of hearsay, the seeds of football had taken root in the state of Michigan. Here though, the Wolverines were somewhat isolated. For twenty years they were obliged to travel to the eastern hotbed where they received a customary pounding. However, by the turn of the century they formed part of what would become a powerhouse group of universities later known as the Big Ten conference.

In 1901 under head coach Fielding H. 'Hurry Up' Yost, they swept aside the likes of Ohio State, Purdue, Illinois and North-western, winning all eleven games and scoring 550 points whilst conceding none. Not surprisingly his lads were known as the 'Point-a-Minute' team. Coincidentally the organisers of the 1902 Tournament Of Roses, a traditional New Year's Day festival in Pasadena, California, had decided to include a game of Football as part of their celebrations. Naturally, Michigan accepted their invitation to play Stanford, whom they beat 49-0, thus becoming the first winners of the oldest and most famous bowl game of all, the Rose Bowl. The modern Rose Bowl game still matches the winners of the Big Ten and Pacific Ten conferences.

It was at this time that there emerged another champion of the game, truly in the mould of the great Walter Camp. Amos Alonzo Stagg spent his playing days at Yale before embarking on a coaching career which was to last for seventy years, at the end of which he had amassed the staggering total of 314 victories (this figure was surpassed in 1981 by the late Paul 'Bear' Bryant of Alabama.) Of these, 254 were gained at the University of Chicago which he left at the age of seventy to 'further' his career at the College of the Pacific on the west coast. Not so much the rules maker, he was more the brilliant tactical innovator, particularly of defensive systems which usually fooled the opposition. He

'Hurry-up' Yost and his 'Point-a-minute' Michigan team in 1901.

introduced the center snap, the man in motion and the idea of having a quick discussion before every down (the huddle). He also wrote the first book describing plays using the familiar arrows and circles. A teetotal, non-smoking man of the highest integrity, he died in 1965 at the age of 102.

He would have known and respected the other great coaches of the day: men such as John Heisman (the Father of the Forward Pass), George W. Woodruff (Pennsylvania), Henry L. Williams (Minnesota), Daniel E. McGugin (Vanderbilt) and Gillmour 'Gloomy Gil' Doble (Washington). To these and many more the game of Football was the honourable and natural expression for America's young men, and meant to be played for the love of it. Yet even as Walter Camp was completing the initial design in 1912, the professionals has arrived and were going to stay . .

'Pudge' Heffelfinger, Yale's
All-American star, in 1892.

CHAPTER 2
FOOTBALL GOES PROFESSIONAL

At the present time, 1983, the National Collegiate Athletic Association (NCAA) and the NFL have a joint agreement which obliges an undergraduate to spend four years in college before being eligible to play Professional Football. Even if he leaves early to go pumping petrol or whatever, he still cannot play professionally until his classmates have completed the four-year course of study. If he is just too stupid to get into college (virtually unknown), again he must wait until his age group has graduated.

Things were different in the 1890s. A student might play college football for, say, six years, graduate and carry his enthusiasm for football into one of the athletic clubs popular with the young men of those days. In a very short time inter-club games were being played, just as hard-fought as those in the colleges – perhaps even more so. Here though, there were no college authorities to impose fines and threaten expulsion and it was often necessary to summon the local police, who would crack the few skulls which remained intact in the attempt to separate the snarling combatants. These early battles took place in towns and cities within striking distance of Pittsburgh, a discreet 400 miles west and to the south of where the college activity was at its most intense.

Very quickly, the clashes assumed such an importance that clubs deliberately sought and recruited former college 'star' players who, of course, were paid for their services. As early as 1892 William W. 'Pudge' Heffelfinger, a former Yale All-American, was paid $500 to play a game in which he scored the only touchdown for the Allegheny Athletic Association in its victory over the Pittsburgh Athletic Club. Other teams such as Greensburgh A.A., Jeannette A.C. and Latrobe rapidly followed suit. Greensburgh in particular were to prosper from the talents of the three warmongering brothers Fiscus. These transactions are a matter of record but there must have been scores of others in which Billy the Bruiser and Albert the Animal would gladly have accepted ten dollars plus all the legs they could bite. Many

Above Latrobe Athletic Club in 1895 – note the skin pads which are not unlike mini batting pads.

Above Lawson Fiscus in 1893.
Right Morgan Athletic Club in 1898 – fore-runners of the St Louis Cardinals.

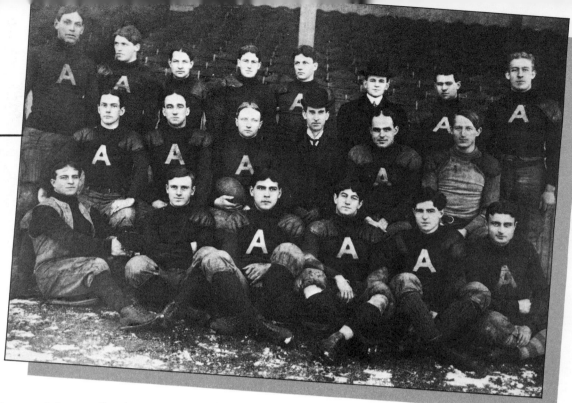

players felt no allegiance to a particular club and would go to work on a game-to-game basis for the highest bidder.

At the turn of the century there were an estimated 300 semi-pros playing for teams which were dotted all the way from the state of New York to Illinois. The origins of the modern Cardinals can be traced back to 1898, since when they have been named successively Morgan A.C., Chicago Normals, Racine Cardinals, Chicago Cardinals and eventually, St. Louis.

Games were now being watched by crowds of 4000 and inevitably attracted the attentions of sports entrepreneurs, notably Connie Mack, W. C. Temple and David J. Berry. In 1902 Mack, who already had his Philadelphia baseball team, collaborated with Temple and Berry in the first of several attempts to form a league. Mack laid claim to the first 'Championship' for his Athletics on the basis of their won-lost record, and later entered a tournament advertised as the 'World Series'. All the games in this four-team competition were played indoors at Madison Square Garden and the very first game was won by Syracuse All Stars, the eventual tournament winners, who beat Philadelphia 6-0.

But the crowds did not increase, there was no money to be made and as the entrepreneurs withdrew the professional circus drifted westward into Ohio. Here, several teams, including Franklin A.C. and Oil City, gathered around the fierce rivalry which was forming between the Massillon Tigers and the Canton Bulldogs. Although no league tables were ever kept, these clashes between the big two were always billed as being for the 'Championship'. The blood flowed freely and so did the money

The legendary Jim Thorpe,
controversial Olympic champion and
supreme all-round sportsman,
demonstrates his punting style
around 1918.

as both players and fans wagered huge sums. There was no
doubt some 'fixing' and certainly one major scandal when the
Massillon newspaper accused Blondy Wallace, the Canton coach,
of persuading his players to throw a game. The question never
was resolved and anyway, Blondy did a moonlight flit back east
and was never heard of again.

Perhaps because of the sour taste left by the fixing and
fiddling, interest in the professional game lay dormant for five
years before being rekindled by the arrival of Jim Thorpe in

1915. He was the hero of the 1912 Olympic Games, where he won two gold medals (decathlon and pentathlon), and he was acknowledged the greatest college player of his time. He could run, pass and apparently punt the ball 'ought of sight'. With Thorpe alone, the Bulldogs had a team but they supported him with the likes of Earle 'Greasy' Neale, Charlie Brinkley, an outstanding goal kicker, and the monster lineman, Howard Buck. They were unstoppable.

The crowds reappeared and new teams emerged but so too did the habits of old. The itinerant professionals again skipped from club to club and it is reported that in one season alone, Knute Rockne (later the famous head coach of Notre Dame) played for six different teams. It was rumoured that even Jim Thorpe feigned injury in one game to raise the betting odds for the next.

Nonetheless, there was the usual talk of forming a league to straighten things out and Ralph Hays, a Canton car dealer, chanced to offer his premises for a meeting. Amongst those, all from the mid-west, who gathered at the car lot of the Hupmobile Agency in Canton, Ohio, were representatives of Chicago Cardinals (later of St. Louis) and a youthful George Stanley Halas of Decatur Staleys (later Chicago Bears). All trace of what went on has disappeared but by its end, about a dozen clubs had agreed to form the American Professional Football Association, with a membership fee set at $100. Jim Thorpe (Canton Bulldogs), still playing and already a legend, lent credibility by becoming the first President, and naturally hopes were high as the teams began the inaugural season. Yet the fact that not one team bothered to pay the membership fee was a forewarning. What few regulations existed were treated with scant disrespect. Only one indisputable fact, the first player transfer (Bob Nash from Akron to Buffalo for $300), is known of a season which ended in shambles and for which no playing results remain.

Of course the formation of a professional league was never going to be easy, since it was always seen to be in conflict with a College Football system, amateur and glorious, which was both well established and in keeping with the social values of the times. It is not too inaccurate a comparison when thinking of that group which parted company with the English Rugby Union, to play its own (semi-pro) brand of the game in the shadows of our northern slag heaps. Though this split occurred in 1895, it was coincident with the American movement when, in 1922, the

George Halas before a game in 1924. He had been present at the meeting in Canton to form a professional league.

professional Rugby League adopted its new name. Sadly for us in the United Kingdom, the differences remain unreconciled between the amateur and professional codes but in the United States all conflict is a thing of the past. Nonetheless in 1920 it would have been a source of pleasure to many when the original men of Canton, men of vision, enthusiasm and some, no doubt, of greed, separated in chaos.

There was need for a man of administrative genius and he arrived in the shape of Joseph F. Carr. He was to dominate the League for twenty years but for the moment, he reconstructed the splintered group, and with charm, persuasion and a will of iron, whipped them into line.

In the 1921 season not all teams played the same number of games but at least records were kept and out of them emerged the first Champions, George Halas's Chicago Staleys (later the Bears). Prior to the season, an application by one J. E. Clair of the Acme Packing Company in Green Bay, had been accepted – the Packers had arrived.

Joseph F. Carr, NFL President, 1921-39.

Below Acme Packers of Green Bay. Curly Lambeau is at the front centre.

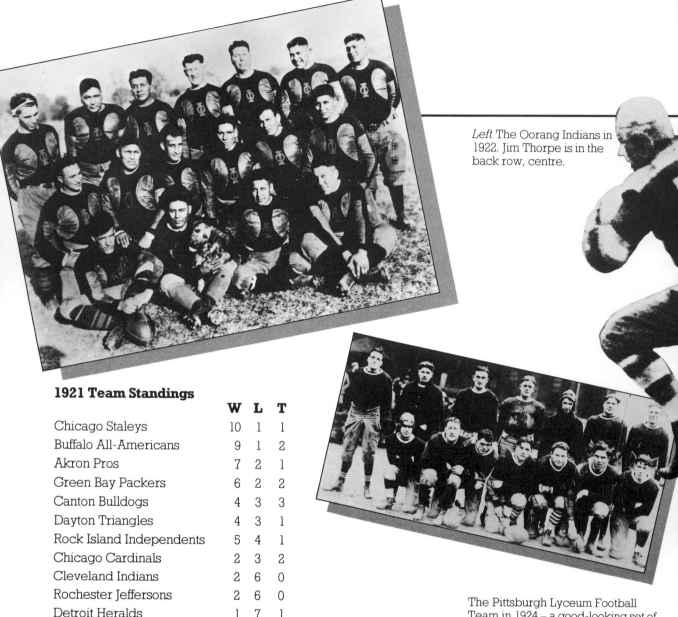

Left The Oorang Indians in 1922. Jim Thorpe is in the back row, centre.

1921 Team Standings

	W	L	T
Chicago Staleys	10	1	1
Buffalo All-Americans	9	1	2
Akron Pros	7	2	1
Green Bay Packers	6	2	2
Canton Bulldogs	4	3	3
Dayton Triangles	4	3	1
Rock Island Independents	5	4	1
Chicago Cardinals	2	3	2
Cleveland Indians	2	6	0
Rochester Jeffersons	2	6	0
Detroit Heralds	1	7	1
Columbus Panhandles	0	6	0
Cincinnati Celts	0	8	0

The Pittsburgh Lyceum Football Team in 1924 – a good-looking set of lads.

It was more a measure of ambition than reality when in 1922 they adopted the new title of National Football League, since the teams were drawn from a mere five states (Illinois, Indiana, Michigan, Ohio and Wisconsin). Yet their evident potential was such that the formidable Amos Alonzo Stagg, then Head Coach of the University of Chicago, threatened that his college conference (the Big Ten) would 'break' the NFL. Nonetheless, the League expanded to include the Oorang Indians, as its name implies a team composed of native Americans. The Apaches though need not have worried for the name Oorang was not, as one might

Red Grange (77) outruns the opposition in 1926 when playing for the Yankees. Note the empty seats – the league folded shortly afterwards through lack of fan support.

think, a rival tribe but rather the trade name of the sponsoring Oorang Dog Kennel Company. Despite recruiting Jim Thorpe, they were dreadful and lasted only the two seasons which saw his former team, Canton Bulldogs, win consecutive Championships. In 1924 the Bulldogs, then based in Cleveland, made it three in a row.

In these early days a squad consisted of only fifteen men – even the 'stars' would play both on offense and defense – and in 1925 it was significant when the roster was increased to sixteen. It was a major factor too when the old ball, which had the aerodynamics of a stewed water melon, was replaced by a panelled version. But more important than these, 'Red' Grange arrived on the scene. 'The Galloping Ghost' from the University of Illinois had for three years terrorised college defenses with his devastating running and now he was to play for George Halas's Bears.

Whereas games had been only of local interest, watched by

3,000 or so, he attracted the attention of a nation and crowds of 40,000, even in the winter of the mid-west, were not uncommon. Indeed, a reported 70,000 turned out in New York to see him play against the Giants who had newly entered the League. Yet ironically and after only one year, it was the departure of a disgruntled Grange which led to the first serious challenge to the authority of the NFL, riding high on his very success. Unable to obtain a satisfactory contract, his agent, C. C. Pyle, took Grange to New York and formed the American Football League. Mind you, he was asking a lot. The 1925 contract gave him essentially half the gate receipts and was worth around $50,000, and this at a time when the average player salary was $1,500 for a full season.

The new league collapsed after only one year, as did several later attempts, yet surprisingly Pyle's personal team, the Yankees, were welcomed into the NFL. However, what may have appeared an act of magnanimity by Joe Carr was more one of commercial expedience – the League was contracting and he needed all the

The Teams in 1932

*Boston Braves
Brooklyn Dodgers
Chicago Bears
Chicago Cardinals
Green Bay Packers
New York Giants
Portsmouth (Ohio) Spartans
Stapleton Stapes
*renamed Boston Redskins
in 1933

Far left Ernie Nevers around 1928 –
he took over a starring mantle from
Red Grange.
Below The Green Bay Packers
champion team of 1929.

attractions he could muster. To make matters worse, Grange suffered a knee injury after which, and to quote him: 'I was just another running back', and it was just as well that another big name, Ernie Nevers, arrived to claim the spotlight. Despite his exploits, which included scoring all 40 points when his Cardinals beat a Bears team including Grange and another powerhouse running back, Bronko' Nagurski, the slide continued, and by 1932 only eight teams remained. With the NFL in redoubt, it was time for a reassessment.

Purely in terms of numbers, the situation was depressing and yet of that tiny group of eight, five teams represented a solid foundation on which to rebuild. The Cardinals and Giants with one Championship each (1925 and 1927 respectively) were in good shape, as were the Bears. Green Bay, whose Head Coach, Earl 'Curly' Lambeau, had first recognised and then exploited the staggering potential of the forward pass, were in tremendous form, coming off three consecutive Championship years (1929-31). They were joined by the Boston Braves who were to find a permanent home in Washington and be renamed the Redskins. In addition, Halas had initiated the process of fence-mending with the colleges by persuading the club owners not to poach college players until after their senior class had graduated. The show would go on . . .

The player roster was increased to 20 for the 1932 season, at the end of which the Bears were tied with Portsmouth Spartans. Naturally, there would have to be a showdown. December in Chicago is always cold but this was a really bad one and the teams jumped at the opportunity to play the NFL's first serious indoor game. (The Bears and Cardinals had played a charity game indoors in 1930). In a packed Chicago Stadium 11,000 saw the Bears win 9-0 but, more significantly, there arose three major innovations.

Firstly, for reasons of player safety in the cramped conditions all plays were started at a point no less than ten yards from the sideline – marking the first step towards the introduction of hashmarks (inbounds lines). This allowed for width in the rushing game. Secondly, the forward pass rule was modified. At the time, a forward pass could be delivered only from at least five yards behind the line of scrimmage and it is argued to this day that the winning pass from Nagurski to Grange violated this rule. This distance requirement was scrapped, leading to much greater freedom for the quarterback and encouraging the pass as an

The NFL Championship game, in which Chicago beat Portsmouth Spartans 9-0 on 18 December 1932, was played indoors at Chicago Stadium.

offensive weapon. Finally, the playoff was such a success that it was permanently adopted in subsequent years, matching the winners of what were to be two new Divisions within the League.

The Bears repeated their 1932 Championship, this time beating the Giants 23-21 in a League expanded by the entry of Pittsburgh and Philadelphia, both of which were to endure.

In early 1934 the Portsmouth Spartans were sold, wrapped up neatly and transferred to Detroit where they took root as the Lions. The Giants gained revenge for their loss of the previous year to the Bears by winning the Championship, but in the most unusual of circumstances. On an ice-covered pitch and at half way losing 10-3, the Giants trotted out for the second half wearing tennis shoes. The dumbfounded Bears, slipping and sliding, could only watch as the Giants literally ran away with the game, 30-13.

Towards the end of 1934 Football was still predominantly a rushing game and even despite Lambeau's successes, his passing alternative was most definitely not in keeping with the game's masculine image. Yet the rulemakers had recognised the potential spectacle of the long pass and it was almost certainly with this in mind that the ball was slimmed down by a full inch to establish the dimensions which have since remained unchanged. Right on cue there appeared a rookie by the name of Don Hutson, who was to exploit this new and elegant prolate spheroid to the full. Naturally he joined the Packers where first Arnie Herber and then Cecil Isbell would fire off their long bombs in the direction of this willowy ghost. For close on ten years he was to murder the League's defenses but not just yet, for 1935 belonged to the Detroit Lions who won their first Championship by beating New York 26-7.

At the suggestion of Bert Bell of Philadelphia, the NFL's administrators took another significant step to regularise their dealings with the colleges in adopting a formal draft system. By this, the pro teams would select college graduates in the order determined by their previous season's won-lost record. In each round the team with the worst record would make the first selection and the League Champions would choose last of all. The system remains to this day.

The formation of a potential rival, again named the American Football League, went largely unnoticed and unconsidered as the Packers, with Hutson beginning to blossom, swept to the 1936 Championship. There was consolation for the defeated Boston Redskins when in the year following, and in their new Washington home, they celebrated with the Championship by beating the Bears 28-21. Their owner, George P. Marshall, had confirmed his belief in the potential of the passing game by installing his own rifleman, quarterback Sammy Baugh, who in his rookie year led the League. Quite a character, Mr Marshall will be remembered not least for having been the first to provide the half-time entertainment we now take for granted.

For the record the Cleveland Rams (later Los Angeles Rams) had entered the League to join the Bears, Cardinals, Lions and Packers in the Western Division, and the AFL threat collapsed after only one year.

By the mid 1930s the NFL had amassed a bewildering array of regulations, and with each new year bringing its own avalanche, the officials on the field (only four at this time) were in danger of

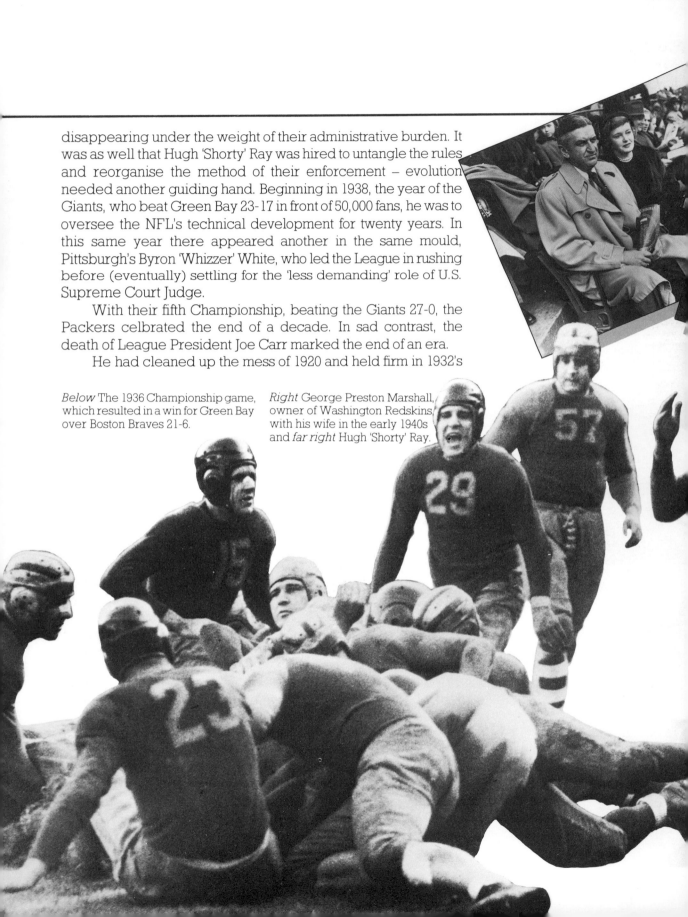

disappearing under the weight of their administrative burden. It was as well that Hugh 'Shorty' Ray was hired to untangle the rules and reorganise the method of their enforcement – evolution needed another guiding hand. Beginning in 1938, the year of the Giants, who beat Green Bay 23-17 in front of 50,000 fans, he was to oversee the NFL's technical development for twenty years. In this same year there appeared another in the same mould, Pittsburgh's Byron 'Whizzer' White, who led the League in rushing before (eventually) settling for the 'less demanding' role of U.S. Supreme Court Judge.

With their fifth Championship, beating the Giants 27-0, the Packers celbrated the end of a decade. In sad contrast, the death of League President Joe Carr marked the end of an era.

He had cleaned up the mess of 1920 and held firm in 1932's

Below The 1936 Championship game, which resulted in a win for Green Bay over Boston Braves 21-6.

Right George Preston Marshall, owner of Washington Redskins, with his wife in the early 1940s and *far right* Hugh 'Shorty' Ray.

darkest moments. His League had remained financially sound despite even the ravages of America's economic Depression and of his 1939 teams, only Brooklyn was to fold, and this for the reasons of different times. In this his last year, attendance topped the one million mark for the first time. Under his watchful eye, the professional game had evolved from the brutal trench warfare of the 1920s to the beginnings of today's aerial spectacular. With the squads now increased to 30 players, specialisation had arrived. He cultivated relations with the NFL's nursery, the colleges, brought in the College Draft, the notion of Divisions and from it, the playoffs.

He died a bare six months before reports of an event, of little significance at the time, which was to lead to the fulfilment of his dream. The National Broadcasting Company had televised the Philadelphia – Brooklyn game and it had been well-received . . .

The NFL in 1940

Western Division	Eastern Division
Chicago Bears	Brooklyn Dodgers
Chicago Cardinals	New York Giants
Cleveland Rams	Philadelphia Eagles
Detroit Lions	Pittsburgh Steelers
Green Bay Packers	Washington Redskins

Carl Storck took over as caretaker President-Secretary in a year which saw the Bears gain their fourth Championship by beating Washington in the first major game to be broadcast on nationwide radio (Mutual Broadcasting System). A mere three weeks earlier, the Redskins had beaten Chicago 7-3 in a regular season contest and were clear favourites to win the title. However in the big one, though the numbers in the score were the same, they were all in favour of Chicago who won by an astonishing 73-0. It brought about an abrupt change in offensive thinking throughout the League.

For several seasons, Halas and his partner, Ralph Jones, had been experimenting with a formation not unlike Camp's original 'T', mostly to the amusement of the other clubs, and before the game he had summoned his old friend Clark Shaughnessy, then waiting to take Stanford to the Rose Bowl. Shaughnessy was one of the first to study film of previous games and he suggested a refinement which he felt would exploit Washington's predictable

33

defense. Essentially, before play commenced, a running back would drift out wide, obliging the defense to adjust its alignment in response. Then, following sleight of hand by the quarterback (now known as 'faking' and 'play action'), the actual play would be redirected to the opposite side against a defense in some confusion. This so-called counter play was worked to perfection by Chicago quarterback Sid Luckman. Even so, the very best offense can not take credit for an opposition score reading zero. Rather, it was a Bear defense, charged up and snarling, which responded in the most appropriate way to George Marshall's taunts made after the previous game.

Not all historians are prepared to acknowledge Shaughnessy's contribution, but by the following year virtually all the clubs, including Washington, had taken up the system.

Still in this same year and no doubt in the hope of skimming some of the NFL's one million fans, yet another rival organisation had a go. Using the familiar name which we can now abbreviate to AFL, this one lasted two years before making contact with the wall.

In 1941, Elmer Layden assumed the position of NFL overlord, under the new title of Commissioner. Himself a former outstanding college running back, he had been one of the fabled 'Four Horsemen of Notre Dame' who ran riot in the early 1920s. Chicago again won the Championship, which was their second of four in a seven-year period, but not without a struggle. By now, some nine years after its formation, the Western Division had become a bloodbath of murderous encounters and not without

Top Action from the 1940 Championship game Chicago 73 Washington 0. George McAfee (5) gains seven yards, and *left* a jubilant Head Coach George Halas celebrates afterwards with some of his players.

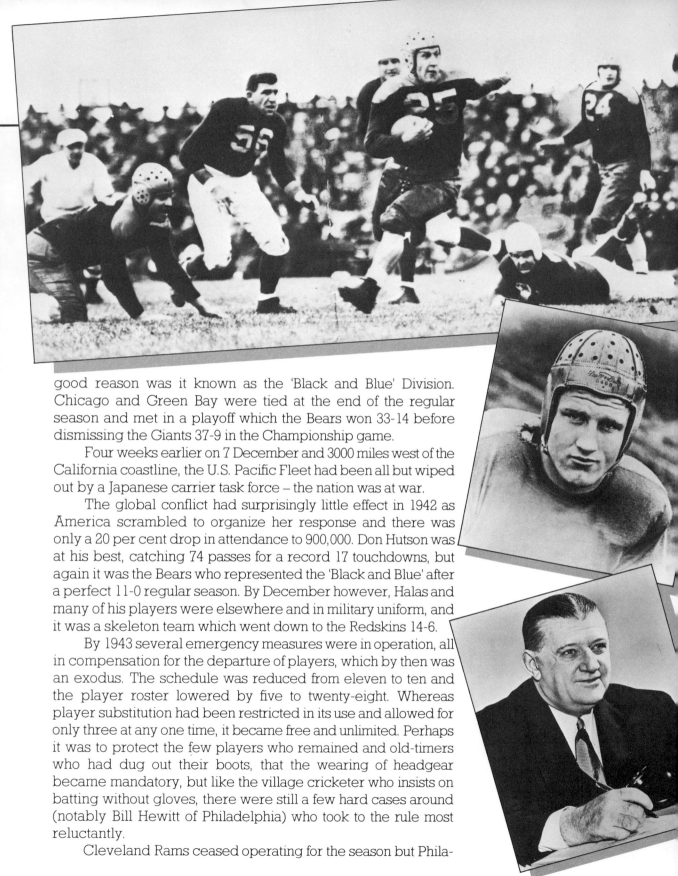

good reason was it known as the 'Black and Blue' Division. Chicago and Green Bay were tied at the end of the regular season and met in a playoff which the Bears won 33-14 before dismissing the Giants 37-9 in the Championship game.

Four weeks earlier on 7 December and 3000 miles west of the California coastline, the U.S. Pacific Fleet had been all but wiped out by a Japanese carrier task force – the nation was at war.

The global conflict had surprisingly little effect in 1942 as America scrambled to organize her response and there was only a 20 per cent drop in attendance to 900,000. Don Hutson was at his best, catching 74 passes for a record 17 touchdowns, but again it was the Bears who represented the 'Black and Blue' after a perfect 11-0 regular season. By December however, Halas and many of his players were elsewhere and in military uniform, and it was a skeleton team which went down to the Redskins 14-6.

By 1943 several emergency measures were in operation, all in compensation for the departure of players, which by then was an exodus. The schedule was reduced from eleven to ten and the player roster lowered by five to twenty-eight. Whereas player substitution had been restricted in its use and allowed for only three at any one time, it became free and unlimited. Perhaps it was to protect the few players who remained and old-timers who had dug out their boots, that the wearing of headgear became mandatory, but like the village cricketer who insists on batting without gloves, there were still a few hard cases around (notably Bill Hewitt of Philadelphia) who took to the rule most reluctantly.

Cleveland Rams ceased operating for the season but Phila-

Above Bill Hewitt of Philadelphia (56) playing without headgear in 1939.
Left 'Bronko' Nagurski, one of the players immortalised in the Pro Football Hall of Fame.
Left below Bert Bell, the NFL Commissioner from 1946 and 1959.

delphia and Pittsburgh, neither of whom was able to field a decent squad, merged under the name of Phil-Pitt Steagles. Looking back, the alliance and its name look ridiculous, and yet the two were linked by goings on of the immediate past. In 1940, their respective owners had exchanged rights of franchise before swapping back in 1941. They did well finishing only one win behind Washington in the Eastern Division. Over in the West, Sid Luckman had the Bears on top again. On one glorious afternoon against the Giants, he threw for seven touchdowns (a record) on the way to becoming the first quarterback to pass for over 400 yards in a single game. It would have rekindled the flames of old to see 'Bronko' Nagurski, who had come out of a six-year retirement because 'there was nobody else', add his final rushing touchdown to Sid's passing five as the Bears said goodbye to the Redskins, 41-21.

In 1944 Cleveland resumed operations, Brooklyn Dodgers became known as the 'Tigers' and a new team, Boston Yanks, entered the NFL. Not to be outdone in the name game, Pittsburgh merged with Chicago Cardinals to be known as Card-Pitt which, unlike the flirtation with Philadelphia, proved barren – they didn't win a game.

Coaching from the bench, which had been happening anyway, was given formal approval though it is unlikely that the legislators could have visualised the modern coach, wired up as he is and having at his disposal both the defensive tendencies of the opposing cornerback and the betting odds for the 2.30 at Kempton.

The fans came back to top the million mark and break the attendance record as 46,000 watched Green Bay beat the Giants 14-7 for the Championship.

The end of the Second World War in 1945 signalled a return to normality, though the wartime emergency measures remained, except for the roster which reverted to 33. Boston Yanks and Brooklyn Tigers, neither of whom had won a game in 1944, merged under the Boston name but were still awful, with only one win. The Steelers were once more of Pittsburgh and with Don Hutson leading the League in his final year, it was business as usual.

Washington won the Eastern Division for the sixth time in ten years but lost out, by the narrowest of margins, to Cleveland Rams, who won their first Championship, 15-14.

Under new Commissioner Bert Bell, the pace began to

quicken. In his very first year (1946) he would be faced with the problems of players gambling and the emergence of yet another rival league. Before these however, Cleveland Rams moved out to Los Angeles (the League now extended from coast to coast) and had the good sense to enlist Ken Washington, the first black player since 1933 (the very first had been Henry McDonald of Rochester Jeffersons in 1912).

The gambling problem arose out of allegations that Frank Filchock and Merle Hapes, of the Giants, had been approached by the 'mob' to 'fix' their Championship game against Chicago. In the end, Hapes was suspended and his team went down 24-14 to the Bears, who then embarked on a sixteen-year trip into the wilderness.

The rival group had the initiative to choose a novel title, the All America Football Conference, and even though its four-year lifetime was dominated by Cleveland Browns, the football was ominously good. In all, the Browns had a record of 47 wins, 4 losses and 3 ties en route to all four Championships. With the likes of Otto Graham, Marion Motley and Lou Groza, they were truly awesome and to be compared with the Bears of the 1940s, the Packers to come and Pittsburgh of the 1970s. But could they do it in the NFL? They were given the chance by Bert Bell who had the foresight to welcome them, together with San Francisco 49ers and Baltimore Colts, when the Conference fell apart at the end of the 1949 season.

The 'Million Dollar Backfield' of St Louis in 1947: Paul Christman (44), Pat Harder (34), Charley Trippi (99) and Elmer Angsman (62).
Right Steve Van Buren scoring the winning touchdown in the Championship Game of 19 December 1948 at Shibe Park. Philadelphia Eagles beat Chicago Cardinals 7-0.
Top right Steve Van Buren, the Eagles running back.

The late 1940s saw the emergence of Philadelphia Eagles who, as winners of the Eastern Division, contested the Championship game in 1947, 1948 and 1949. In the first, they went down 28-21 to the Cardinals, who had momentarily surfaced in the West on the strength of their 'Million Dollar Backfield' of Paul Christman, Pat Harder, Charley Trippi and Elmer Angsman. But Philadelphia too had its wrecking crew and, led by Steve Van Buren, they closed out the decade with consecutive Championships. In the first they gained revenge 7-0 against the Cardinals and in 1949, beat Los Angeles 14-0 . . .

The Teams in 1950

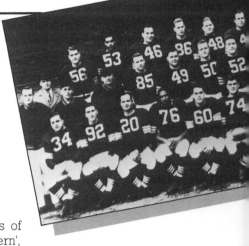

*American Conference

Chicago Cardinals
Cleveland Browns
New York Giants
Philadelphia Eagles
Pittsburgh Steelers
Washington Redskins

*National Conference

Baltimore Colts
Chicago Bears
Detroit Lions
Green Bay Packers
Los Angeles Rams
*New York Yanks
San Francisco 49ers.

*The NFL just loves changing names and they used the titles of 'American' and 'National' before reverting to 'Eastern' and 'Western', though still Conferences, in 1952. In rapid sequence, the New York Yanks had been Boston Yanks then New York Bulldogs before in 1952, moving to Dallas where they became extinct after one year.

Above The Cleveland Browns Championship-winning team of 1950.
Below Action from the Championship Game. Cleveland Browns beating the Detroit Lions.
Right Pete Rozelle, the current NFL Commissioner, photographed when he took office in 1960.
Right below Lamar Hunt, founder of the AFL and owner of Kansas City Chiefs.

As if to confirm the wisdom of Bert Bell's invitation and to silence a few doubters around the League, the Cleveland Browns won the Championship in their very first year, beating the Rams 30-28 with a last-minute Lou Groza field goal. The win was to be

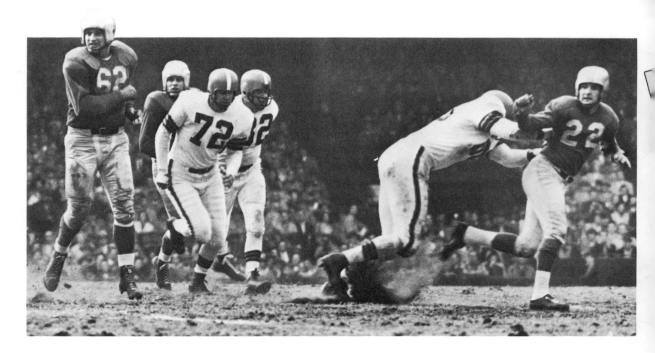

the first of three (1950, 1954 and 1955) in an eight-year period during which they contested the Championship game no fewer than seven times. By drafting Jim Brown (1957) who was to emulate Don Hutson but as a running back, they would prosper well into the 1960s. The Colts too made their mark (after sitting out the 1951 and 1952 seasons), coming out on top in both 1958 and 1959 with quarterback 'Ice Cool' John Unitas at the controls. In between, Detroit Lions had their only period of dominance, winning the Championship three times (1952, 1953 and 1957) in four attempts. With their solitary successes, the Rams (1951) and Giants (1956) made up the group of five teams which shared out the gravy.

But more and more fans were sharing in the spectacle as Los Angeles, in 1950, just before Washington and the rest, contracted to have their games televised to local audiences. In 1951, the Du Mont network beamed the Championship game coast to coast and by 1956, CBS were presenting selected regular season games on the same scale. Those who tuned in might well testify that the NFL had anticipated the space age by decking out the players with domed plastic helmets. In 1954 a face cage was added, presumably to protect a player's teeth but if you consider it to be a muzzle, there's an alternative interpretation.

Stadia were filling up and the slightly less than two million spectators of 1950 had become more than three million by 1959, averaging 43,000 per game. Hugh 'Shorty' Ray, the NFL's technical mentor, passed away in 1956 and the death of Commissioner Bert Bell in 1959 was accepted with equal sadness. What Joe Carr had planted, 'Shorty' Ray had propagated, while Bert Bell kept the blooms in order.

In every sense, new Commissioner Pete Rozelle took control of a going concern and yet he, too, would have to deal with the recurring smear of gambling, added to which there would be the new problem of drug abuse. The unforgiving eye of television brought the game's inherent violence into the living rooms of millions. Something had to be done about it. Furthermore, and predictably, there was to be the inevitable challenge from a rival group and in this one, the gloves came off at a very early stage.

Unable to obtain an NFL franchise, Lamar Hunt of the powerful Texas family did what any man of such means might: he formed his own league, and though not yet hammering at the gates, they could be heard in the distance, as in January 1960, Rozelle took office . . .

The Teams in 1960

AFL

Western Conference
*Dallas Texans
Denver Broncos
*L.A. Chargers
Oakland Raiders

Eastern Conference
Boston Patriots
Buffalo Bills
Houston Oilers
*N.Y. Titans

NFL

Western Conference
Baltimore Colts
Chicago Bears
*Dallas Cowboys
Detroit Lions
Green Bay Packers
L.A. Rams
San Francisco 49ers

Eastern Conference
Cleveland Browns
N.Y. Giants
Philadelphia Eagles
Pittsburgh Steelers
*St. Louis Cardinals
Washington Redskins

*Dallas Texans became Kansas City Chiefs in 1963
*Los Angeles Chargers moved to San Diego in 1961
*New York Titans were renamed the Jets in 1963
*Dallas Cowboys entered NFL in 1960
*The Cardinals moved from Chicago to St. Louis in 1960

It all started pleasantly enough as the two Leagues agreed, verbally, not to 'tamper' with each other's players. But, before long, they were battling in the courts. The key word in the charges levelled by the AFL was conspiracy, in the matters of League expansion, dealings with television companies, player signings and monopoly. On all counts, the AFL lost both the 1962 verdict and their appeal a year later.

Then came the bidding war, as clubs from both Leagues sought to attract the 'star' college players to their ranks. New York Jets pulled off a coup by signing Alabama's Joe Namath who was to quarterback them to Super Bowl victory, but the NFL still garnered the lion's share of talent in a struggle which reached its peak in 1966, when the two spent a total of $7,000,000. Later in the same year, probably for reasons of good commercial sense, the hatchet was buried and the two Leagues agreed to join forces.

The new organisation, which would retain the title of National Football League, with Pete Rozelle as its Commissioner, was to

Left Joe Namath, whose signing was a coup for the New York Jets and the AFL.

Below Paul Hornung (5) running for Green Bay Packers and having his path cleared by a good block by a fellow Packer.

come into effect for the 1970 season (four years ahead). Until then the two Leagues would keep their separate identities. But before this, at the end of the 1966 season, the respective Champions would meet in the so-called Championship Game. The name Super Bowl was given only to the fourth of these, but these days everyone refers to the first inter-League game as Super Bowl I. Some AFL owners accepted the merger only with reluctance. They had learned to survive, despite the costs of competition and litigation. Furthermore, they would each have to pay a 'joining fee' of somewhere around $2,000,000. And their average attendance, though still 15,000 below the NFL's 47,000, had doubled in five years, while they too had their television contract (with ABC). Nonetheless when the day came they all fell into line.

When ABC signed a five-year contract in 1960 to televise selected AFL games, it would have been with fingers crossed, since the new League was an unknown quantity. The other two major companies, NBC and CBS, had put their money with the NFL and were on to a sure thing. NBC took the early Championship games for $600,000 each, but it was CBS who really took the plunge in 1964 by paying $16,000,000, rising to $19,000,000 by

1966, for one game each week throughout the season. By 1969, the share of television money received by each club amounted to one third of its total revenue. Already there were cynics who felt that television was running Football.

They were answered by Rozelle who showed exactly who was in charge. Recognising the potential bonanza for Football, he steadily persuaded the big three companies to accept a pattern of coverage which would maximise the benefits for his expanded League. In time for the NFL-AFL merger, the companies were paying to televise every single game of the season – not just the glamour games.

Rozelle also showed strength when faced with the gambling scandal of 1963. He exercised his right to apply summary justice by imposing indefinite suspensions on the two miscreants, Paul Hornung of Green Bay and Alex Karras of Detroit, who had placed bets on their own teams and in other games. In addition, five other Detroit players were given $2,000 fines and their club received a $4,000 rap on the knuckles. Having made his point, he lifted the suspensions a year later.

The 1960s saw few rule changes. Notably, in 1965 the number of officials was increased to six (a fifth had been added in 1947) and the roster steadily crept up to 40. In 1963 the NFL honoured its former great players, administrators and owners, by establishing the Pro Football Hall Of Fame, appropriately in Canton, Ohio. Election to this group of heroes, currently numbering 119 and all depicted in bronze, represents the ultimate in achievement. Aspiring players must have been retired for five years before coming under consideration for entry.

On the field, and firstly in the NFL, the Green Bay Packers were the team of the decade. Not since 1944 had they won a Championship, but under coach Vince Lombardi, they fought their way to the 1960 game, losing narrowly 17-13 to Philadelphia before driving to the Championship in five of the next seven years, and in the last two, contesting the Super Bowl. Of this era, no fewer than eight players would later find their way into the Hall Of Fame alongside their beloved coach Lombardi, in honour of whom the Super Bowl trophy is named.

Their five-game sequence was broken firstly by Chicago with a 14-10 victory over the Giants in 1963, to register coach Halas's sixth and last Championship win. Spare a thought for the poor Giants who, with this loss, made it three in as many years. All the while, Cleveland's Jim Brown had been mercilessly

Top left The legendary Vince
Lombardi, the Green Bay Packers
Head Coach, in the 1960s.
Left The Vince Lombardi Trophy,
awarded to the Super Bowl winners.
Bottom Left A touchdown by Dave
Smith from a short pass over the
centre by George Blanda, as the
Houston Oilers beat L. A. Chargers in
the Championship of 1960.
Bottom right George Blanda (16) flips
a short pass to running back Charley
Tolar (44) in the AFL Championship
Game in 1962.

pounding away, topping the League in rushing almost as of right,
and he led his team to an easy 27-0 victory over Baltimore in the
1964 game. In 1968 the Colts, by now a formidable outfit, turned
the tables with a 34-0 drubbing of the Browns, who again lost in
the following year, this time to Minnesota 27-7.

In its early years the AFL was regarded as a bit of a joke by
the purists, as offensive players racked up astronomical statistics
against defenses which barely existed. Yet to the unsophisticated
TV fan it was riveting stuff. Surprises were common, and none
more embarrassing than the one suffered by NBC television
over the famous 'Heidi Game'. In a key New York-Oakland
confrontation with one minute remaining and the Jets leading
32-29, the controller switched to the network presentation of
'Heidi', a story for children, and as this delicate flower skipped
across her Alpine meadow, the Raiders came back with two
touchdowns to win the game 43-32.

In the ten year existence of the AFL, six clubs won Championships. Houston began with the first two (1960 and 1961),
Buffalo also had consecutive wins (1964 and 1965) and San Diego
(1963), Oakland (1967) and New York (1968) won one each.
Lamar Hunt's Kansas City did best with three wins, 1962 (then
named Dallas Texans), 1966 and 1969. The 1966 win earned them
the dubious honour of representing the AFL in the first Super

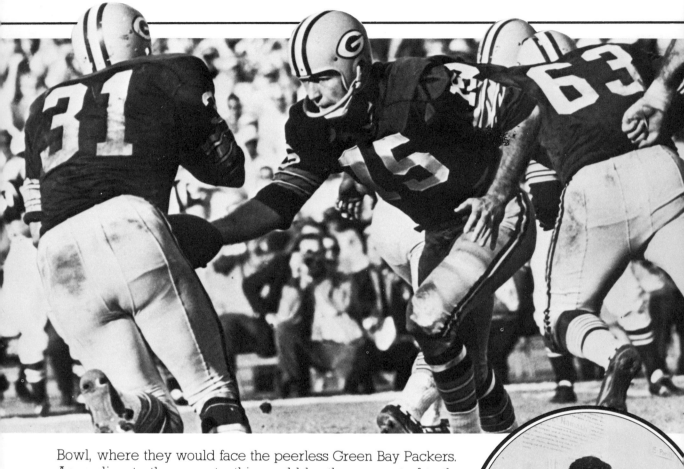

Bowl, where they would face the peerless Green Bay Packers. According to the experts, this would be the moment of truth, when the yawning gap between the establishment and the upstarts would be exposed.

They were not far wrong as the Packers stomped the Chief 35-10. The same was true the following year when the Raiders took a 33-14 thrashing, again at the hands of Green Bay. Super Bowl III however was a different story when New York Jets of the AFL, led by quarterback 'Broadway' Joe Namath, pulled off a shocking 16-7 victory over Baltimore, who had been favourites to win by seventeen points. A year later, Kansas City evened the score with a 23-7 victory over the NFL's Minnesota Vikings.

Honour was satisfied and respect for the AFL established just in time for the merger, which duly took place in 1970. The two former Leagues were renamed Conferences and in order to establish a balance (13 teams in each), three former NFL teams, Baltimore, Cleveland and Pittsburgh, joined the ten former AFL teams.

The Teams in 1970

AFC

Eastern Division
Baltimore Colts
Boston Patriots
Buffalo Bills
*Miami Dolphins
New York Jets
Central Division
*Cincinnati Bengals
Cleveland Browns
Houston Oilers
Pittsburgh Steelers
Western Division
Denver Broncos
Kansas City Chiefs
Oakland Raiders
San Diego Chargers

NFC

Eastern Division
Dallas Cowboys
New York Giants
Philadelphia Eagles
St. Louis Cardinals
Washington Redskins
Central Division
Chicago Bears
Detroit Lions
Green Bay Packers
*Minnesota Vikings
Western Division
*Atlanta Falcons
Los Angeles Rams
*New Orleans Saints
San Francisco 49ers

AFC
*Miami joined AFL in 1966
*Cincinnati joined AFL in 1968
**Seattle Seahawks (AFC West)
 joined NFL in 1976

NFC
*Minnesota joined NFL in 1961
*Atlanta joined NFL in 1966
*New Orleans joined NFL in 1967
**Tampa Bay Buccaneers (NFC
 Central) joined NFL in 1976.

Bert Starr (15) hands off to Jim Taylor in Super Bowl I. Fred Thurston is 63. The Packers beat the Chiefs 35-10.

Joe Namath celebrates victory in Super Bowl III with his father (right) and Coach Ewbank. New York Jets shocked Baltimore 16-7.

By 1970, millions of Americans found themselves committed to a six-hour stretch of televised Football every Sunday, followed by a game specially rescheduled for Monday evening. It was to assist the television viewer that a player's name first appeared in large capitals on the back of his shirt. More important rule changes were designed to encourage the passing style of play and to control violence.

The player roster rose as high as 47 in 1974, before settling down to the current 45. A seventh official (and there could be more) was introduced in 1978 when the season expanded from fourteen to sixteen games.

Quarterbacks prospered from the extra security given by linemen, now able to use their hands in protection blocking, and it was made illegal to impede a receiver beyond a point five yards downfield from the line of scrimmage. Whereas in 1970 passing and rushing yardage had been roughly equal, by 1982 passing accounted for two thirds of the total gain.

Throughout the NFL's history, defensive thugs have taken every opportunity to lay into the 'star' offensive players. This would take the form of roughing up the quarterback during a sack, jumping on top of a rusher who was clearly downed and

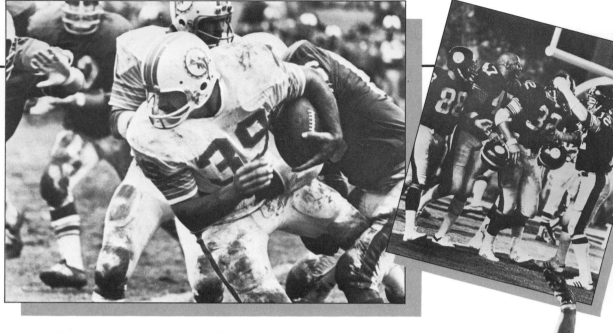

Above left Larry Csonka grinds out the yards for Miami in 1972. *Above centre* Terry Bradshaw (12) with Franco Harris (32), Lynn Swan (88) and Mel Blount (47) after beating Dallas in Super Bowl XIII. *Above right* O. J. takes off. *Left* The Smurfs (Washington Receivers) go through their routine after winning Super Bowl XVII.

unnecessary physical contact with a receiver after having forced him over the sideline. All these were outlawed: for those madmen who would perpetuate the carnage, a one-game suspension is now virtually automatic.

In 1969 O. J. 'Juice' Simpson was drafted by Buffalo. He began quietly at first before 'exploding' in 1973 for 2003 rushing yards, surpassing even Jim Brown's 1863, the record until then. Considered by many to be the greatest-ever, he left the game in 1979 only 1076 short of Brown's all-time record of 12,312 and alas, with only his Heisman Trophy on the sideboard.

It was Baltimore who celebrated the new beginning and erased the embarrassment of their loss to New York with a 16-13 Super Bowl V win over Dallas. For five years the Cowboys had been simmering: indeed, they came close to beating Green Bay in their 1966 and 1967 Championship encounters. But it was in the 1971 season, when they defeated Miami 24-3 to win Super Bowl VI, that they became known by that name peculiar to Football teminology, 'The Perennial Powerhouse'. To win the Super Bowl, a team usually has to beat Dallas somewhere along the way.

Miami bounced back with consecutive wins, over Washington 24-7 in Super Bowl VII and Minnesota 24-7 in game VIII. Already they were being compared to Green Bay of the 1960s, when, quite suddenly, three of their offensive giants, Paul Warfield,

Larry Csonka and Jim Kiick, defected to the newly formed World Football League. It was no surprise when this venture, conspicuous for its extravagance, collapsed after one season, abandoning its disillusioned players to fend for themselves.

Pittsburgh stifled Minnesota 16-6 in Super Bowl IX before going on to squeeze past Dallas in a 21-17 thriller for Super Bowl X, and it seemed as if the AFC teams were taking turns to humble Minnesota when Oakland outplayed them 32-14 in Super Bowl XI.

The Cowboys were back in 1977, easily disposing of Denver 27-10, and in the following year faced Pittsburgh in a rematch of Super Bowl X. In a 66-point spectacular, the Steelers held on despite a late 14-point Cowboy rally to win 35-31. Pittsburgh went on to register their fourth win in as many appearances and, by sheer nerve, overcame a brave Los Angeles Rams 31-19.

Super Bowl XV was the comeback story of the year as quarterback Jim Plunkett who had lain discarded for over two years, led the Raiders to a 27-10 triumph over the Philadelphia Eagles. There were two new teams in Super Bowl XVI when the surprising 49ers beat Cincinnati 26-21 to take home San Francisco's first ever Championship in any major professional sport.

United Kingdom television viewers had the pleasure of watching as the courageous Redskins, with not a little help from John Riggins, came from behind three times to overcome Miami 27-17 in Super Bowl XVII.

The year 1982 will be forever remembered for the 57-day players' strike in support of their claim to a half share of the new television windfall which guarantees each club $75,000,000 over five years (double their revenue from all other sources). By its end, seven weeks of the regular season had been lost and although salaries and benefits had improved substantially, it was by little more than had been offered, even before the season began. Still, in this electronic age there aren't many openings for a 20-stone lineman, and most of the players were glad to go back to work.

One loses count of the rival organisations which have challenged the NFL over the past 63 years. In the summer of 1983 the United States Football League is playing its eighteen-week schedule. Being a Spring-Summer League, of course 'there would be no competition with the NFL', but all that went out of the window when the USFL drafted a bucketful of top college players, including the most glittering jewel of all, Georgia's Herschel Walker.

The more things change, the more they stay the same . . .

CHAPTER 3
CHAMPIONS 1921-82

National Football League
1921-69 *(Until 1932 based solely on regular season play)*

1921 Chicago Staleys
1922 Canton Bulldogs
1923 Canton Bulldogs
1924 Cleveland Bulldogs
1925 Chicago Cardinals
1926 Frankford Yellowjackets
1927 New York Giants
1928 Providence Steamroller
1929 Green Bay Packers
1930 Green Bay Packers
1931 Green Bay Packers

The Canton Bulldogs, NFL Champions in 1922: Roy Lyman, B. Guy Chamberlin, Louis Smythe, Joe Williams, Cecil Griggs, Ben Jones, Wilbur Henry, Larry Conover, Harry Robb, Norman Speck, Rudolph Comstock, Wallace Elliot, Robert Osborne, Oscar Hendrian, Elmer Carroll and Walcott Roberts.

1932	Chicago Bears 9 Portsmouth Spartans 0	1951	Los Angeles Rams 24 Cleveland Browns 17
1933	Chicago Bears 23 New York Giants 21	1952	Detroit Lions 17 Cleveland Browns 7
1934	New York Giants 30 Chicago Bears 13	1953	Detroit Lions 17 Cleveland Browns 16
1935	Detroit Lions 26 New York Giants 7	1954	Cleveland Browns 56 Detroit Lions 10
1936	Green Bay Packers 21 Boston Braves 6	1955	Cleveland Browns 38 Los Angeles Rams 14
1937	Washington Redskins 28 Chicago Bears 21	1956	New York Giants 47 Chicago Bears 7
1938	New York Giants 23 Green Bay Packers 17	1957	Detroit Lions 59 Cleveland Browns 14
1939	Green Bay Packers 27 New York Giants 0	1958	Baltimore Colts 23 New York Giants 17
1940	Chicago Bears 73 Washington Redskins 0	1959	Baltimore Colts 31 New York Giants 16
1941	Chicago Bears 37 New York Giants 9	1960	Philadelphia Eagles 17 Green Bay Packers 13
1942	Washington Redskins 14 Chicago Bears 6	1961	Green Bay Packers 37 New York Giants 0
1943	Chicago Bears 41 Washington Redskins 21	1962	Green Bay Packers 16 New York Giants 7
1944	Green Bay Packers 14 New York Giants 7	1963	Chicago Bears 14 New York Giants 10
1945	Cleveland Rams 15 Washington Redskins 14	1964	Cleveland Browns 27 Baltimore Colts 0
1946	Chicago Bears 24 New York Giants 14	1965	Green Bay Packers 23 Cleveland Browns 12
1947	Chicago Cardinals 28 Philadelphia Eagles 21	1966	Green Bay Packers 34 Dallas Cowboys 27
1948	Philadelphia Eagles 7 Chicago Cardinals 0	1967	Green Bay Packers 21 Dallas Cowboys 17
1949	Philadelphia Eagles 14 Los Angeles Rams 0	1968	Baltimore Colts 34 Cleveland Browns 0
1950	Cleveland Browns 30 Los Angeles Rams 28	1969	Minnesota Vikings 27 Cleveland Browns 7

American Football League 1960-69

1960	Houston Oilers 24 Los Angeles Chargers 16		1965	Buffalo Bills 23 San Diego Chargers 0
1961	Houston Oilers 10 San Diego Chargers 3		1966	Kansas City Chiefs 31 Buffalo Bills 7
1962	Dallas Texans 20 Houston Oilers 17		1967	Oakland Raiders 40 Houston Oilers 7
1963	San Diego Chargers 51 Boston Patriots 10		1968	New York Jets 27 Oakland Raiders 23
1964	Buffalo Bills 20 San Diego Chargers 7		1969	Kansas City Chiefs 17 Oakland Raiders 7

Conference Champions 1970-82

NFC

1970	Dallas Cowboys 17 San Francisco 49ers 10
1971	Dallas Cowboys 14 San Francisco 49ers 3
1972	Washington Redskins 26 Dallas Cowboys 3
1973	Minnesota Vikings 27 Dallas Cowboys 10
1974	Minnesota Vikings 14 Los Angeles Rams 10
1975	Dallas Cowboys 37 Los Angeles Rams 7
1976	Minnesota Vikings 24 Los Angeles Rams 13
1977	Dallas Cowboys 23 Minnesota Vikings 6
1978	Dallas Cowboys 28 Los Angeles Rams 0
1979	Los Angeles Rams 9 Tampa Bay Buccaneers 0
1980	Philadelphia Eagles 20 Dallas Cowboys 7
1981	San Francisco 49ers 28 Dallas Cowboys 27
1982	Washington Redskins 31 Dallas Cowboys 17

AFC

1970	Baltimore Colts 27 Oakland Raiders 17
1971	Miami Dolphins 21 Baltimore Colts 0
1972	Miami Dolphins 21 Pittsburgh Steelers 17
1973	Miami Dolphins 27 Oakland Raiders 10
1974	Pittsburgh Steelers 24 Oakland Raiders 13
1975	Pittsburgh Steelers 16 Oakland Raiders 10
1976	Oakland Raiders 24 Pittsburgh Steelers 7
1977	Denver Broncos 20 Oakland Raiders 17
1978	Pittsburgh Steelers 34 Houston Oilers 5
1979	Pittsburgh Steelers 27 Houston Oilers 13
1980	Oakland Raiders 34 San Diego Chargers 27
1981	Cincinnati Bengals 27 San Diego Chargers 7
1982	Miami Dolphins 14 New York Jets 0

Super Bowl 1966-82

SB	Winner		Loser		Stadium	Attendance
I	Green Bay	35	Kansas City	10	Los Angeles Coliseum	61,946
II	Green Bay	33	Oakland	14	Miami Orange Bowl	75,546
III	New York Jets	16	Baltimore	7	Miami Orange Bowl	75,389
IV	Kansas City	23	Minnesota	7	New Orleans Tulane Stadium	80,562
V	Baltimore	16	Dallas	13	Miami Orange Bowl	79,204
VI	Dallas	24	Miami	3	New Orleans Tulane Stadium	81,023
VII	Miami	14	Washington	7	Los Angeles Coliseum	90,182
VIII	Miami	24	Minnesota	7	Houston Rice Stadium	71,882
IX	Pittsburgh	16	Minnesota	6	New Orleans Tulane Stadium	80,997
X	Pittsburgh	21	Dallas	17	Miami Orange Bowl	80,187
XI	Oakland	32	Minnesota	14	Pasadena Rose Bowl	103,438
XII	Dallas	27	Denver	10	New Orleans Superdome	75,583
XIII	Pittsburgh	35	Dallas	31	Miami Orange Bowl	79,484
XIV	Pittsburgh	31	Los Angeles Rams	19	Pasadena Rose Bowl	103,985
XV	Oakland	27	Philadelphia	10	New Orleans Superdome	76,135
XVI	San Francisco	26	Cincinnati	21	Pontiac Silverdome	81,270
XVII	Washington	27	Miami	17	Pasadena Rose Bowl	103,667

CHAPTER 4
HOW THE
SEASON WORKS

The National Football League consists of twenty-eight teams divided equally into two Conferences, the American Football Conference (AFC) and the National Football Conference (NFC). Each of these is subdivided into three Divisions on a geographical basis.

AFC

Western Division	Central Division	Eastern Division
Denver Broncos	Cincinnati Bengals	Baltimore Colts
Kansas City Chiefs	Cleveland Browns	Buffalo Bills
*Los Angeles Raiders	Houston Oilers	Miami Dolphins
San Diego Chargers	Pittsburgh Steelers	New England Patriots
Seattle Seahawks		New York Jets

*Prior to the 1982 season, Los Angeles Raiders were known as the Oakland Raiders.

NFC

Western Division	Central Division	Eastern Division
Atlanta Falcons	Chicago Bears	Dallas Cowboys
Los Angeles Rams	Detroit Lions	Philadelphia Eagles
New Orleans Saints	Green Bay Packers	St. Louis Cardinals
San Francisco 49ers	Minnesota Vikings	New York Giants
	Tampa Bay Buccaneers	Washington Redskins

The Schedule (Fixture List)

A team plays home and away against each team in its own Division, the balance of the schedule being made up of games against teams within its own Conference together with two to four against teams from the rival Conference. In all, sixteen regular season games are played.

The schedule, which in part is determined by the results of the previous season, is not quite so haphazard as might appear. Indeed it has been carefully designed to allow for the inter-

Conference games on a rotating basis whilst maintaining, as far as possible, a common schedule for teams from the same Division. Thus, teams placed first and fourth (in order of merit from the previous season) face a full sixteen common opponents, though whilst one may play, say the Packers at home, the other might play away. The same is true for the second and third placed teams. Additionally, all four teams will play at least twelve common opponents. The bottom team in a five-team Division is given a little help in that it is guaranteed home and away games against the other fifth placed team in its own Conference plus one game with each of the fifth placed teams from the rival Conference. In this sense its schedule is less severe and reflects the NFL policy of trying to bring together evenly matched teams.

A typical schedule, that of Pittsburgh Steelers for the 1983 season, appears below.

Pittsburgh Steelers (AFC Central Division)

4 Sept	DENVER	AFC West
11 Sept	at Green Bay	NFC Central
18 Sept	at Houston	AFC Central
25 Sept	NEW ENGLAND	AFC East
2 Oct	HOUSTON	AFC Central
10 Oct	at Cincinnati	AFC Central
16 Oct	CLEVELAND	AFC Central
23 Oct	at Seattle	AFC West
30 Oct	TAMPA BAY	NFC Central
6 Nov	SAN DIEGO	AFC West
13 Nov	at Baltimore	AFC West
20 Nov	MINNESOTA	NFC Central
24 Nov	at Detroit	NFC Central
4 Dec	CINCINNATI	AFC Central
10 Dec	at New York Jets	AFC East
18 Dec	at Cleveland	AFC Central

The Schedule is summarised as follows:

Six games within the Division
Three games against teams from the AFC Eastern Division
Three games against teams from the AFC Western Division
Four games against teams from the NFC Central Division

The overall structure of their 1984 schedule will differ only in that their four inter-Conference games will be against teams from tne NFC Western Division and in 1985 they will play the NFC Eastern Division.

There are very few drawn games (ties) in the regular season since, if the scores are level at the end of normal time, the teams play a fifteen-minute period of 'sudden death' overtime in which the team scoring first, wins. If however there is no scoring during this period, the result is a tie (draw).

In playoff games the teams play periods of 'sudden death' overtime until one of them scores.

The Playoffs

On completion of the regular seaon, each Conference holds an elimination competition. The teams involved in this are the three Division winners together with the winner of the Wild Card game, contested by those two teams who, other than the Division winners, have the best playing records. The so-called playoffs produce two Conference Champions who go at it in the Super Bowl for the NFL Championship, and with it the Vince Lombardi Trophy.

Last season (1982) was ruined by the players' strike, and only nine of the sixteen games were played. The playoff series too was a hastily arranged affair, and as a consequence it makes good sense to refer back to the results of the 1981 season for illustration of the way the system normally works. The final standings then for the AFC were as listed below:

Eastern	W	L	D	Central	W	L	D	Western	W	L	D
Miami	11	4	1	Cincinnati	12	4	0	San Diego	10	6	0
New York Jets	10	5	1	Pittsburgh	8	8	0	Denver	10	6	0
Buffalo	10	6	0	Houston	7	9	0	Kansas City	9	7	0
Baltimore	2	14	0	Cleveland	5	11	0	Oakland	7	9	0
New England	2	14	0					Seattle	6	10	0

Miami and Cincinnati advance to the playoffs as clear Division winners. However, in the West there is the problem of discriminating between San Diego and Denver (who have identical 10-6 records) for the Division Championship. Before leaping into this, it is appropriate to point out that it is often necessary to separate two teams within the same Conference. For this, reference is made to one of two sets of criteria, depending on whether the two teams are from the same Division or from different Divisions. These criteria are listed below and known as Tie-Breaking Procedures.

A: Two Teams From The Same Division

1. Head-to-head (best record in games played between the two clubs)
2. Best record in games played within the Division
3. Best record in games played within the Conference
4. Best record in common games
5. Best net points scored in Division games
(just like goal difference in soccer)
6. Best net points in all games

B: Two Teams From Different Divisions

1. Head-to-head (best record in games played between the two clubs)
2. Best record in games played within the Conference
3. Best net points in all games
4. Best net touchdowns in all games

Firstly the San Diego-Denver problem, for which we consult the criteria listed under A since the teams are from *the same* Division.

1. Head-to-head: In the regular season, each team won one of the two games played between the clubs. Separation is not possible on this basis, hence we move to number 2.
2. Best record in games within the Division: San Diego's record in Division games was 6-2, whereas Denver's was 5-3. The tie is broken. In particular, San Diego was named Division Champions and advance to the the playoffs.

We still need to identify the two teams which will contest the Wild Card game, to produce the fourth playoff team. A 10-5-1 record is better than a 10-6-0 and means that New York will be one of the teams. To discriminate between Buffalo and Denver (identical 10-6-0 records), we consult the criteria listed under B since the two are from *different* Divisions.

1. Head-to-head: Buffalo beat Denver on the only occasion they met during the regular season and therefore become the other Wild Card team. (It really wasn't Denver's year!)

Playoff Results

Wild Card Game:	Buffalo 31	New York 27
Conference Semi-Finals:	San Diego 41	Miami 38
	Cincinnati 27	Buffalo 21
Conference Championship:	Cincinnati 27	San Diego 7

Cincinnati advance to the Super Bowl as AFC Champions.

The Super Bowl is often compared with the Football Association Cup Final in England, but clearly this is an oversimplification. True, the Super Bowl is the culmination of an elimination competition, and yet the teams involved are those who have demonstrated their consistency by establishing near enough the best regular season records.

Unlike the Cup Final, which is always played in the same stadium, the Super Bowl venue changes from year to year, and

Tampa Bay Stadium – site of Super Bowl XVIII.

since the site is chosen three years in advance, it is possible for one of the teams to be playing at home. In the selection of the location, clearly the financial potential is involved, but it is of perhaps greater importance that the spectacle should not be marred by sub-zero weather conditions. Stadia in the states of California, Florida and Louisiana, together with those which are completely enclosed, are ideal for the purpose.

The All Pro Team

The major periodicals and news services (A.P. and U.P.I.) each produce what they consider to be the best team selected from the whole League. There is little variance in these and few would argue with the squad listed below.

Wide Receivers	Wes Chandler	San Diego
	James Lofton	Green Bay
Tight End	Kellen Winslow	San Diego
Tackles	Anthony Munoz	Cincinnati
	Marvin Powell	N.Y. Jets
Guards	John Hannah	New England
	R. C. Thielemann	Atlanta
Center	Mike Webster	Pittsburgh
Quarterback	Ken Anderson	Cincinnati
Running Backs	Earl Campbell	Houston
	Tony Dorsett	Dallas
Defensive Ends	Mark Gastineau	N.Y. Jets
	Lee Roy Selmon	Tampa Bay
Defensive Tackles	Randy White	Dallas
	Dan Hampton	Chicago
Outside Linebackers	Ted Hendricks	L.A. Raiders
	Robert Brazile	Houston
Middle Linebacker	Randy Gradishar	Denver
Cornerbacks	Lester Hayes	L.A. Raiders
	Everson Walls	Dallas
Safeties	Nolan Cromwell	L.A. Rams
	Kenny Easley	Seattle
Punter	Luke Prestridge	Denver
Kicker	Rafael Septien	Dallas
Punt Returner	Rick Upchurch	Denver
Kick Returner	Mike Nelms	Washington

The Pro Bowl

At the end of each season, representative teams from the two Conferences play the Pro Bowl game, at a location selected less for its Football fervour than the hospitality of its hotels and beaches. The team rosters emerge from a poll involving the players, coaches, administrators and sports journalists, and of course represent the very best players from each Conference. The players involved in last year's Pro Bowl (1982), played in Hawaii, are listed opposite

Right Joe Theismann setting up to pass in the 1982 Pro Bowl. Other players (wearing their club helmets) are: Tony Dorsett (33, Cowboys), Larry McCarren (54, Packers), Kent Hill (71, Rams) and Jimmie Giles (88, Buccaneers).

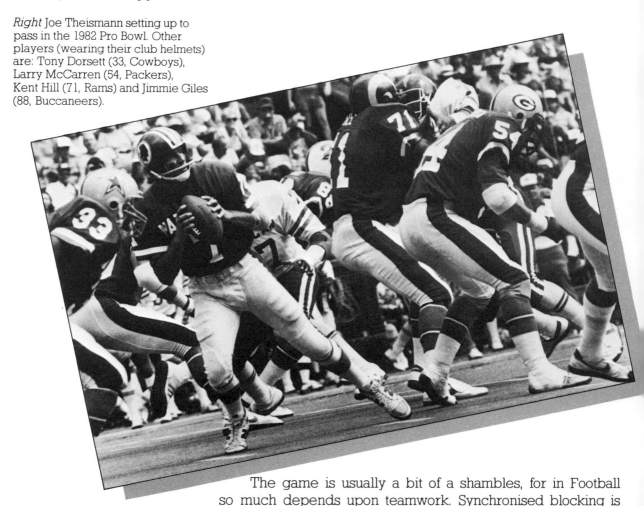

The game is usually a bit of a shambles, for in Football so much depends upon teamwork. Synchronised blocking is markedly absent, and with receivers running unfamiliar pass routes, receptions too are few. Thankfully though, the heavies do pull their punches and injuries, too, are few in a jamboree worth seeing, for everyone has his dream team. With last year's 20-19 win, the NFC maintained its lead with eight victories to the AFC's five.

	AFC		NFC	
Wide Receivers	Wes Chandler	San Diego	James Lofton	Green Bay
	Cris Collinsworth	Cincinnati	Dwight Clark	San Francisco
	Wesley Walker	N.Y. Jets	Charlie Brown	Washington
	John Stallworth	Pittsburgh	John Jefferson	Green Bay
Tight Ends	Kellen Winslow	San Diego	Jimmie Giles	Tampa Bay
	Dan Ross	Cincinnati	Paul Coffman	Green Bay
Tackles	Anthony Munoz	Cincinnati	Mike Kenn	Atlanta
	Marvin Powell	N.Y. Jets	Pat Donovan	Dallas
	Larry Brown	Pittsburgh	Keith Dorney	Detroit
Guards	John Hannah	New England	R. C. Thielemann	Atlanta
	Doug Wilkerson	San Diego	Randy Cross	San Francisco
	Ed Newman	Miami	Kent Hill	L. A. Rams
Centers	Mike Webster	Pittsburgh	Jeff Van Note	Atlanta
	Joe Fields	N.Y. Jets	Larry McCarren	Green Bay
Quarterbacks	Dan Fouts	San Diego	Joe Theismann	Washington
	Ken Anderson	Cincinnati	Danny White	Dallas
Running Backs	Marcus Allen	L. A. Raiders	William Andrews	Atlanta
	Freeman McNeil	N.Y. Jets	Tony Dorsett	Dallas
	Andra Franklin	Miami	Billy Sims	Detroit
	Chuck Muncie	San Diego	George Rogers	New Orleans
Defensive Ends	Mark Gastineau	N.Y. Jets	Lee Roy Selmon	Tampa Bay
	Art Still	Kansas City	Ed Jones	Dallas
	Ben Williams	Buffalo	Dennis Harrison	Philadelphia
Defensive Tackles	Fred Smerlas	Buffalo	Randy White	Dallas
	Gary Johnson	San Diego	Doug English	Detroit
	Bob Baumhower	Miami	Dan Hampton	Chicago
Outside Linebackers	Ted Hendricks	L.A. Raiders	Lawrence Taylor	N.Y. Giants
	Rober Brazile	Houston	Hugh Green	Tampa Bay
	Chip Banks	Cleveland	Matt Blair	Minnesota
Middle Linebackers	Jack Lambert	Pittsburgh	Harry Carson	N.Y. Giants
	Randy Gradishar	Denver	Bob Breunig	Dallas
Cornerbacks	Mike Haynes	New England	Everson Walls	Dallas
	Lester Hayes	L.A. Raiders	Mark Haynes	N.Y. Giants
	Gary Green	Kansas City	Ronnie Lott	San Francisco
Safeties	Donnie Shell	Pittsburgh	Nolan Cromwell	L.A. Rams
	Gary Barbaro	Kansas City	Tony Peters	Washington
	Kenny Easley	Seattle	Dwight Hicks	San Francisco
Punter	Luke Prestridge	Denver	Dave Jennings	N.Y. Giants
Kicker	Rolf Benirschke	San Diego	Mark Moseley	Washington
Kick Returner	Rick Upchurch	Denver	Mike Nelms	Washington

CHAPTER 5
THE YEAR OF THE REDSKINS

In 1981, under new Head Coach Joe Gibbs, Washington lost their first five games before coming back strongly to end the season with an 8-8 record. Several times in the past they had come close, but not since 1942 had they won an outright Championship . . .

In the 1982 season opener, the Redskins needed a field goal in overtime by Mark Moseley to beat Philadelphia 37-34 in a wild one. Yet their form of late 1981 was confirmed – the complexities of Gibbs's offensive system had been mastered. Over in the rival Conference, Don Shula's Miami dispatched an error-prone New York Jets 45-28.

In week two, alarm bells around the League began to ring as John Riggins racked up 136 rushing yards, powering the Redskins to a 21-13 victory over Tampa Bay. Surprisingly the Dolphins had trouble with Baltimore who led for some time before going under 24-20 to a Vigorito touchdown. The teams were even, each with two wins, as the shutters went up and the players drifted into what would be a 57-day strike.

The Redskins resumed with another victory as quarterback Joe Theismann systematically picked away at the Giants, who were on the wrong end of a 27-17 result. First it had been Moseley, then Riggins and now Theismann – the 'Skins were beginning to look genuine. Miami too continued to roll although needing a late von Schamann field goal to beat Buffalo 9-7.

The Redskins drove on, completing the double over Philadelphia 12-7, to remain the only undefeated team in the entire NFL. The Dolphins had succumbed to Tampa Bay, largely against an unremitting rushing offense. It was this weakness, this unresolved puzzle, which was to bedevil Bill Arnsparger, the doyen of defensive stategists, to the very end.

For Miami, game five against a pass-happy Minnesota was no problem as their defensive backs gleefully intercepted three Tommy Kramer passes in a 22-14 victory. But in Washington there was a resounding thump as the Redskins came down to earth, losing 24-10 to the Cowboys, who make a habit of treating this particular fixture with some seriousness.

John Riggins (44) gets going, supported by George Starke (74) for Washington Redskins against Detroit in a 21-19 victory.

It was a more circumspect Washington squad which held
on to win close games, firstly against St Louis 12-7 and then the
Giants 15-14, in weeks six and seven. On the way, Mark Moseley
established an NFL record of 21 consecutive field goals, a
sequence he was to extend to 23. Miami, with the help of a
last-second field goal, again beat the Jets, but before this had lost
to New England in the most bizarre of circumstances. On a
snow-covered pitch and in a game nicknamed 'The Snow Bowl',
the teams were scoreless as John Smith of New England came
out to attempt a late field goal. At Coach Meyer's behest Mark
Henderson, a convicted burglar on day release from the local

'pen', drove his snow plough onto the pitch, clearing away the snow for Smith's game-winning kick. The rulemakers had made no allowance for this (they quickly did) and the score had to stand. With incredulity, but in the manner of the gentleman he is, Shula accepted the result without complaint.

Now assured of reaching the playoffs, both teams needed to complete the season free from injury. The Redskins, having regrouped, loosened up to beat New Orleans 27-10 and then the Cardinals, 28-0, with astonishing ease. Miami too were impressive, overcoming a ten-point deficit to beat Buffalo 27-10, before hammering the luckless Colts 34-7.

The Playoffs

The jubilation of Washington's entry into the playoffs was soured by the loss of their ace wide receiver, Art Monk. He was replaced by the diminutive Alvin Garrett, who had spent most of his three-year career watching from the sidelines – one remembers asking: 'Alvin who?'. He replied with three touchdowns as the Lions fumbled, stumbled and finally were humbled 31-7 out of the competition. Minnesota fell 21-7 to a display of awesome rushing power by the man himself, John Riggins. For good measure, Garrett chipped in with touchdown number four. Then the Cowboys. Riggins again firstly bruised then dented and eventually destroyed the finest defensive line in Football, whilst from the sideline, an injured Danny White of Dallas could only watch through tears, more of frustration than pain, as the young Gary Hogeboom threw the interceptions which lost the title game 27-17.

In the AFC, Miami avenged their 'Snow Bowl' defeat, beating New England 28-13 in quarterback David Woodley's most impressive showing to date. Then another score was settled – the epic 1981 playoff loss – as Miami finally came good. Tony Nathan dismembered the Charger defense whilst an embarrassing five pass interceptions asphyxiated the Dan Fouts – Wes Chandler passing axis. It takes the very best to beat San Diego 34-13. In the Championship game, Miami linebacker A. J. Duhe held the fort whilst his offense scored fourteen unanswered points as the Dolphins beat the Jets for the third time in the season.

The Super Bowl

Miami spent the days leading up to the game as favourites to win by three points. It was argued that good coaching and disciplined

Jack Kent Cook, the Redskins' owner, with Joe Theismann and a smiling John Riggins after the thrilling victory in Super Bowl XVII.

application would be enough to counter the likes of Theismann, Riggins, Alvin Who?, an offensive line ('The Hogs') which lacked big game experience and a defense which was noticeably short of pace. An offense based on the rushing of Franklin and Nathan would score just enough points for the 'Killer Bees', Bokamper, Baumhower, Betters, Brudzinski and the brothers Blackwood, to defend. But Miami, too, had weaknesses: possibly the passing offense and definitely in defense against the rush.

The first score came literally out of the blue which had replaced the Rose Bowl's grey skies. David Woodley found Jimmy Cefalo, cutting in from the right, with a pass for a 76-yard touchdown for the Dolphins (0-7). Undeterred, the Redskins fought back, but Moseley's field goal was quickly matched by his opposite number von Schamann (3-10). Again the Redskins came back with an Alvin Who? touchdown (his fifth in the playoffs) to level the score 10-10, with less than two minutes until half time. What followed on the very next play would have broken the spirits of lesser men. After a quick fade to the left behind two key blockers, Fulton Walker sliced through the Redskin special team, now in total disarray, returning the kickoff 98 yards for the Super Bowl's longest ever touchdown play (10-17). At half time the Washington squad, still in a state of shock, headed for the locker room knowing that, for the third time, they would have to come from behind.

Unlike many running backs, John Riggins thrives on hard work – he gains strength as the game wears on – and this was never more apparent than in the third quarter as he repeatedly steam-hammered the Dolphin line, now beginning to buckle. Moseley's second field goal narrowed the deficit to four points (13-17). With only ten minutes remaining and on a do-or-die 4th down play (4th and 1), it was in the best traditions of this noble game when Riggins smashed over left tackle before sweeping down the sideline for the 43-yard touchdown which carried Washington into the lead (20-17). Joe Theismann connected with Charlie Brown for the touchdown which put the game beyond doubt at 27-17.

It was with his own brand of 'Rigginomics' that the big man, this one-time malcontent, had carried the three-point underdogs to a famous ten-point victory. His 166 yards on 38 attempts, including a 43-yard touchdown run, established three Super Bowl records, earned him the title of Most Valuable Player and his own special place in the annals of the game.

CHAPTER 6

A FOOTBALL MISCELLANY

Television Football

The armchair fan has never had it so good. Every Sunday, complete with magazines and a dozen beers ready and waiting in the refrigerator, he can settle down to seven hours of viewing, confident that he won't miss a thing. Between them, CBS and NBC have their cameras at every game and at convenient moments will switch to the network centre for the best action from around the League. ABC pioneered the novelty of the 'Monday Night' game in 1970. With their own unique styles, Frank 'The Giff' Gifford (former Giants) is the 'straight man' whilst Howard Cosell interjects with his controversial comments. In between, 'Dandy' Don Meredith (former Cowboys) cracks a few jokes, sings the odd song, and then makes the point that everyone else has missed. It's a lovely way to forget the Monday blues.

The real 'nuts' have their mates dotted around the nation, videotaping every game, and by the following weekend they will have viewed 42 hours of Football. Of course during the week, there are the post-game analyses, game previews, highlights from the past, Super Bowl repeats. And we must not forget six hours of college football every Saturday. Yet despite this saturation TV coverage, attendances average 60,000 per game, with over 95% of all tickets sold. There is one minuscule concession Football makes to TV. After a time-out, play does not restart until the adverts have been completed. This naturally upsets some purists but it involves a mere 20-seconds or so wait for the fans actually at the game.

Amazingly there remain the detractors of television, who choose to ignore the fact that, by subtle camera positioning, the home-viewer sees far more than he possibly could by being in the crowd. Occasionally, even the excellent officials are caught out and there is the distinct possibility that the 1980s will see the use of instant replays in adjudicating crucial plays where the official is unsighted. This is not American gimmickry reducing referees to gadget-laden robots – similar aids are being suggested for umpires in the conservative game of cricket.

Needless to say, the Super Bowl is the television highlight of

the year. Eighty-five technicians operating fifteen video machines and twenty cameras, not to mention the air crew of the Goodyear Blimp, bring the picture not only to 112 million viewers (half the population) in the USA but to the rest of the world.

In case you were wondering, a TV commercial during the Super Bowl costs one million dollars a minute.

Salaries

One thing to emerge from the 1982 strike was an incremental salary scale starting at $30,000 and rising in lumps to a maximum after eighteen years of $200,000. Very few will remain on this basic scale but rather they negotiate individual contracts with the owners. The actual amounts aren't exactly posted on a bulletin board but it is well known that a top running back, such as Chicago's Walter Payton, who will gain 1000 rushing yards in a year, earns $600,000. This breaks down to $37,500 a game, or $600 for every yard gained, and he gains on average four yards ($2,400) every time he touches the ball. This is in addition to his income from other sources. Indeed all the stars have their fast-food chains, real estate businesses, health centres and the like. A player on a successful Super Bowl squad earns an extra $72,000 for a mere three playoff games – and if he is not a first-stringer he might not even get on to the field.

The Head Coaches do less well, earning around $300,000 of the $1.5 million it costs to pay a coaching staff of twelve.

Mob Names

Monsters Of The Midway – Chicago Bears of the early thirties
The Fearsome Foursome – Successive Los Angeles Ram defensive lines
Doomsday Defense – Dallas Cowboys defense of the late sixties
The Over The Hill Gang – Washington Redskins team of the early seventies
The No Name Defense – Miami Dolphins defensive squad of the early seventies
The Purple Gang – Minnesota Vikings defensive line of the early seventies
The Electric Company – Buffalo Bills offensive line of the early seventies
The Steel Curtain – Pittsburgh Steeler defensive line of 1974-1979
The 'Aints – New Orleans Saints after losing the first fourteen games of 1980

Above Walter 'Sweetness' Payton, of Chicago Bears
Below Pittsburgh's 'Steel Curtain' taking instructions from Jack Lambert (58).

The Orange Crush – Denver Broncos defensive line of 1977
Air Coryell and The Air Force – San Diego's current passing offense
The Killer Bees – Miami Dolphin defense in 1982
The Hogs – Washington Redskins offensive line
The Smurfs – Washington Redskins pass receivers
The Crunch Bunch – New York Giants linebackers
The New York Sack Exchange – New York Jets defensive linemen

Player Nicknames

Old Timers

Harold 'Red' Grange, Chicago Bears, 1920s
Bronislau 'Bronko' Nagurski, Chicago Bears, 1920s and 1930s
Earle 'Greasy' Neale, Canton Bulldogs, 1920s
Elroy 'Crazy Legs' Hirsch, Los Angeles Rams, 1950s
Dick 'Night Train' Lane, Los Angeles Rams, 1950s
David 'The Deacon' Jones, Los Angeles Rams, 1960s
Daryle 'The Mad Bomber' Lamonica, Oakland Raiders, 1960s
'Dandy' Don Meredith, Dallas Cowboys, 1960s
'Broadway' Joe Namath, New York Jets, 1960s
'Mean' Joe Greene, Pittsburgh Steelers, 1970s
O. J. 'The Juice' Simpson, Buffalo Bills, 1970s
Roger 'The Dodger' Staubach, Dallas Cowboys, 1970s
Jack 'Monster Man' Tatum, Oakland Raiders, 1970s
Alonzo 'Dr Death' Thomas, Oakland Raiders, 1970s

Active Players

Billy 'White Shoes' Johnson, Atlanta
Walter 'Sweetness' Payton, Chicago
Ed 'Too Tall' Jones, Dallas
Harvey 'Too Mean' Martin, Dallas
Earl 'The Hammer' Campbell, Houston
Robert 'Dr Doom' Brazile, Houston
Ted 'Mad Stork' Hendricks, L.A. Raiders
Vascero Diaz 'Vagas' Ferguson, New England
Ken 'The Snake' Stabler, New Orleans
Johnny 'Lam' Jones, New York Jets
Ron 'The Polish Rifle' Jaworski, Philadelphia
Lyvonia 'Stump' Mitchell, St. Louis
Gary 'Big Hands' Johnson, San Diego
Jack 'Hacksaw' Reynolds, San Francisco
Joe 'Big Sky' Montana, San Francisco

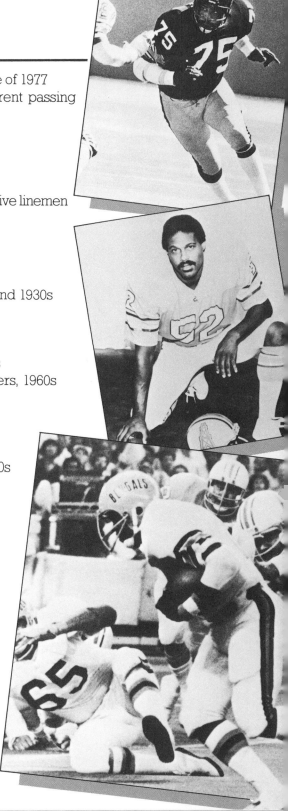

Left top 'Mean' Joe Greene of Pittsburgh Steelers.
Left centre Robert 'Dr Doom' Brazille of Houston Oilers.
Below Brazille returns an interception.
Bottom 'Dr Doom' homes in.

The Coldest Game

Until 1982 it was generally accepted that the coldest game had been the famous 'Ice Bowl' in 1967, when Green Bay beat Dallas 21-17 with a last second touchdown run by Bart Starr to win the NFL Championship. But by comparison with the Cincinnati-San Diego AFC Championship game in 1982, the −20°C of the 'Ice Bowl' would have been sub-tropical. Wind chill helped bring the temperature down to −35°C; the Chargers were used to San Diego's 27°C. Fans were passing out, the ball was like a heavy brick, and Ken Anderson, Cincinnati's quarterback, was frost-bitten in one ear. Not surprisingly, the Bengals won 27-7.

The Longest Game

When the playoffs are reached, the NFL does not mess around with replays. The teams have to play to a finish. In 1971 Miami defeated Kansas City 27-24 with a field goal, 7 minutes and 40 seconds into the second period of overtime. The whole game took 82 minutes and 40 seconds, easily the longest on record.

The Closest Super Bowl

At the Orange Bowl in 1971, the scores were level with 5 seconds remaining as Jim O'Brien (a rookie) addressed the ball for a field goal attempt from the Dallas 25-yard line. His 32-yard kick gave Baltimore a 16-13 victory over Dallas to win Super Bowl V.

The Shortest Pass

In the Dallas-Washington game in 1960, on a play two inches from the Washington goal line, Eddie LeBaron dropped back and tossed a three-yard touchdown pass to Dick Bielski. But since all scoring plays are measured from the original line of scrimmage, the pass was a two-incher, the shortest on record.

Most Embarrassing Moment

It is the ultimate achievement of his career if a defensive lineman can recover an opponent's fumble and take it into the end zone for a touchdown. On 16 October 1964, Jim Marshall of the Minnesota Vikings got his chance. Barely pausing to gather the ball after a Bill Kilmer fumble and after a quick glance to the end zone, 66 yards away, he made his run for that glorious touchdown. The trouble is he didn't realise he was running the wrong way and ended up conceding a two point safety to the opposition. Fortunately for him his team beat the 49ers 27-22.

CHAPTER 7

HEROES OF THE GRIDIRON

It would take volumes to do justice to the many heroes who have graced Football. Here are but seven, together with my reasons for their selection.

(1) 'Red' Grange was the personality of the 1920s whose involvement gave enormous impetus to the professional movement.

(2) Sammy Baugh was instrumental in the transition from the running and sometimes passing 'tailback' to the passing and sometimes running 'quarterback'.

(3) Don Hutson made an art form out of pass receiving.

(4) Elroy Hirsch showed that the 'bomb' pass could be a standard form of offense.

(5) Jim Brown was the best running back.

(6) O. J. Simpson was nearly the best running back.

(7) George Blanda kicked field goals and threw touchdown passes for 26 years.

Harold Edward 'Red' Grange (Chicago Bears, 1925, 1929-34, N.Y. Yankees 1926-27)

The college hero with the shock of flame-coloured hair attracted the crowds in their hundreds of thousands to see him play Pro Football. 'Red' Grange first came to national prominence as a junior (third year student) at the University of Illinois. On 24 October 1924, when they met the Michigan Wolverines, he produced his most awesome performance. In response to coach 'Hurry Up' Yost, who had boasted that he had the answer to this upstart running back, he returned the opening kickoff 95 yards for a touchdown, following which there were to be three more of 67, 56 and 44 yards – the only occasions he touched the ball and still in the first quarter. He was replaced for the second quarter but returned later to rush for a fifth touchdown and throw for a sixth. Hitherto he had been known locally as 'The Wheaton Iceman', or plainly as 'Red', but it was after this staggering display that Grantland Rice, the most respected sports journalist of the day, was moved to eulogise him as 'The Galloping Ghost', and the name stuck.

Already touched with immortality he left college a year

A pensive Red Grange in 1932.

later, already under the wing of an agent, C. C. 'Cash and Carry' Pyle, who saw to it that he would play for George Halas's Bears for $5,000 a game or half the gate receipts, whichever was the greater – they took the 'gate'. By the season's end it was confirmed that he was eminently marketable, though it was equally clear that he would never approach the standards he had established in college. Nonetheless the people loved him and the Bears embarked on a nationwide tour of eighteen games, squeezed into six short weeks. The adoring fans flocked in and the 70,000 which had turned up in New York were matched 3000 miles away in Los Angeles and finally, up the Pacific coast in Seattle.

At this stage Grange was a physical wreck but the well-earned rest was still some way off, for 'C.C.' had other plans (he was raking in one third of everything). There would be a movie, *One Minute to Play*, and endorsements covering everything from cars to candy bars. The movie alone brought in $500,000 – the modern Pros are only now approaching earnings of this size.

After a contractual disagreement with the Bears (Pyle and Grange wanted half ownership of the team), Pyle took Grange to New York in an abortive attempt to form a new league, but by 1927 he was back in the NFL, now playing for Pyle's Yankees. Against the Bears he suffered a (non-contact) knee injury which banished for ever any illusions of invincibility. He spent 1928 recuperating and appearing on the vaudeville circuit before playing out his career with the Bears, for whom he still managed to produce the occasional big day, including the winning touchdown reception in the 1932 Championship game.

In truth he was certainly inferior to Ernie Nevers (Cardinals) and perhaps even to Frank Rapp (Columbus), a forgotten name, yet our three-time All-American hero was quite rightly an automatic selection for charter membership of the Hall Of Fame in 1963. He spends a happy retirement in his Florida home and can justifiably reflect that, but for his endorsement of the game in those early hectic years, Professional Football might not have survived.

Sammy Baugh (Washington Redskins, 1937-52)
Sammy Baugh was the quarterback of the Washington Redskins and led the League in overall pass rating (taking account of his completed passes, touchdowns, total distance etc.) six times in a sixteen-year career. A bald statement, yet to imagine a present day Joe Theismann transposed back in time some forty years or

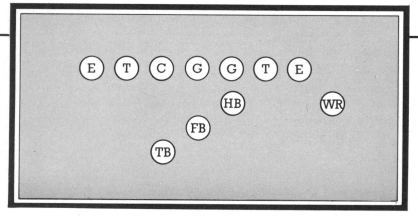

Diagram showing the Single Wing Formation. TB = Tailback;
FB = Fullback; HB = Halfback; WB = Wingback.

Above The 1942 NFL Championship
Game. Sammy Baugh (33) the
Washington quarterback, protected
by Ed Cifers (43) and Clyde Shugart
(51), prepares to throw a pass.
Washington beat Chicago Bears 14-6.

so would be quite wrong, for in Sammy's day throwing the
pigskin was an entirely different matter.

It is only by chance that he came into Pro Football, since all
the heroes of a boy growing up in Sweetwater, Texas, in the early
1930s would be throwing a white ball on a baseball diamond.
Indeed Sammy was signed up by the St. Louis Cardinals baseball
organisation, and though it is doubtful that he would have made it
in the major leagues, he was nonetheless good enough to earn
the nickname of 'Slingin' Sammy. But Washington owner George
Marshall had seen something in this 6ft 2in, 13-stone athlete at
Texas Christian University and persuaded him to play tailback
for the Redskins.

In those days Football was still largely a rushing game and
the Pros used a lop-sided formation known as the single wing.
The center would snap the ball to either the tailback or the
fullback, leaving the one who didn't get the ball to block for the
other and only as a surprise tactic would the tailback throw a
forward pass. It was a rough business for, even after the pass had
been thrown, defensive players would follow through and savage
the passer.

It is, then, an understatement to say that Baugh had to be
tough to survive. But survive he did and by 1940, still using the
single-wing formation, he was acknowledged to be the League's
best. But there was even better to come as the NFL legislated
greater protection for the quarterback and the single wing was
abandoned for the T formation, with which the Bears had given
Washington the 73-0 drubbing of 1940. Now, in the more familiar
position of quarterback, Baugh's real genius, as measured by the
speed, accuracy and timing of his passes, emerged. Additionally

he was a 'two-way' player, as were most until the 1950s. His lifetime punting average of 45.1 yards is unlikely to be bettered, he led the League with eleven interceptions as a defensive back in 1943, and he shares still a League record of having made four interceptions in one game. Entry into the Hall Of Fame was a formality.

However, things weren't always rosy. In the 1945 Championship game against the Rams, he hit his own goal posts with a pass from inside the end zone. The two point safety, as it was in those days, made the difference in a 14-15 loss. Again, in his very last game, he was sent off for taking a swing at a Cardinal tackler. Happily though, he now finds peace raising cattle on his Texas ranch and, one imagines, watching the modern thoroughbred quarterback throwing for 300 yards, just knowing that he could double the distance.

Don Hutson (Green Bay Packers 1935-45)

On his very first play in Professional Football, Don Hutson scored with an 83-yard pass reception and, in so doing, established a standard he was to maintain for a total of eleven glorious years. He had given fair warning with touchdowns covering distances of 67 and 54 yards when leading Alabama to a 29-13 victory over Stanford in the 1935 Rose Bowl a few months earlier. Evidently it wasn't heeded.

Hutson had learned his trade in college, in the days when the forward pass was a last resort or, at best, a shock tactic. This is not surprising for the ball was still rather plump, and though it was more conducive to passing than in the very early days of the game, the modern type of bullet pass with only a slight arc in its flight was out of the question. Added to the difficulty, the receiver (the 'end') would take up a position in the congested area close to what we now know as the interior offensive line, in the spot occupied by the modern day tight end. (The greater freedom arising out of the 'split end' position would evolve over the next ten years.) Were these problems not enough, the 'end' could be legally impeded, not just at the line of scrimmage but at all times during his downfield run.

Understandably then, in 1935 even with the ball size newly slimmed down, a mere 26 receptions were sufficient to win the League receiving title. All changed dramatically in 1936, when both the number of receptions and passing yardage increased by 50 per cent, with the Arnie Herber-Don Hutson combination leading the way. Then, with Cecil Isbell supplying the ammunition, there followed a seemingly endless sequence of League titles. Except for when injury intervened, he was the very best in all aspects of pass receiving and scoring throughout his career. Yet the statistics can only hint at the true picture of a man whose blistering speed, lightning reflexes and rock-safe though soft and sensitive hands, turned pass receiving into an art form.

It seems superfluous to add that he was quite a fair defensive back with eight pass interceptions in 1943 and, in percentage terms, led the League in field goals that same year. Naturally, he was one of that elite group of seventeen who made up the charter membership of the Hall Of Fame in 1963.

Elroy 'Crazy Legs' Hirsch (Chicago Rockets (AAFC) 1946-48, Los Angeles Rams 1949-57)

Elroy first came to the attention of the Rams as a running back in

Don Hutson, in his other role of defensive back, returning an interception 85 yards for a touchdown in 1943, one of three touchdowns he scored that day.

the 1946 All Star game, a traditional fixture matching the previous year's NFL Champions against the team comprising the best players drawn from the colleges (last played in 1976). For reasons best known to himself, he had a three-year flirtation with the Rockets of the AAFC and he must have been surprised when the Rams, already knee-deep in running backs, with Paul 'Tank' Younger, Dick Hoerner and 'Vitamin' T. Smith, took him on. But coach Clark Shaughnessy, who had helped engineer the famous Bears Championship win of 1940, had another trick up his sleeve.

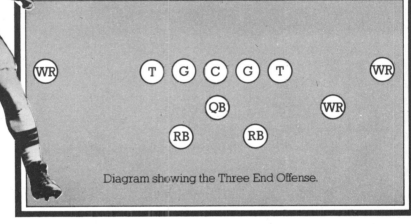

Diagram showing the Three End Offense.

Elroy 'Crazy Legs' Hirsch in the clear and making a touchdown reception in 1951.

He was planning to open up with a novel type of offense using three receivers, two out wide and one in the so-called slot, and Hirsch would be joining Tom Fears and later, Bob Boyd, in the new formation.

Before long, that unique rubbery-legged style (hence the nickname) would be both a familiar and dreaded sight to defensive backs, usually from the rear and going away. Without doubt, his best season was 1951 when he became known as the man who introduced the long 'bomb' reception as a standard offensive option. His 17 touchdowns equalled Hutson's record for a season, set in 1942, but with the difference that Hirsch's averaged over 50 yards per score, a feat never likely to be repeated or even approached. Of course the system required the involvement of others. Tom Fears, who some would assert to be Hirsch's equal if not better, would be hurtling down the opposite sideline to catch his share of the bombs delivered by Bob Waterfield and Norm Van Brocklin, who alternated in the quarterback position. All four would eventually be elected to the Hall Of Fame.

The Hollywood film producers found the combination of his handsome profile and national acclaim irresistable and he was on hand to play the part of himself in the 1953 production of *Crazy Legs: All American.* (Bob Waterfield went one better by marrying Jane Russell.) He retired in 1957 and took over the post of Rams general manager for a year before returning to his home state of Wisconsin, where he became the University's Athletic Director. By courtesy of Channel 4 Television, UK viewers were privileged to have a glimpse of 'Crazy Legs', who was the Honoured Guest for Super Bowl XVII.

Jim Brown (Cleveland Browns 1957-65)

Jim Brown might well never have played Pro Football, for even as a high school boy his natural sporting talents had attracted the attention of the New York Yankees baseball organisation and shortly before leaving college, he rejected offers of a heavy-weight boxing career. Thankfully though, he brought his 6ft 2in, 16½-stone frame into the NFL, which he then proceeded to dominate for the next nine years.

Already at that time the list of 'All Time Great' running backs was growing, and Brown's targets had been set by the likes of Bill Osmanski and 'Bronko' Nagurski (Bears), Bill Paschal (Giants), Steve Van Buren (Philadelphia), Joe Perry (49ers) and latterly, Marion Motley, whose achievements with the Cleveland Browns he would hope to emulate. This he did and a whole lot more.

Rushing yardage in Football is not unlike runs scored in cricket. A 100-yard performance is equivalent to scoring a century and has the same influence on the outcome of the game. In a nine-year career, Jim Brown never missed a game (118) and in 58 of these he scored his 'century', four of which he converted to a double century, with a top score of 237 (twice). He averaged 104 yards per game in amassing a staggering 12,312 yards, or over five yards every time he touched the ball. Mind you, 'stagger' is the one thing he did not do. Hovering behind the line of scrimmage, he would search for the slightest chink of daylight before crashing through and once into open field, quite simply, no one could catch him. A hundred and six of these rampaging runs would end in touchdowns, to which he added a further twenty on pass receptions.

Everything he did established records, not by a bit but by miles. O.J. Simpson came close and both Franco Harris (Pittsburgh) and Walter Payton (Chicago) could conceivably surpass

his yardage total, but surely nobody will amass more yards in quite the same style as Jim Brown.

He left the game, physically intact, not an ounce heavier, with the same 32-inch hip measurement and caught a plane for Hollywood. He was the marine captain in *Ice Station Zebra,* lit the fuses in *The Dirty Dozen* and did a little frolicking with Racquel Welch in an epic, south of the border. Now where *did* I put those boots?

O. J. 'Juice' Simpson (Buffalo Bills 1969-77, San Francisco 49ers 1978-79)
No discussion of the game's heroes could ever be complete without mention of the great O. J., who came so close to emulating the peerless Jim Brown. He left the University of Southern California, Heisman Trophy in hand, *en route* to Buffalo, who, unfortunately for him, were the worst team in Football (hence their number one position in the College Draft). Surprisingly their coach at the time John Rauch, saw him in the dual role of running back/pass receiver and for three years he was to languish before the arrival of Lou Saban, who announced: 'We go with the O. J. rush'.

The new Head Coach immediately set about the task of organising the whole team effort to prise open the gaps for 'The Juice'. Reggie McKenzie already installed in one of the guard positions, was joined by Joe Delamielleure in the other, and even Simpson's co-running back, Jim Braxton, would act merely as a blocker. Rookie quarterback Joe Ferguson was told: 'Hand it to

Left Jim Brown of the Cleveland Browns rips off the yards.
Right O. J. playing for San Francisco in 1978.

O. J.', who promptly ripped off the 1251 yards which won the 1972 League rushing title.

By the following year the League's defenses were ready and waiting but it mattered little for this was to be Simpson's greatest ever year, by the end of which, and with his very last carry of the season, he cracked the 2000-yard barrier. It was typical of the man that his first words to the assembled sports-writers were in praise of his offensive linemen, 'The Electric Company', who had done as they promised they would: they turned on the 'Juice'.

Twice more (in 1975 and 1976) he led the League but the pressure was beginning to tell and it was a pale shadow of the original O. J. who left for his home town of San Francisco, where he played out the last two years of his career.

His season's best of 2003 yards rushing is still unchallenged, as is his 1975 touchdown total of 23, but he retired still over 1000 yards adrift of his ultimate goal, Jim Brown's 12,312.

Simpson, too, acts in the movies but hasn't yet found a way of getting the girl. Indeed, any way you look at it he will always have to settle for second place behind the greatest ever. But then, there's no shame in that.

George Blanda setting up to pass against Kansas City during a game in 1975.

George Blanda (Chicago Bears 1949, 1950-58, Baltimore 1950, Houston 1960-66, Oakland 1967-75)
Most of the old pros will tell you that by the time they'd worked out the game, the legs and a few more bits had gone and they would retire thinking what might have been. George Blanda was different, although even he could hardly have known that a ten-year career, kicking for the Bears, would later be seen merely as an apprenticeship for the real thing to come. He did all right at Chicago, playing on the 1956 NFL Championship team and 'retiring' with a Chicago points record of 541 which still stands. For him, kicking was not enough, yet he could never displace Ed Brown and Johnny Lujack to do what he loved the most, quarterback the team. He could well have been cutting his lawn and pondering what next to do, when the AFL started up and the Houston Oilers needed a quarterback.

George answered the call, and how. The 'master' set about exploiting the AFL's naive pass defenses and in a seven-year stay amassed statistics unheard of at the time. He threw for 19,149 yards and 165 touchdowns (including a 95-yarder), tacked on 299 extra points and kicked 91 field goals (one of 55 yards), all of

which remain as Oiler records. More than these he was the team leader, coaxing them to the first two AFL Championships and only losing the third to an overtime field goal.

By this time (seventeen years) he had truly earned his retirement, but the Raiders needed a kicker to tide them over. No doubt thinking that kicking would be a rather pleasant way to stay in Football and still secretly knowing that he could quarterback any team, off he went to the West coast and the city of Oakland.

The interim period turned out to be nine years, during which 'Superfoot' led the team in scoring seven times and more than occasionally put his trusty arm to good use. At the time, Daryle 'The Mad Bomber' Lamonica was the starting quarterback, but he was prone to injury and his form would often fall away abruptly towards the end of a game. On would come the man (by now the trot had become a trundle) and with the odd touchdown pass in between field goals, he would keep the Raiders alive. It was during his stay with the Raiders that in 1970, with last-minute game-saving heroics in four successive weeks, he became a television celebrity. After 26 years, at the age of 48, and assured of induction to the Hall Of Fame, he called it a day but that kind face is still to be seen in commercials, extolling the virtues of Desenex foot powder – and somehow you believe him.

CHAPTER 8
NFL ALL-TIME RECORDS

REGULAR SEASON PLAY

Career Best

SEASONS PLAYED	26	George Blanda, Chicago Bears 1949, 1950-58, Baltimore 1950, Houston 1960-66, Oakland 1967-75
GAMES PLAYED	340	George Blanda
POINTS	2002	George Blanda (9-TD, 943-EP, 335-FG)
EXTRA POINTS	943	George Blanda
FIELD GOALS	335	George Blanda

TOUCHDOWNS

Rushing and Pass Receiving	126	Jim Brown, Cleveland Browns 1957-65 (106-R, 20-PR)
Rushing	106	Jim Brown
Pass Receiving	99	Don Hutson, Green Bay 1935-38, 1940-44
Passes Thrown	342	Fran Tarkenton, Minnesota 1961-66, 1972-78, N. Y. Giants 1967-71
By Interception Return	9	Ken Houston, Houston 1967-72, Washington 1973-80
By Punt Return	8	Jack Christiansen, Detroit 1951-58
By Kick Return	6	Ollie Matson, Chicago Cards 1952, 1954-58, L.A. Rams 1959-62, Detroit 1963, Philadelphia 1964
		Gale Sayers, Chicago Bears 1965-71
		Travis Williams, Green Bay 1967-70, L.A. Rams 1971
By Fumble Recovery Return	4	Bill Thompson, Denver 1969-81

YARDAGE

Rushing	12,321	Jim Brown
Pass Receiving	11,834	Don Maynard, N.Y. Giants 1958, N.Y. Jets 1960-72, St. Louis 1973
Passing	47,003	Fran Tarkenton

HOW MANY TIMES

Pass Receptions	649	Charley Taylor, Washington 1964-75, 1977
Passes Completed	3686	Fran Tarkenton
Interceptions	81	Paul Krause, Washington 1964-67, Minnesota 1968-79

MOST SEASONS LEADING LEAGUE

Points	5	Don Hutson, Green Bay 1940-44
		Gino Cappelletti, Boston 1961, 1963-66
Extra Points	8	George Blanda, Chicago Bears 1956, Houston 1961-62, Oakland 1967-69, 1972, 1974
Field Goals	5	Lou Groza, Cleveland Browns 1950, 1952-54, 1957
Touchdowns	8	Don Hutson, Green Bay 1935-38, 1941-44
Touchdowns, Rushing	5	Jim Brown, Cleveland Browns 1957-59, 1963, 1965
Touchdowns, Pass Receiving	9	Don Hutson, Green Bay 1935-38, 1940-44
Touchdowns, Passes Thrown	4	John Unitas, Baltimore 1957-60
		Len Dawson, Dallas Texans 1962, Kansas City 1963, 1965-66
Yards, Rushing	8	Jim Brown, Cleveland Browns 1957-61, 1963-65
Yards, Pass Receiving	7	Don Hutson, Green Bay 1936, 1938-39, 1941-44
Yards, Passing	5	Sonny Jurgensen, Philadelphia 1961-62, Washington 1966-67, 1969
Pass Receptions	8	Don Hutson, Green Bay 1936-37, 1939, 1941-45
Passes Completed	5	Sammy Baugh, Washington 1937, 1943, 1945, 1947-48

SEASON BEST

POINTS	176	Paul Hornung, Green Bay 1960 (15-TD, 41-EP, 15-FG)
EXTRA POINTS	64	George Blanda, Houston 1961
FIELD GOALS	34	Jim Turner, N.Y. Jets 1968
TOUCHDOWNS		
Rushing and Pass Receiving	23	O. J. Simpson 1975 (16-R, 7-PR)
Rushing	19	Jim Taylor, Green Bay 1962
		Earl Campbell, Houston 1979
		Chuck Muncie, San Diego 1981
Pass Receiving	17	Don Hutson, Green Bay 1942
		Elroy 'Crazy Legs' Hirsch, L.A. Rams 1951
		Bill Groman, Houston 1961
Passes Thrown	36	George Blanda, Houston 1961
		Y. A. Tittle, N.Y. Giants 1963
By Interception Return	4	Ken Houston, Houston 1971
		Joe Kearney, Kansas City 1972
By Punt Return	4	Jack Christiansen, Detroit 1951
		Rick Upchurch, Denver 1976
By Kick Return	4	Travis Williams, Green Bay 1967
By Fumble Recovery Return	2	By many players

(continued overleaf)

YARDAGE

Rushing	2,003	O. J. Simpson, Buffalo 1973
Pass Receiving	1,746	Charley Hennigan, Houston 1961
Passing	4,802	Dan Fouts, San Diego 1981

HOW MANY TIMES

Pass Receptions	101	Charley Hennigan, Houston 1964
Passes Completed	360	Dan Fouts, San Diego 1981
Interceptions	14	Dick 'Night Train' Lane, L.A. Rams 1952

GAME BEST

POINTS	40	Ernie Nevers (6-TD, 4-EP), Chicago Cards. v Chicago Bears 1929
EXTRA POINTS	9	Pat Harder, Chicago Cards. v N.Y. Giants 1948
		Bob Waterfield, L.A. Rams v Baltimore 1950
		Charlie Gogolak, Washington v N.Y. Giants 1966
FIELD GOALS	7	Jim Bakken, St. Louis v Pittsburgh 1967

TOUCHDOWNS

Rushing and Pass Receiving	6	Ernie Nevers (6-R), Chicago Cards. v Chicago Bears 1929
		Dub Jones (4-R, 2-PR), Cleveland Browns v Chicago Bears 1951
		Gale Sayers (4-R, 1-PR, 1-K Ret), Chicago Bears v San Francisco 1965
Rushing	6	Ernie Nevers, Chicago Cards. v Chicago Bears 1929
Pass Receiving	5	Bob Shaw, Chicago Cards. v Baltimore 1950
		Kellen Winslow, San Diego v Oakland 1981
Passes Thrown	7	Sid Luckman, Chicago Bears v N.Y. Giants 1943
		Adrian Burk, Philadelphia v Washington 1954
		George Blanda, Houston v N.Y. Titans 1961
		Y. A. Tittle, N.Y. Giants v Washington 1962
		Joe Kapp, Minnesota v Baltimore 1969

YARDAGE

Rushing	275	Walter Payton, Chicago Bears v Minnesota 1977
Pass Receiving	303	Jim Benton, Cleveland v Detroit 1945
Passing	554	Norm Van Brocklin, L.A. Rams v N.Y. Yanks 1951

HOW MANY TIMES

Pass Receptions	18	Tom Fears, L.A. Rams v Green Bay 1950
Passes Completed	42	Richard Todd, N.Y. Jets v San Francisco 1980
Interceptions	4	By many players

LONGEST

Touchdown Rushing	99 yards	Tony Dorsett, Dallas v Minnesota 1982
Touchdown Pass Receiving	99 yards	Andy Farkas (from Filchock) Washington v Pittsburgh 1939
		Bobby Mitchell (from Izo) Washington v Cleveland 1963
		Pat Studstill (from Sweetan) Detroit v Baltimore 1966
		Gerry Allen (from Jurgensen) Washington v Chicago 1968
Field Goal	63 yards	Tom Dempsey, New Orleans v Detroit 1970
Punt Return (All TDs)	98 yards	Gil LeFebvre, Cincinnati v Brooklyn 1933
		Charlie West, Minnesota v Washington 1968
		Dennis Morgan, Dallas v St. Louis 1974
Kick Return (All TDs)	106 yards	Al Carmichael, Green Bay v Chicago Bears 1956
		Noland Smith, Kansas City v Denver 1967
		Roy Green, St. Louis v Dallas 1979
Interception Return (All TDs)	102 yards	Bob Smith, Detroit v Chicago Bears 1949
		Eric Barnes, N.Y. Giants v Dallas 1961
		Gary Barbaro, Kansas City v Seattle 1977
		Louis Breeden, Cincinnati v San Diego 1981
Fumble Recovery Return (TD)	104 yards	Jack 'Monster Man' Tatum, Oakland v Green Bay 1972

CLUB RECORDS

Most Championships	11	Green Bay, 1929-31, 1936, 1939, 1944, 1961-62, 1965-67
	8	Chicago Bears, 1921, 1932-33, 1940-41, 1943, 1946, 1963
	4	N.Y. Giants, 1927, 1934, 1938, 1956
		Detroit, 1935, 1952-53, 1957
		Cleveland Browns, 1950, 1954-55, 1964
		Baltimore, 1958-59, 1968, 1970
		Pittsburgh, 1974-75, 1978-79
Most Consecutive Games Won (inc. playoffs)	18	Chicago Bears, 1933-34 and 1941-42
		Miami, 1972-73
Most Consecutive Games Won (exc. playoffs)	17	Chicago Bears, 1933-34
Most Consecutive Games Lost	26	Tampa Bay, 1976-77
Most Points In A Season	513	Houston, 1961
Fewest Points in A Season	37	Cincinnati/St. Louis, 1934
Most Points In A Game	72	Washington v N.Y. Giants, 1966
Most Points (Both Teams) In A Game	113	Washington v N.Y. Giants, 1966
Fewest Points (Both Teams) In A Game	0	Many Teams, last time N.Y. Giants v Detroit, 1943

ALL-TIME STATISTICS
(Active players in capitals)

ALL-TIME LEADING RUSHERS

	Yrs.	Att.	Yds.	Av.	TD
1. Jim Brown	9	2,359	12,312	5.2	106
2. O. J. Simpson	11	2,404	11,236	4.7	61
3. FRANCO HARRIS	11	2,602	10,943	4.2	86
4. WALTER PAYTON	8	2,352	10,204	4.3	72
5. Joe Perry	16	1,929	9,723	5.0	71
6. Jim Taylor	10	1,941	8,597	4.4	83
7. JOHN RIGGINS	11	2,038	8,089	4.0	58
8. Larry Csonka	11	1,891	8,081	4.3	64
9. Leroy Kelly	10	1,727	7,274	4.2	74
10. TONY DORSETT	6	1,545	7,015	4.5	45
11. EARL CAMPBELL	5	1,561	6,995	4.5	57
12. John Henry Johnson	13	1,571	6,803	4.3	48
13. Lawrence McCutcheon	10	1,521	6,578	4.3	26
14. Lydell Mitchell	9	1,675	6,534	3.9	30
15. Floyd Little	9	1,641	6,323	3.8	43
16. MARK VAN EEGHEN	9	1,557	6,293	4.0	35
17. Don Perkins	8	1,500	6,217	4.1	42
18. Ken Willard	10	1,622	6,105	3.8	45
19. Calvin Hill	12	1,452	6,083	4.2	42
20. Chuck Foreman	8	1,556	5,950	3.8	53

ALL-TIME LEADING RECEIVERS

	Yrs.	No.	Yds.	Ave.	TD
1. Charley Taylor	13	649	9,110	14.0	79
2. Don Maynard	15	633	11,834	18.7	88
3. Ray Berry	13	631	9,275	14.7	68
4. Fred Biletnikoff	14	589	8,974	15.2	76
5. HAROLD JACKSON	15	572	10,260	17.9	75
6. Lionel Taylor	10	567	7,195	12.7	45
7. HAROLD CARMICHAEL	12	551	8,463	15.4	76
8. Lance Alworth	11	542	10,266	18.9	85
9. CHARLIE JOINER	14	531	9,021	17.0	47
10. Bobby Mitchell	11	521	7,954	15.3	65
11. Billy Howton	12	503	8,459	16.8	61
12. Tommy McDonald	12	495	8,410	17.0	84
Ahmad Rashad	10	495	6,831	13.8	44
14. Don Hutson	11	488	7,991	16.4	99
15. Jackie Smith	16	480	7,918	16.5	40
16. Art Powell	10	479	8,046	16.8	81
17. Boyd Dowler	12	474	7,270	15.4	40
18. Pete Retzlaff	11	452	7,412	16.4	47
19. Roy Jefferson	12	451	7,539	16.7	52
20. Haven Moses	13	448	8,091	18.1	56

ALL-TIME LEADING SCORERS

	Yrs.	TD	EP	FG	Total
1. George Blanda	26	9	943	335	2,002
2. Lou Groza	21	1	810	264	1,608
3. Jim Turner	16	1	521	304	1,439
4. JAN STENERUD	16	0	457	317	1,408
5. Jim Bakken	17	0	534	304	1,380
6. Fred Cox	15	0	519	282	1,365
7. Gino Cappelletti	11	42	350	176	1,130
8. Don Cockroft	13	0	432	216	1,080
9. Garo Yepremian	14	0	444	210	1,074
10. Bruce Gossett	11	0	374	219	1,031
11. Sam Baker	15	2	428	179	977
12. Lou Michaels	13	1	386	187	955
13. MARK MOSELEY	12	0	316	209	943
14. Roy Gerela	11	0	351	184	903
15. Bobby Walston	12	46	365	80	881
16. Pete Gogolak	10	0	344	173	863
17. Errol Mann	11	0	315	177	846
18. Don Hutson	11	105	172	7	823
19. Paul Hornung	9	62	190	66	760
20. Tony Fritsch	11	0	287	157	758

ALL-TIME PASSING LEADERS BY OVERALL RATING

	Yrs.	Att.	Comp.	Yds.	TD	Int.	Rating
1. Otto Graham	10	2,626	1,464	23,584	174	135	86.64
2. Roger Staubach	11	2,958	1,685	22,700	153	109	83.41
3. Sonny Jurgensen	18	4,262	2,433	32,224	255	189	82.63
4. Len Dawson	19	3,741	2,136	28,711	239	183	82.55
5. KEN ANDERSON	12	3,848	2,254	28,057	172	133	81.75
6. Bart Starr	16	3,149	1,808	24,718	152	138	80.49
7. Fran Tarkenton	18	6,467	3,686	47,003	342	266	80.38
8. DAN FOUTS	10	3,533	2,053	27,145	162	153	79.77
9. BERT JONES	10	2,551	1,430	18,190	124	101	78.21
10. Johnny Unitas	18	5,186	2,830	40,239	290	253	78.19
11. Frank Ryan	13	2,133	1,090	16,042	149	111	77.63
12. KEN STABLER	13	3,412	2,061	25,611	183	199	77.28
13. Bob Griese	14	3,429	1,926	25,092	192	172	77.14
14. Norm Van Brocklin	12	2,895	1,553	23,611	173	178	75.09
15. Sid Luckman	12	1,744	904	14,686	137	132	75.02
16. Don Meredith	9	2,308	1,170	17,199	135	111	74.83
17. Roman Gabriel	16	4,498	2,366	29,444	201	149	74.32
18. Y. A. Tittle	17	4,395	2,247	33,070	242	248	74.30
19. Earl Morrall	21	2,689	1,379	20,809	161	148	74.12
20. BRIAN SIPE	9	2,943	1,653	20,147	128	126	74.10

ALL-TIME PASSING RECORDS

Total Touchdown Passes — No.

1. Fran Tarkenton	342	9. TERRY BRADSHAW	210	16. Craig Morton	183
2. Johnny Unitas	290	10. JIM HART	205	KEN STABLER	183
3. Sonny Jurgensen	255	11. Roman Gabriel	201	18. Babe Parilli	176
4. John Hadl	244	12. Norm Snead	196	19. Otto Graham	174
5. Y. A. Tittle	242	Bobby Layne	196	20. Norm Van Brocklin	173
6. Len Dawson	239	14. Bob Griese	192	Charley Conerly	173
7. George Blanda	236	15. Sammy Baugh	186	Joe Namath	173
8. John Brodie	214				

Total Passes Attempted	No.	Total Passes Completed	No.	Total Yards Passing	No.
1. Fran Tarkenton	6,467	1. Fran Tarkenton	3,686	1. Fran Tarkenton	47,003
2. Johnny Unitas	5,186	2. Johnny Unitas	2,830	2. Johnny Unitas	40,239
3. JIM HART	4,978	3. JIM HART	2,540	3. JIM HART	34,047
4. John Hadl	4,687	4. John Brodie	2,469	4. John Hadl	33,513
5. Roman Gabriel	4,498	5. Sonny Jurgensen	2,433	5. Y. A. Tittle	33,070
6. John Brodie	4,491	6. Y.A. Tittle	2,427	6. Sonny Jurgensen	32,224
7. Y.A. Tittle	4,395	7. Roman Gabriel	2,366	7. John Brodie	31,548
8. Norm Snead	4,353	8. John Hadl	2,363	8. Norm Snead	30,797
9. Sonny Jurgensen	4,262	9. Norm Snead	2,276	9. Roman Gabriel	29,444
10. George Blanda	4,007	10. KEN ANDERSON	2,254	10. Len Dawson	28,711
11. TERRY BRADSHAW	3,893	11. Len Dawson	2,136	11. KEN ANDERSON	28,057
12. KEN ANDERSON	3,848	12. KEN STABLER	2,061	12. TERRY BRADSHAW	27,917
13. Craig Morton	3,786	13. DAN FOUTS	2,053	13. Craig Morton	27,908
14. Joe Namath	3,762	Craig Morton	2,053	14. Joe Namath	27,633
15. Len Dawson	3,741	15. TERRY BRADSHAW	2,020	15. DAN FOUTS	27,145
16. Bobby Layne	3,700	16. Bob Griese	1,926	16. George Blanda	26,920
17. DAN FOUTS	3,533	17. ARCHIE MANNING	1,915	17. Bobby Layne	26,768
18. ARCHIE MANNING	3,460	18. George Blanda	1,911	18. KEN STABLER	25,611
19. Bob Griese	3,429	19. Joe Namath	1,886	19. Bob Griese	25,092
20. KEN STABLER	3,412	20. Bobby Layne	1,814	20. Bart Starr	24,718

INDEX OF PLAYERS LISTED IN ALL-TIME STATISTICS

(continued opposite)

FRITSCH Tony, Dallas (1971-73, 1975), Houston (1976-81),
New Orleans (1982)
GABRIEL Roman, Los Angeles Rams (1962-72),
Philadelphia (1973-77)
GERELA Roy, Houston (1969-70), Pittsburgh (1971-78)
GOGOLAK Pete, Buffalo (1964-65), N.Y. Giants (1966-74)
GOSSETT Bruce, Los Angeles Rams (1964-68),
San Francisco (1970-74)
GRAHAM Otto, Cleveland (1946-55)
GRIESE Bob, Miami (1967-80)
GROZA Lou, Cleveland (1946-59 and 1961-67)
HADL John, San Diego (1962-72), Los Angeles Rams
(1973-74)
HARRIS Franco, Pittsburgh (1972-)
HART Jim, St. Louis (1966-)
HILL Calvin, Dallas (1969-74), Washington (1976-77),
Cleveland (1978-81)
HORNUNG Paul, Green Bay (1957-62 and 1964-66)
HOWTON Billy, Green Bay (1952-58), Cleveland (1959),
Dallas (1960-63)
HUTSON Don, Green Bay (1935-45)
JACKSON Harold, Los Angeles Rams (1968 and 1973-77),
Philadelphia (1969-72), New England (1978-81),
Minnesota (1982-)
JEFFERSON Roy, Pittsburgh (1965-69), Baltimore (1970),
Washington (1971-76)
JOHNSON John Henry, San Francisco (1954-56), Detroit
(1957-59), Pittsburgh (1960-65), Houston (1966)
JOINER Charlie, Houston (1969-72), Cincinnati (1973-75),
San Diego 1976-)
JURGENSEN Sonny, Philadelphia (1957-63), Washington
(1964-74)
KELLY Leroy, Cleveland (1964-73)
LAYNE Bobby, Chicago (1948), N.Y. Giants (1949),
Detroit (1950-58), Pittsburgh (1958-62)
LITTLE Floyd, Denver (1967-75)
LUCKMAN Sid, Chicago (1939-50)
MANN Errol, Green Bay (1968), Detroit (1969-76),
Oakland (1976-78)
MANNING Archie, New Orleans (1971-82), Houston
(1982-)
MAYNARD Don, N.Y. Jets (1960-72), St. Louis (1973)
McCUTCHEON Lawrence, Los Angeles Rams (1972-79),
Denver (1980), Seattle (1980), Buffalo (1981)
McDONALD Tommy, Philadelphia (1957-63),
Dallas (1964), Los Angeles Rams (1965-66),
Atlanta (1967), Cleveland (1968)
MEREDITH Don, Dallas (1960-68)
MICHAELS Lou, Los Angeles Rams (1958-60), Pittsburgh
(1961-63), Baltimore (1964-69), Green Bay (1971)
MITCHELL Bobby, Cleveland (1958-61), Washington
(1962-68)
MITCHELL Lydell, Baltimore (1972-77), San Diego
(1978-79)

MORRALL Earl, San Francisco (1956), Pittsburgh
(1957-58), Detroit (1958-64), N.Y. Giants (1965-67),
Baltimore (1968-71), Miami (1972-76)
MORTON Craig, Dallas (1965-74), N.Y. Giants (1974-76),
Denver (1977-82)
MOSELEY Mark, Philadelphia (1970), Houston (1971-72),
Washington (1974-)
MOSES Haven, Buffalo (1968-72), Denver (1972-81)
NAMATH Joe, N.Y. Jets (1965-76), Los Angeles Rams (1977)
PARILLI Babe, Green Bay (1952-53 and 1956-58),
Cleveland (1956), Oakland (1960), New England
(1961-67), N.Y. Jets (1968-69)
PAYTON Walter, Chicago (1975-)
PERKINS Don, Dallas (1961-68)
PERRY Joe, San Francisco (1948-60 and 1963), Baltimore
(1961-62)
POWELL Art, Philadelphia (1959), N.Y. Jets (1960-62),
Oakland (1963-66), Buffalo (1967)
RASHAD Ahmad, St. Louis (1972-73), Buffalo (1974-75),
Minnesota (1976-82)
RETZLAFF Pete, Philadelphia (1956-66)
RIGGINS John, N.Y. Jets (1971-75), Washington (1976-79
and 1981-)
RYAN Frank, Los Angeles Rams (1958-61), Cleveland
(1962-68), Washington (1969-70)
SIMPSON O. J., Buffalo (1969-77), San Francisco (1978-79)
SIPE Brian, Cleveland (1974-)
SMITH Jackie, St. Louis (1963-77), Dallas (1978)
SNEAD Norm, Washington (1961-63), Philadelphia
(1964-70), Minnesota (1971), N.Y. Giants (1972-74
and 1976)
STABLER Ken, Oakland (1970-79), Houston (1980-81),
New Orleans (1982-)
STARR Bart, Green Bay (1956-71)
STAUBACH Roger, Dallas (1969-79)
STENERUD Jan, Kansas City (1967-79), Green Bay (1980-)
TARKENTON Fran, Minnesota (1961-66 and 1972-78),
N.Y. Giants (1967-71)
TAYLOR Charley, Washington (1964-77)
TAYLOR Jim, Green Bay (1958-66), New Orleans (1967)
TAYLOR Lionel, Chicago (1959), Denver (1960-66),
Houston (1967-68)
TITTLE Y. A., Baltimore (1948-51), San Francisco
(1951-60), N.Y. Giants (1961-64)
TURNER Jim, N.Y. Jets (1964-70), Denver (1971-79)
UNITAS John, Baltimore (1956-72), San Diego (1973)
VAN BROCKLIN Norm, Los Angeles Rams (1949-57),
Philadelphia (1958-60)
VAN EEGHEN Mark, Oakland (1974-81), New England
(1982-)
WALSTON Bobby, Philadelphia (1951-62)
WILLARD Ken, San Francisco (1965-73)
YEPREMIAN Garo, Miami (1970-78), New Orleans (1979),
Tampa Bay (1980-81)

AMERICAN FOOTBALL CONFERENCE

Conference Standings 1982

Los Angeles Raiders	9	1	0	260	200
Miami Dolphins	7	2	0	198	131
Cincinnati Bengals	7	2	0	232	137
Pittsburgh Steelers	6	3	0	204	146
San Diego Chargers	6	3	0	288	221
New York Jets	6	3	0	245	166
New England Patriots	5	4	0	143	157
Cleveland Browns	4	5	0	140	182
Buffalo Bills	4	5	0	150	154
Seattle Seahawks	4	5	0	127	147
Kansas City Chiefs	3	6	0	176	184
Denver Broncos	2	7	0	148	226
Houston Oilers	1	8	0	136	245
Baltimore Colts	0	8	1	113	236

Teams with identical won-lost records were separated by a specially devised tie-breaker just for the 1982 strike-shortened season.

Playoff Results 1982

1st Round
Los Angeles 27   Cleveland Browns 10
Miami Dolphins 28   New England Patriots 13
New York Jets 44   Cincinnati Bengals 17
San Diego Chargers 31   Pittsburgh Steelers 28

2nd Round
New York Jets 17   Los Angeles Raiders 14
Miami Dolphins 34   San Diego Chargers 13

Championship Game
Miami Dolphins 14   New York Jets 0

AFC Individual Ratings 1982

Passing

		Att.	Comp.	%	Yds.	TD	Lg.	Int.	Rating
Anderson	Cincinnati	309	218	70.6	2495	12	56	9	95.5
Fouts	San Diego	330	204	61.8	2889	17	44	11	93.6
Todd	New York Jets	261	153	58.6	1961	14	56	8	87.3
Grogan	New England	122	66	54.1	930	7	62	4	84.2
Bradshaw	Pittsburgh	240	127	52.9	1768	17	74	11	81.4
Plunkett	L.A. Raiders	261	152	58.2	2035	14	52	15	77.3
Kenney	Kansas City	169	95	56.2	1192	7	51	6	77.0
De Berg	Denver	223	131	58.7	1405	7	51	11	67.2
Nielsen	Houston	161	87	54.0	1005	6	46	8	64.6
Woodley	Miami	179	98	54.7	1080	5	46	8	63.4
Pagel	Baltimore	221	111	50.2	1281	5	53	7	62.4
Zorn	Seattle	245	126	51.4	1540	7	50	11	62.1
Manning	Houston	132	67	50.8	880	6	54	8	61.8
Sipe	Cleveland	185	101	54.6	1064	4	40	8	61.0
McDonald	Cleveland	149	73	49.0	993	5	56	8	59.5
Ferguson	Buffalo	264	144	54.5	1597	7	47	16	56.3

Receiving

		No.	Yds.	Ave.	Lg.	TD
Winslow	San Diego	54	721	13.4	40	6
Chandler	San Diego	49	1032	21.1	66	9
Collinsworth	Cincinnati	49	700	14.3	50	1

(continued opposite)

(receiving continued)

		No.	Yds.	Ave.	Lg.	TD
Newsome	Cleveland	49	633	12.9	54	3
Ross	Cincinnati	47	508	10.8	28	3
Christensen	L.A. Raiders	42	510	12.1	50	4
Marshall	Kansas City	40	549	13.7	44	3
Walker	N.Y. Jets	39	620	15.9	56	6
Allen	L.A. Raiders	38	401	10.6	51	3
Parros	Denver	37	259	7.0	24	2
Casper	Houston	36	573	15.9	38	6
Watson	Denver	36	555	15.4	41	2
Joiner	San Diego	36	545	15.1	43	0
Largent	Seattle	34	493	14.5	45	3
White	Cleveland	34	283	8.3	36	0
Johnson	Cincinnati	31	267	8.6	25	0
Harris	Pittsburgh	31	249	8.0	20	0
Branch	L.A. Raiders	30	575	19.2	51	4
Morgan	New England	28	584	20.9	75	3
Lewis	Buffalo	28	443	15.8	39	2
Feacher	Cleveland	28	408	14.6	46	3
Carson	Kansas City	27	494	18.3	51	2
Stallworth	Pittsburgh	27	441	16.3	74	7
Upchurch	Denver	26	407	15.7	51	3
Bailey	Houston	26	367	14.1	27	0
Butler	Buffalo	26	336	12.9	47	4
Willhite	Denver	26	227	8.7	27	0
Brammer	Buffalo	25	225	9.0	22	2
Muncie	San Diego	25	213	8.5	39	1
Augustyniak	N.Y. Jets	24	189	7.9	15	0

Rushing

		No.	Yds.	Ave.	Lg.	TD
McNeil	N.Y. Jets	151	786	5.2	48	6
Franklin	Miami	177	701	4.0	25	7
Allen	L.A. Raiders	160	697	4.4	53	11
Cribbs	Buffalo	134	633	4.7	62	3
Collins	New England	164	632	3.9	54	1
Johnson	Cincinnati	156	622	4.0	21	7
Harris	Pittsburgh	140	604	4.3	21	2
Muncie	San Diego	138	569	4.1	27	8
Campbell	Houston	157	538	3.4	22	2
Pruitt	Cleveland	143	516	3.6	17	3
Brooks	San Diego	87	430	4.9	48	6
Leaks	Buffalo	97	405	4.2	17	5
Van Eeghen	New England	82	386	4.7	17	0
Delaney	Kansas City	95	380	4.0	36	0
Willhite	Denver	64	325	5.1	23	2

(continued overleaf)

(rushing continued)

		No.	Yds.	Ave.	Lg.	TD
McMillan	Baltimore	101	305	3.0	13	1
Parros	Denver	77	277	3.6	14	1
King	L.A. Raiders	69	264	3.8	21	2
Winder	Denver	67	259	3.9	18	1
White	Cleveland	69	259	3.8	18	3
Dixon	Baltimore	58	249	4.3	32	1
Jackson B.	Kansas City	86	243	2.8	18	3
Pollard	Pittsburgh	62	238	3.8	18	2
Nathan	Miami	66	233	3.5	15	1
Dickey	Baltimore	66	232	3.5	25	1
Woodley	Miami	36	207	5.8	29	2
Alexander	Cincinnati	64	207	3.2	18	1
Smith	Seattle	63	202	3.2	19	0
Brown	Buffalo	41	187	4.6	19	0
Doornink	Seattle	45	178	4.0	46	0

Kicking (Extra Points & Field Goals)		EP	EP Att.	FG	FG Att.	Pts.
Benirschke	San Diego	32	34	16	22	80
Lowery	Kansas City	17	17	19	24	74
Von Schamann	Miami	21	22	15	20	66
Breech	Cincinnati	24	25	14	18	66
Bahr	L.A. Raiders	32	33	10	16	62
Leahy	N.Y. Jets	26	31	11	17	59
Anderson	Pittsburgh	22	23	10	12	52
Karlis	Denver	15	16	11	13	48
Johnson	Seattle	13	14	10	14	43
Bahr	Cleveland	17	17	7	16	38
Herrera	Buffalo	11	13	8	14	35
Kempf	Houston	16	18	4	6	28
Miller	Baltimore	9	11	6	11	27
Wood	Baltimore	6	6	6	10	24
Smith	New England	6	7	5	8	21

Kickoff Returns		No.	Yds.	Ave.	Lg.	TD
Mosley	Buffalo	18	487	27.1	66	0
Pruitt	L.A. Raiders	14	371	26.5	55	0
Smith R.	New England	24	567	23.6	98	1
Bohannon	Pittsburgh	14	329	23.5	57	0
Manning	Denver	15	346	23.1	34	0
Brooks	San Diego	33	749	22.7	47	0
Walker	Cleveland	13	295	22.7	36	0
Hancock	Kansas City	27	609	22.6	68	0
Tate	Cincinnati	14	314	22.4	55	0
Ivory	Seattle	10	224	22.4	30	0

(continued opposite)

(kickoff returns continued)

		No.	Yds.	Ave.	Lg.	TD
Walker	Miami	20	433	21.7	32	0
Roaches	Houston	21	441	21.0	45	0
Sohn	N.Y. Jets	15	306	20.4	27	0
Harper	N.Y. Jets	18	361	20.1	37	0
Verser	Cincinnati	16	320	20.0	33	0
Willhite	Denver	17	337	19.8	26	0
Hall	Cleveland	22	430	19.5	32	0
Allen	Houston	15	292	19.5	38	0
Anderson	Baltimore	27	517	19.1	33	0
Montgomery	L.A. Raiders	17	312	18.4	39	0

Punting

		No.	Yds.	Lg.	Ave.	Ret yds.	Net Ave.
Prestridge	Denver	45	2026	65	45.0	227	37.9
Camarillo	New England	49	2140	76	43.7	191	37.7
Cater	Buffalo	35	1328	61	37.9	30	36.5
Guy	L.A. Raiders	47	1839	57	39.1	71	36.3
West	Seattle	48	1835	52	38.2	69	35.5
Goodson	Pittsburgh	49	1981	66	40.4	182	35.1
Stark	Baltimore	46	2044	60	44.4	226	34.7
Orosz	Miami	35	1353	61	38.7	77	34.2
James	Houston	43	1741	56	40.5	195	34.1
McInally	Cincinnati	26	999	53	38.4	34	34.0
Ramsey	N.Y. Jets	36	1350	54	37.5	153	32.1
Cox	Cleveland	48	1877	52	39.1	216	31.4
Parsley	Houston	24	926	51	38.6	135	31.3
Gossett	Kansas City	33	1366	56	41.4	247	30.9

Punt Returns

		No.	Yds.	Ave.	Lg.	TD
Upchurch	Denver	15	242	16.1	78	2
Brooks	San Diego	12	138	11.5	29	0
Johns	Seattle	19	210	11.1	37	0
Woods	Pittsburgh	13	142	10.9	20	0
Vigorito	Miami	20	192	9.6	59	0
Smith	New England	16	139	8.7	19	0
Hancock	Kansas City	20	103	8.6	30	0
Harper	N.Y. Jets	23	184	8.0	24	0
Sydnor	Pittsburgh	22	172	7.8	21	0
Pruitt	L.A. Raiders	27	209	7.7	25	0
Fuller	Cincinnati	17	95	5.6	13	0
Mosley	Buffalo	11	61	5.5	16	0
Roaches	Houston	19	104	5.5	25	0
Walker	Cleveland	19	101	5.3	14	0
Holt	Buffalo	10	45	4.5	21	0

Predictions 1983

East

New York Jets
Miami Dolphins*
Buffalo Bills
New England Patriots
Baltimore Colts

Central

Pittsburgh Steelers
Cincinnati Bengals
Houston Oilers
Cleveland Browns

West

Los Angeles Raiders
San Diego Chargers*
Seattle Seahawks
Denver Broncos
Kansas City Chiefs

*Wild Card Teams

By season's end, the Chargers defense should just about know each other's first names and will be good enough to restrict the Raiders to 24 points in winning a close AFC Championship Game, as a prelude to losing in Super Bowl XVIII to Dallas.

AFC TEAMS 1983

AFC Eastern Division

BALTIMORE COLTS AFC East

Address P.O. Box 2000, Owings Mills, Maryland 21117.
Stadium Memorial Stadium, Baltimore.
  Capacity 60,714. *Playing Surface* Grass.
Team Colours Royal Blue, White and Silver.
Head Coach Frank Kush – second year.
Championships Super Bowl 1970; NFL 1958, '59, '68;
  Conference 1970; Division 1970, '75, '76, '77.
History AAFC 1947-49. NFL 1950, 1953-69. AFC 1970-

The Colts made little impact in the AAFC and when it collapsed in 1949, they were absorbed into the NFL, only to go out of business after one year. They resurfaced in 1953, now with Carroll Rosenbloom in charge and, under Head Coach Weeb Ewbank, won consecutive NFL Championships in 1958 and '59, each time at the expense of the Giants. With John Unitas, Ray Berry and Lennie Moore at their best, the Colts were always a threat but it would be eleven years before their next success, in Super Bowl V over Dallas. The 1970s saw four more play-off appearances without reward and by 1980 they were well into decline. If 1981 was a bad year with only two wins, 1982 was worse, when they could manage only a tie, coming dead last in the entire NFL. Even with the benefit of prime draft selections, Frank Kush will be hard pressed to approach parity in this fiercely competitive division.

Offense

With his overall number one selection in the College Draft, Kush took the most exciting quarterback prospect to enter the NFL in a decade, Stanford's John Elway. But the one team Elway did not want to play for was the Colts, and after the usual two weeks of rhetoric, he was traded to Denver. In return, Baltimore obtained Chris Hinton (offensive tackle, selected overall fourth in the draft), Mark Hermann (a good quarterback prospect) and Denver's 1984 1st round draft option – a good deal for the Colts. Hinton must help an offensive line which is in need of remedial treatment everywhere. Quarterback protection is respectable (only 20 sacks yielded), but the scrimmage domination so necessary for any kind of offensive momentum is non-existent. Under the circumstances, rookie quarterback Mike Pagel (who was surprisingly preferred to Art Schlichter, now under suspension for gambling, did well to come through his baptism of fire. There are problems at wide receiver where the only one of quality, Ray Butler, is seeking a transfer, which would leave the inexperienced Matt Bouza as the senior man. The possibilities for a rushing offense are much more attractive, with the power of Randy McMillan and the speed of Curtis Dickey. Zachary Dixon, who averaged 4.3 yards per attempt in 1982, will see action in relief of Dickey.

Defense

The defense is in tatters and it is widely accepted that several players have morale problems – a sad commentary on this proud Club. Donnell Thompson (defensive end) will soldier on, alas without George Achica who has gone to USFL. Johnie Cooks at linebacker is expected to improve after a rookie year which began with so much promise, but ended with his head just above water. Here though, there is quality in Barry Krauss and Sanders Shiver (both former first round picks). There is a glimmer of hope at defensive back where rookie Jim Burroughs showed his speed with a 94-yard interception return.

Special Teams

Dan Miller (kicker) replaced Mike Wood late in the season and still has to prove himself. Rohn Stark had an excellent 44.4 yard punting average. Larry Anderson (ex-Pittsburgh) adds a touch of class, returning both kicks and punts.

Baltimore Colts (AFC East)

No.	Name	Pos.	Ht.	Wt.	Age	NFL Yr.	College
26	Anderson, Kim*	CB	5-11	182	26	4	Arizona State
30	Anderson, Larry*	S/KR	5-11	188	26	6	Lousiana Tech.
87	Bailey, Elmer	WR	6-0	195	25	4	Minnesota
81	Beach, Pat	TE	6-4	245	23	2	Washington
85	Bouza, Matt*	WR	6-3	205	25	2	California
52	Bracelin, Greg*	LB	6-1	215	26	4	California
45	Burroughs, James*	CB	6-1	190	25	2	Michigan State
80	Butler, Ray*	WR	6-3	197	27	4	USC
98	Cooks, Johnie*	LB	6-4	240	24	2	Mississippi State
73	Crosby, Cleveland	DE	6-4	250	27	2	Arizona
75	Crouch, Terry*	G	6-1	275	24	2	Oklahoma
34	Delaney, Jeff	S	6-1	197	26	4	Pittsburgh
33	Dickey, Curtis*	RB	6-1	205	26	4	Texas A & M

(continued opposite)

Curtis Dickey, the Baltimore Rocket.

> **In the team lists the asterisks (*) denote prospective starters.**

1983 Schedule

4 Sept	at New England	1:00
11 Sept	DENVER	4:00
18 Sept	at Buffalo	1:00
25 Sept	CHICAGO	2:00
2 Oct	at Cincinnati	1:00
9 Oct	NEW ENGLAND	2:00
16 Oct	BUFFALO	2:00
23 Oct	MIAMI	2:00
30 Oct	at Philadelphia	1:00
6 Nov	at New York Jets	4:00
13 Nov	PITTSBURGH	2:00
20 Nov	at Miami	1:00
27 Nov	at Cleveland	1:00
4 Dec	NEW YORK JETS	4:00
11 Dec	at Denver	2:00
18 Dec	HOUSTON	2:00

Baltimore Colts (AFC East) – continued

No.	Name	Pos.	Ht.	Wt.	Age	NFL Yr.	College
31	Dixon, Zachary	RB	6-1	204	27	5	Temple
53	Donaldson, Ray*	C	6-3	263	25	4	Georgia
72	Durham, Steve	DE	6-5	258	24	2	Clemson
28	Franklin, Cleveland	RB	6-2	220	28	6	Baylor
25	Glasgow, Nesby*	S	5-11	185	26	5	Washington
68	Hart, Jeff*	T	6-5	272	29	7	Oregon State
42	Hatchett, Derrick*	CB	6-0	186	24	4	Texas
27	Hemphill, Darryl	DB	6-0	195	23	2	West Texas State
88	Henry, Bernard	WR	6-1	180	23	2	Arizona State
88	Herrmann, Mark	QB	6-4	184	24	3	Purdue
63	Hudson, Nat	G	6-3	270	25	3	Georgia
62	Huff, Ken*	G	6-5	253	30	9	North Carolina
57	Humiston, Mike	LB	6-3	238	24	3	Weber State
92	Hunter, James	DE/DT	6-4	245	25	2	USC
94	Jenkins, Fletcher*	DE/DT	6-2	247	23	2	Washington
51	Jones, Ricky	LB	6-2	222	28	7	Tuskegee
55	Krauss, Barry*	LB	6-4	238	26	5	Alabama
86	McCall, Reese	TE	6-6	243	27	6	Auburn
32	McMillan, Randy*	RB	6-1	226	24	3	Pittsburgh
48	Meacham, Lamont	CB	6-0	170	22	2	W. Kentucky
1	Miller, Dan	K	5-10	172	22	2	Miami
49	Odom, Cliff	LB	6-2	225	24	3	Texas-Arlington
60	Padjen, Gary	LB	6-2	240	25	2	Arizona State
18	Pagel, Mike*	QB	6-2	200	22	2	Arizona State
83	Sherwin, Tim*	TE	6-5	239	25	3	Boston College
54	Shiver, Sanders*	LB	6-2	230	28	8	Carson-Newman
96	Simmons, Dave	LB	6-4	220	26	3	North Carolina
79	Sinnott, John*	OT	6-4	275	25	3	Brown
84	Smith, Holden	WR	6-2	190	24	2	California
3	Stark, Rohn	P	6-3	195	24	2	Florida State
90	Taylor, Hosea	DE	6-5	250	24	3	Houston
99	Thompson, Donnell*	DE	6-5	252	24	3	North Carolina
64	Utt, Ben	OG	6-4	255	24	2	Georgia Tech.
69	Wisniewski, Leo*	DT	6-1	251	23	2	Penn. State
38	Wright, Johnnie	RB	6-1	205	24	2	South Carolina

1983 Draft

Round	Name	Pos.	Ht.	Wt.	College
1	Hinton, Chris	OG	6-4	272	Northwestern
2	Maxwell, Vernon	LB	6-1	228	Arizona State
4	Smith, Phil	WR	6-2	190	San Diego State
5	Abramowitz, Sid	OT	6-4½	270	Tulsa
6	Feasel, Grant	C	6-6½	245	Abilene Christian
7	Moore, Alvin	RB	5-11	192	Arizona State
9	Mills, Jim	T	6-7½	265	Hawaii
9	Rose, Chris	T	6-4½	244	Stanford
10	Hopkins, Ronald	DB	5-10	185	Murray State
11	Taylor, Jim Bob	QB/RB	6-2	196	Georgia Tech.
12	Williams, Karl	WR	5-10	170	Texas Southern

BUFFALO BILLS AFC East

Address One Bills Drive, Orchard Park, New York 14127.
Stadium Rich Stadium, Buffalo.
   Capacity 80,020. *Playing Surface* AstroTurf.
Team Colours Scarlet Red, Royal Blue and White.
Head Coach Kay Stephenson – first year.
Championships AFL 1964, '65; Division 1980.
History AFL 1960-69. AFC 1970-

In 1959, thwarted in his attempts to set up in Miami, Ralph C. Wilson Jr. took his Bills to Buffalo as one of the seven charter members of the AFL. They won consecutive Championships in 1964 and '65, narrowly missing a hat-trick by losing to Kansas City the following year. This loss however, marked the beginning of a downward trend which was to last seven years before, in 1974, they once more reached the playoffs. Despite the presence of the remarkable O.J. Simpson at running back, they could proceed no further. As the opposition worked out the Simpson oriented offense, the Bills returned to the cellar.

Under the patient guidance of Chuck Knox, they regrouped and now are always to be considered as play-off prospects. This being so, it was all the more surprising that Knox departed for Seattle, leaving his former assistant, Kay Stephenson, to take charge for 1983. His first problem will be to re-motivate the dozen or so players who are reported to be seeking transfers.

Offense
The offensive line maintained its high traditions, yielding only twelve quarterback sacks (third best, NFL) and prising holes for the running backs. McKenzie has gone to Seattle but there is ample reserve strength. Running back Joe Cribbs is particularly adept at picking his way through the pile of bodies at the line of scrimmage and, given any sort of a gap, will rip off the yards against the best defense. Both Curtis Brown and Roosevelt Leaks averaged over four yards per carry in 1982 but should Cribbs depart (he is one of the dissenters), the venom of the Buffalo rush will go with him. Quarterback Joe Ferguson would like to forget last season (rated last in the NFL) and, after a ten-year career, is unlikely to improve. Nonetheless, he will be valuable in ensuring the smooth introduction of second-year man, Matt Kofler. Wide receiver Jerry Butler has searing pace and Frank Lewis has the experience of twelve years but may be under pressure from Perry Tuttle. There is need for two good tight ends in several modern formations and Kay Stephenson gave a clue to his philosophy by using his first draft option to take Tony Hunter.

Defense
With the 'Bermuda Triangle' of Fred Smerlas (tackle), Jim Haslett and Shane Nelson (linebackers) at its centre, the defense is ominously good, rating seventh and second against the rush and pass respectively. Even so, despite the fact that only Isiah Robertson is approaching retirement, Stephenson selected eight defensive players out of his twelve draft options. Surprisingly, the defense registered only twelve quarterback sacks, yet this could be the secret of success – quick reaction after waiting to allow the opposition to show its hand.

Special Teams
Kicker Efren Herrera has vast experience and though Greg Cater's punts are short, the special team tacklers do an excellent job of smothering the punt returner. It demonstrates the difference between returning kicks and punts, when a player, Mike Mosley, can top the NFL in the former but struggle near the bottom in the latter.

1983 Schedule

Date	Opponent	Time
4 Sept	MIAMI	1:00
11 Sept	at Cincinnati	1:00
18 Sept	BALTIMORE	1.00
25 Sept	HOUSTON	1:00
3 Oct	NEW YORK JETS	9:00
9 Oct	at Miami	1:00
16 Oct	at Baltimore	2:00
23 Oct	NEW ENGLAND	1:00
30 Oct	NEW ORLEANS	1:00
6 Nov	at New England	1:00
13 Nov	at New York Jets	1:00
20 Nov	LOS ANGELES RAIDERS	1:00
27 Nov	at Los Angeles Rams	1:00
4 Dec	at Kansas City	12:00
11 Dec	SAN FRANCISCO	1:00
18 Dec	at Atlanta	1:00

Buffalo Bills (AFC East)

No.	Name	Pos.	Ht.	Wt.	Age	NFL Yr.	College
84	Barnett, Buster	TE	6-5	225	24	3	Jackson State
73	Borchardt, Jon*	OT	6-5	255	26	5	Montana State
86	Brammer, Mark*	TE	6-3	235	25	4	Michigan State
47	Brown, Curtis	RB	5-10	203	28	7	Missouri
80	Butler, Jerry*	WR	6-0	178	25	5	Clemson
7	Cater, Greg	P	6-0	191	26	4	Chattanooga
29	Clark, Mario*	CB	6-2	195	29	8	Oregon
20	Cribbs, Joe*	RB	5-11	190	25	4	Auburn
63	Cross, Justin	OT	6-6	262	24	2	Western State
70	Devlin, Joe*	OT	6-5	250	29	8	Iowa
12	Ferguson, Joe*	QB	6-1	195	33	11	Arkansas
85	Franklin, Byron	WR	6-1	179	25	3	Auburn
22	Freeman, Steve*	S	5-11	185	30	9	Mississipi State
53	Grant, Will*	C	6-4	248	29	6	Kentucky
55	Haslett, Jim*	LB	6-3	232	27	5	Indiana, Pa.
1	Herrera, Efren	K	5-9	190	32		UCLA
87	Holt, Robert	WR	6-1	174	23	2	Baylor
25	Hooks, Roland	RB	6-0	195	30	8	N. Carolina State
97	Irvin, Darrell*	DE	6-4	255	25	4	Oklahoma

(continued opposite)

Buffalo Bills (AFC East) – *continued*

Joe Cribbs eyes up the opposition.

No.	Name	Pos.	Ht.	Wt.	Age	NFL Yr.	College
91	Johnson, Ken	DE	6-5	253	28	5	Knoxville
72	Jones, Ken*	OT	6-5	250	30	8	Arkansas State
52	Keating, Chris	LB	6-2	223	25	5	Maine
10	Kofler, Matt	QB	6-2	193	23	2	San Diego State
42	Kush, Rod	S	6-0	188	26	4	Omaha
48	Leaks, Roosevelt*	RB	5-10	225	30	9	Texas
82	Lewis, Frank*	WR	6-1	196	36	13	Grambling
60	Lumpkin, Joey	LB	6-2	230	23	2	Arizona State
61	Lynch, Tom	G	6-5	250	28	7	Boston College
54	Marve, Eugene*	LB	6-3	230	23	2	Saginaw State
33	McKnight, Ted	RB	6-1	212	29	7	Minnesota-Duluth
34	Moore, Booker	RB	5-11	229	24	2	Penn State
88	Mosley, Mike	WR	6-1	186	25	2	Texas A & M
59	Nelson, Shane*	LB	6-1	225	28	7	Baylor
38	Nixon, Jeff*	S	6-3	190	26	5	Richmond
62	Parker, Ervin*	LB	6-5	240	25	4	S. Carolina State
89	Piccone, Lou	WR	5-9	175	33	10	W. Liberty State
40	Riddick, Robb	RB	6-0	195	26	3	Millersville
51	Ritcher, Jim	C-G	6-3	251	25	4	N. Carolina State
26	Romes, Charles*	CB	6-1	190	28	7	N. Carolina Central
99	Roopenian, Mark	DT/DE	6-4	252	25	2	Boston College
57	Sanford, Lucius	LB	6-2	216	27	6	Georgia Tech.
76	Smerlas, Fred*	DT	6-3	270	26	5	Boston College
81	Tuttle, Perry	WR	6-0	178	24	2	Clemson
41	Villapiano, Phil	LB	6-2	225	34	13	Bowling Green
65	Vogler, Tim	C	6-3	245	26	5	Ohio State
77	Williams, Ben*	DE	6-3	245	28	8	Mississippi
27	Williams, Chris	CB	6-0	197	24	2	Louisiana State
23	Williams, Van	RB	6-0	208	23	2	Carson-Newman

1983 Draft

Round	Name	Pos.	Ht.	Wt.	College
1	Hunter, Tony	TE	6-4	237	Notre Dame
2	Talley, Darryl	LB	6-4	219	West Virginia
4	Junkin, Trey	LB	6-1½	217	Louisiana Tech.
4	Payne, Jimmy	DE	6-3½	255	Georgia
5	Vandenboom, Matt	S	6-3½	207	Wisconsin
7	Brown, Gurnest	DE/DT	6-3	260	Maryland
8	Durham, James	S/CB	6-0	190	Houston
9	Parker, George	RB	5-8½	180	Norfolk State
10	Tharpe, Richard	DE	6-3	240	Louisville
12	Dawkins, Julius	WR	6-1½	190	Pittsburgh

MIAMI DOLPHINS AFC East

Address 3550 Biscayne Boulevard, Florida 33137.
Stadium Orange Bowl, Miami.
  Capacity 75,459. *Playing Surface* Grass.
Team Colours Aqua and Orange
Head Coach Don Shula – fourteenth year.
Championships Super Bowl 1972, '73;
  Conference 1971, '72, '73, '82;
  Division 1971, '72, '73, '74, '79, '81.
History AFL 1966-69. AFC 1970-

Under Don Shula Miami made a startling rise to prominence in 1970. He had been acquired from the Head Coaching job at Baltimore and, after a transaction not without controversy, Pete Rozelle felt the need to transfer Miami's first round option in the College Draft to the Colts. Victories in two Super Bowls quickly followed as Shula underlined his reputation as the best coach in the game. He has continued to the present time, inevitably reaching the playoffs with a squad noticeably lacking star players. Indeed, even his early Super Bowl winning team was nicknamed in part, 'The No Name Defense'.

Nowadays he has his 'Killer Bees' defense, which almost kept out the Redskins in Super Bowl XVII, and arguably the League's best defensive strategist, Bill Arnsparger. It will require their combined talents to hold off the Jets and Bills in the AFC East.

Offense

The offensive line, which is good anyway, will benefit from the return of All Pro guard Ed Newman (injured for the playoffs) with Jeff Toews reverting to a reserve role. Only Bob Kuechenberg can be considered as 'getting on a bit' and there is adequate back-up in Roy Foster and Cleveland Green. The running backs should be even more impressive in 1983. The blockbusting Andra Franklin evokes memories of the great Larry Csonka, smashing up the middle, whilst

the speedy Tony Nathan explores the outside route. They are strengthened by the return of David Overstreet, originally a first round draft choice but who chose to play in the Canadian League. There is a problem at quarterback, where David Woodley has not fulfilled his promise, despite the confidence of Don Shula. Rated 23rd in the NFL, he played like it in the Super Bowl (the 'bomb' to Cefalo excepted). He will be under pressure from draftee Dan Marino and the veteran Don Strock (if the latter has the patience to wait around once more). The wide receivers have suffered from a poor supply of passes and are nowhere in the conference ratings. Still, Harris has re-enlisted for a salary reported to be $350,000 and Jimmy Cefalo turns what few passes he catches into sizeable gains (17 at an average of 21 yards in 1982).

Defense

Against the pass, the defense is awesome (NFL best). Linebacker A. J. Duhe joins in with Bokamper, Baumhower and Betters, the front three of the six 'Killer Bees', to mount a savage rush, often placing opposing quarterbacks in a hopeless position. Nineteen times passes were intercepted (NFL best), the majority by prowling defensive backs, including the Blackwood brothers, lying in wait. Amazingly, against the rushing offense, they are the NFL's worst, as Riggins confirmed in the Super Bowl. Being denied access to Bill Arnsparger's secret playbook, one can only surmise that the violent pass rush leaves too few in reserve to handle the ball carrier. The drafting of two defensive linemen, Mike Charles and Charles Benson, could well signify a tactical change to a four-man front as a possible solution.

Special Teams

Von Schamann is a fine kicker but punter Tom Orosz is below average. Tommy Vigorito has an excellent punt return average and there is no problem returning kicks in which Fulton Walker will be hoping to repeat his Super Bowl effort of 98 yards on one play.

Miami Dolphins (AFC East)

No.	Name	Pos.	Ht.	Wt.	Age	NFL Yr.	College
70	Barnett, Bill	DE	6-4	260	27	4	Nebraska
73	Baumhower, Bob*	DT	6-5	260	28	7	Alabama
34	Bennett, Woody	RB	6-2	222	28	5	Miami
75	Betters, Doug*	DE	6-7	260	27	6	Nevada-Reno
72	Bishop, Richard	DT	6-1	260	33	8	Louisville
47	Blackwood, Glenn*	S	6-0	186	26	5	Texas
42	Blackwood, Lyle*	S	6-1	188	32	11	Texas Christian
58	Bokamper, Kim*	DE	6-6	250	28	7	San Jose State
56	Bowser, Charles	LB	6-3	224	23	2	Duke
59	Brudzinski, Bob*	LB	6-4	230	28	7	Ohio State
81	Cefalo, Jimmy*	WR	5-11	188	26	6	Penn State
76	Clark, Steve	DE	6-4	255	23	2	Utah
63	Dennard, Mark*	C	6-1	252	27	5	Texas A & M
33	Diana, Rich	RB	5-9	220	22	2	Yale
77	Duhe, A. J.*	LB	6-4	248	27	7	Louisiana State
85	Duper, Mark	WR	5-9	184	24	2	Northwest Louisiana

Miami offense of the 1980s: Andra Franklin (37), Eddie Hill (31), Tim Fox (48).

(continued opposite)

1983 Schedule

Date	Opponent	Time
4 Sept	at Buffalo	1:00
11 Sept	NEW ENGLAND	1:00
19 Sept	at Los Angeles Raiders	6.00
25 Sept	KANSAS CITY	1:00
2 Oct	at New Orleans	3:00
9 Oct	BUFFALO	1:00
16 Oct	at New York Jets	1:00
23 Oct	at Baltimore	2:00
30 Oct	LOS ANGELES RAMS	1:00
6 Nov	at San Francisco	1:00
13 Nov	at New England	1:00
20 Nov	BALTIMORE	1:00
28 Nov	CINCINNATI	9:00
4 Dec	at Houston	12:00
10 Dec	ATLANTA	4:00
16 Dec	NEW YORK JETS	9:00

Miami Dolphins (AFC East) – *continued*

No.	Name	Pos.	Ht.	Wt.	Age	NFL Yr.	College
61	Foster, Roy	DT/OG	6-4	275	23	2	USC
37	Franklin, Andra*	RB	5-10	225	24	3	Nebraska
79	Giesler, Jon*	OT	6-4	260	26	5	Michigan
74	Green, Cleveland	OT	6-3	262	25	5	Southern
84	Hardy, Bruce*	TE	6-4	230	27	6	Arizona State
82	Harris, Duriel*	WR	5-11	176	28	8	New Mexico State
88	Heflin, Vince	WR/KR	6-0½	185	24	2	Central State, Ohio
53	Hester, Ron	LB	6-1	218	24	2	Florida State
31	Hill, Eddie	RB	6-2	210	26	5	Memphis State
11	Jensen, Jim	QB	6-4	212	24	3	Boston University
49	Judson, William	CB	6-1	181	24	2	S. Carolina State
40	Kozlowski, Mike	S	6-0	198	27	4	Colorado
67	Kuechenberg, Bob*	OG	6-2	255	35	14	Notre Dame
68	Laakso, Eric*	OT	6-4	265	26	6	Tulane
44	Lankford, Paul	CB	6-1	178	25	2	Penn State
86	Lee, Ronnie	TE	6-3	236	26	5	Baylor
28	McNeal, Don*	CB	5-11	192	25	4	Alabama
89	Moore, Nat	WR	5-9	188	31	10	Florida
22	Nathan, Tony*	RB	6-0	206	26	5	Alabama
64	Newman, Ed*	OG	6-2	255	32	11	Duke
3	Orosz, Tom	P	6-1	204	23	3	Ohio State
	Overstreet, David	RB	5-10	202	25	1	Oklahoma
78	Poole, Ken	DE	6-3	251	24	3	Northeast Louisiana
54	Potter, Steve	LB	6-3	235	25	3	Virginia
55	Rhone, Earnie*	LB	6-2	224	30	8	Henderson
80	Rose, Joe	TE	6-3	230	26	4	California
52	Shull, Steve	LB	6-1	220	25	4	William & Mary
48	Small, Gerald*	CB	5-11	192	27	6	San Jose State
57	Stephenson, Dwight	C	6-2	255	25	4	Alabama
10	Strock, Don	QB	6-5	220	32	10	Virginia Tech.
60	Toews, Jeff	OG	6-3	255	25	5	Washington
32	Vigorito, Tommy	PR/RB	5-10	197	23	3	Virginia
5	Von Schamann, Uwe	K	6-0	188	27	5	Oklahoma
41	Walker, Fulton	KR/DB	5-10	193	25	3	West Virginia
16	Woodley, David*	QB	6-2	204	24	4	Louisiana State

1983 Draft

Round	Name	Pos.	Ht.	Wt.	College
1	Marino, Dan	QB	6-3	215	Pittsburgh
2	Charles, Mike	DT	6-4½	283	Syracuse
3	Benson, Charles	DE	6-3	256	Baylor
6	Roby, Reggie	P	6-2½	240	Iowa
7	Woetzel, Keith	LB	6-2	230	Rutgers
8	Clayton, Mark	WR	5-9	170	Louisville
9	Brown, Mark	LB	6-1½	217	Purdue
10	Reed, Anthony	RB	5-9½	225	S. Carolina State
11	Lukens, Joe	CG	6-2½	255	Ohio State

NEW ENGLAND PATRIOTS AFC East

Address Schaefer Stadium, Route 1, Foxboro,
  Massachusetts 02035.
Stadium Schaefer Stadium, Foxboro.
  Capacity 61,297. *Playing Surface* Super Turf.
Team Colours Red, Blue and White.
Head Coach Ron Meyer – second year.
Championships 1978.
History AFL 1960-69. AFC 1970-
  (Known as Boston Patriots until 1971)

The first sixteen years for the Patriots were pretty dismal even in an AFL where the competition was somewhat less than severe. However, beginning in 1976, they reeled off five net winning seasons, in two of which (1976 and '78) they reached the playoffs though going out in the first round. By 1981, the pre-season analysts were taking serious note of a club which had joined the big guns – yet they were to confound everyone by finishing dead last in the entire NFL. They simply weren't that bad, but such is Football that slight weaknesses are quickly identified and exploited, as was their vulnerability against the rushing offense. Head Coach Ron Erhardt had to go, and under his replacement, Ron Meyer, the Patriots bounced back, reaching the 1982 playoffs. Honour at least is restored but further progress up the ladder in the fiercely competitive AFC East will be difficult.

Offense
In 1982, the offense played its full part in restoring Patriot pride, rating fourth in both rushing and passing per attempt. The offensive line established consistent form around All Pro John Hannah (whose retirement will be felt) to the extent that quarterbacks were sacked only fifteen times and rushing improved enormously. Running back Tony

Collins gave fair warning for 1983 by finishing fifth in the AFC whilst Mark Van Eeghen must have produced some red faces in the Raider organisation which released him prior to the season. Mosi Tatupu is now a genuine shock weapon. Quarterback Steve Grogan (creaking knees) may not bootleg much these days but the rifle arm remains. On the other end of his passes, Stanley Morgan (wide receiver) clocked up 20.9 yards per reception, including a 75-yarder. The other receiver position is a problem which one or both of the draftees, Darryal Wilson and Stephen Starring, will hope to solve. Tight end Don Hasselbeck plays with a suspect shoulder but is a classy long pass threat.

Defense
The most heralded rookie defensive end for some years, Ken Sims, started catastrophically but rapidly improved as the season wore on and, together with Lester Williams (also a rookie), solved the problem of the defensive line. Clayton Weishuhn (yet another rookie) was a sensation at linebacker alongside the veteran Steve Nelson, for whom such praise is the norm. There are no problems at defensive back (except for the opposition) with Mike Haynes, a perennial Pro Bowler, virtually impassable at left corner-back. Ray Clayborn and Rick Sanford responded to his example and Roland James more than compensated for the departure of Tim Fox to San Diego.

Special Teams
John Smith (an Englishman) now rates as one of the best kickers in the game and thankfully he has recovered from the injury which kept him out for the early part of the season. Never was he seen to be more composed than when standing aside during the 'Snow Plough' incident against Miami, and of course he kicked the winning field goal. Rich Camarillo booms his punts for a 43.7-yard average. Ricky Smith returns both punts and kicks, the latter to good effect, including a 98-yarder against the Jets.

New England Patriots (AFC East)

No.	Name	Pos.	Ht.	Wt.	Age	NFL Yr.	College
85	Adams, Julius*	DE	6-4	263	33	12	Texas Southern
55	Blackmon, Don*	LB	6-3	235	24	3	Tulsa
88	Bradshaw, Morris*	WR	6-1	195	30	10	Ohio State
58	Brock, Pete*	C	6-5	260	29	8	Colorado
81	Brown, Preston	WR	5-10	184	25	4	Vanderbilt
3	Camarillo, Rich	P	5-11	189	23	3	Washington
12	Cavanaugh, Matt	QB	6-1	200	26	6	Pittsburgh
65	Clark, Steve	OT/DE	6-5	260	23	3	Kansas State
26	Clayborn, Ray*	CB	6-1	190	28	7	Texas
96	Collins, Ken	LB	6-3	236	22	2	Washington State
33	Collins, Tony*	RB	5-11	202	24	3	East Carolina
44	Cowan, Larry	RB	5-11	190	23	2	Jackson State
91	Crump, George	DE	6-4	260	22	2	East Carolina
75	Cryder, Bob	OG	6-4	265	26	6	Alabama
87	Dawson, Lin	TE	6-3	235	24	3	N. Carolina State
47	Dombroski, Paul	DB	6-0	185	25	4	Linfield
43	Ferguson, Vagas	RB	6-1	194	25	4	Notre Dame
10	Flick, Tom	QB	6-1	190	25	3	Washington

John Smith kicking a field goal.

(continued opposite)

New England Patriots (AFC East) – continued

No.	Name	Pos.	Ht.	Wt.	Age	NFL Yr.	College
59	Golden, Tim	LB	6-2	220	23	2	Florida
14	Grogan, Steve*	QB	6-4	208	30	9	Kansas State
67	Haley, Darryl	OT	6-4	279	23	2	Utah
80	Hasselbeck, Don*	TE	6-7	245	28	7	Colorado
40	Haynes, Mike*	CB	6-2	195	29	8	Arizona State
70	Henson, Luther	DT/DE	6-0	275	24	2	Ohio State
76	Holloway, Brian*	OT	6-7	273	24	3	Stanford
51	Ingram, Brian	LB	6-4	230	23	2	Tennessee
38	James, Roland*	S	6-2	189	25	4	Tennessee
83	Jones, Cedric	WR	5-11	183	23	2	Duke
74	Jordan, Shelby*	OT	6-7	260	31	8	Washington, Missouri
19	Kerrigan, Mike	QB	6-3	190	23	2	Northwestern
22	Lee, Keith	DB	5-11	192	25	3	Colorado State
31	Marion, Fred	S	6-2	196	24	2	Miami
50	McGrew, Larry*	LB	6-4	231	25	4	USC
86	Morgan, Stanley*	WR	5-11	180	28	7	Tennessee
57	Nelson, Steve*	LB	6-2	230	31	10	North Dakota State
98	Owens, Dennis	DT	6-1	252	23	2	North Carolina State
25	Sanford, Rick*	S	6-1	192	26	5	South Carolina
77	Sims, Kenneth*	DE	6-5	279	23	2	Texas
1	Smith, John	K	6-0	185	34	10	Southampton, England
27	Smith, Ricky	KR/CB	6-0	174	23	2	Alabama State
78	Spears, Ron	DE	6-6	252	23	2	San Diego State
30	Tatupu, Mosi	RB	6-0	229	27	6	USC
56	Tippett, Andre	LB	6-3	231	23	2	Iowa
82	Toler, Ken	WR	6-2	195	24	3	Mississippi
34	Van Eeghen, Mark*	RB	6-2	220	31	10	Colgate
24	Weathers, Robert	RB	6-2	217	23	2	Arizona
53	Weishuhn, Clayton*	LB	6-2	218	23	2	Angelo State
62	Wheeler, Dwight	C/OT	6-3	255	28	5	Tennessee State
72	Williams, Lester*	DT	6-3	272	23	2	Miami
61	Wooten, Ron*	OG	6-4	257	24	3	North Carolina
54	Zamberlin, John	LB	6-2	239	27	5	Pacific Lutheran

1983 Draft

Round	Name	Pos.	Ht.	Wt.	College
1	Eason, Tony	QB	6-3	208	Illinois
2	Wilson, Darryal	WR	5-11½	180	Tennessee
3	Starring, Stephen	WR	5-10	172	McNeese State
3	Moore, Steve	OG/C	6-4	287	Tennessee State
4	Rembert, Johnny	LB	6-2	235	Clemson
5	Creswell, Smiley	DE	6-4	248	Michigan State
5	Lewis, Darryl	TE	6-5½	216	Texas-Arlington
6	Bass, Mike	K	5-10½	220	Illinois
8	Lippett, Ronnie	DB	5-10½	180	Miami, Florida
9	Williams, Ricky	RB	5-11	200	Langston, Oklahoma
10	Williams, James	TE	6-1	225	Wyoming
10	Williams, Toby	DE	6-3	248	Nebraska
11	Parker, Steve	WR/KR	5-9	160	Abilene-Christian
11	Eason, Calvin	DB	5-10½	185	Houston
12	Kelly, Waddell	RB	5-9	200	Arkansas State
12	Ekern, Andy	OT	6-6	260	Missouri

NEW YORK JETS AFC East

Address 598, Madison Avenue, New York, N.Y. 10022.
Stadium Shea Stadium, New York City.
  Capacity 60,372. *Playing Surface* Grass.
Team Colours Kelly Green and White.
Head Coach Joe Walton – first year.
Championships Super Bowl 1968; AFL 1968.
History AFL 1960-69. AFC 1970-
  (Known as New York Titans until 1963)

Jet History really starts with the arrival of Weeb Ewbank in 1963. He was already recognised as a brilliant coach (formerly Baltimore) but his master stroke, which was to bring Super Bowl victory in 1969, was in drafting quarterback Joe Namath of Alabama. This remarkable player, known as 'Broadway Joe', directed his team to a shock victory over Baltimore, the pride of the NFL. They were to come close in the following season, losing to Kansas City in the AFC semi-final. From this point however, the Jets went steadily downhill. Ewbank went, as did Namath's knees, and it was only in 1981 that they once more challenged for a title. With a regular season record of 10-5-1, they lost a close Wild Card game with Buffalo 27-31. After last year's 14-0 loss in the AFC Championship game to Miami, there can be no doubt that the Jets are back in business.

Offense

An offensive line including All Pro Marvin Powell and Pro Bowl center Joe Fields rates with the best, and as Ward, Alexander and Waldemore reach full maturity in 1983 should set the standard for the rest in the AFC. Their efforts were rewarded by running back Freeman McNeil, who won the NFL rushing title with 786 yards at the remarkable average of 5.2 yards per attempt. Whilst the opposition adjusts to counter his beautiful swerving runs, Augustyniak, Dierking, Harper and Crutchfield take turns adding the balance which makes the rushing offense second only to the mighty Cowboys. Richard Todd, finally in sole ownership of the quarterback position, provides New Yorkers with their first genuine successor to 'Broadway' Joe Namath, whistling his passes to Wesley Walker and Johnny 'Lam' Jones. Walker, who is legally blind in his left eye, gave us a double dose on Channel 4 last year as, first, he barbecued Detroit and then, with greater subtlety, he exposed the Raider weaknesses. Olympic gold medallist Jones (4 × 100m relay in Montreal, 1976) doesn't yet have the hands to match his speed and for the time being will share time with Derrick Gaffney.

Defense

Joe Klecko returns from injury to take his place at defensive end alongside Marty Lyons, Abdul Salaam and the ferocious Mark Gastineau in the 'New York Sack Exchange'. Gastineau celebrates every quarterback sack with his own variety of war dance, found irritating by some, not least the quarterback. Greg Buttle, Stan Blinka and Lance Mehl are a murderous bunch at linebacker, with the promising Bob Crable stepping in on obvious passing downs. Of the defensive backs, Bobby Jackson and Darrol Ray maintain the standard, but Jerry Holmes and Ken Schroy do have their lapses. Yet they are not over exposed in a defense which rates fourth in the AFC against both rushing and passing.

Special Teams

The kicking game needs attention. Pat Leahy missed five extra points and Chuck Ramsey averaged a paltry 37.5 yards punting. Bruce Harper bears the brunt of punt returning with modest success but his partnership with Kurt Sohn, returning kicks, is below average.

1983 Schedule

Date	Opponent	Time
4 Sept	at San Diego	1:00
11 Sept	SEATTLE	4:00
18 Sept	at New England	1.00
25 Sept	LOS ANGELES RAMS	4:00
3 Oct	at Buffalo	9:00
9 Oct	at Cleveland	1:00
16 Oct	MIAMI	1:00
23 Oct	ATLANTA	1:00
30 Oct	at San Francisco	1:00
6 Nov	BALTIMORE	4:00
13 Nov	BUFFALO	1:00
21 Nov	at New Orleans	8:00
27 Nov	NEW ENGLAND	1:00
4 Dec	at Baltimore	4:00
10 Dec	PITTSBURGH	12:30
16 Dec	at Miami	9:00

New York Jets (AFC East)

No.	Name	Pos.	Ht.	Wt.	Age	NFL Yr.	College
60	Alexander, Dan*	OG	6-4	260	28	7	Louisiana State
35	Augustyniak, Mike*	RB	5-11	220	27	3	Purdue
31	Barber, Marion	RB	6-3	224	23	3	Minnesota
83	Barkum, Jerome*	TE	6-4	227	33	12	Jackson State
78	Bennett, Barry	DT	6-4	257	27	6	Concordia
64	Bingham, Guy	OL	6-3	255	25	4	Montana
54	Blinka, Stan*	LB	6-2	234	25	5	Sam Houston State
51	Buttle, Greg*	LB	6-3	235	29	8	Penn State
88	Coombs, Tom	TE	6-3	230	24	2	Idaho
50	Crable, Bob	LB	6-3	228	23	2	Notre Dame
55	Crosby, Ron	LB	6-3	227	28	6	Penn State
45	Crutchfield, Dwayne	RB	6-0	235	23	2	Iowa State
25	Dierking, Scott	RB	5-10	220	28	7	Purdue
65	Fields, Joe*	C	6-2	253	29	9	Widener
38	Floyd, George	S	5-11	190	22	2	East Kentucky
81	Gaffney, Derrick	WR	6-1	182	28	6	Florida
99	Gastineau, Mark*	DE	6-5	276	26	5	E. Central Oklahom
94	Guilbeau, Rusty	DE	6-4	250	24	2	McNeese State
42	Harper, Bruce	KR/RB	5-8	177	28	7	Kutztown State

(continued opposit

New York Jets (AFC East) – *continued*

No.	Name	Pos.	Ht.	Wt.	Age	NFL Yr.	College
47	Holmes, Jerry*	CB	6-2	175	25	4	West Virginia
40	Jackson, Bobby*	CB	5-10	180	26	6	Florida State
27	Johnson, Jesse	DB	6-3	188	26	4	Colorado
89	Jones, Bobby	WR	5-11	185	28	7	No College
80	Jones, Johnny 'Lam'*	WR	5-11	183	25	4	Texas
73	Klecko, Joe*	DE	6-3	272	29	7	Temple
5	Leahy, Pat	K	6-0	189	32	10	St. Louis
71	Luscinski Jim	OT/OG	6-5	275	24	2	Norwich
29	Lynn, Johnny	CB	6-0	195	26	4	UCLA
93	Lyons, Marty*	DT	6-5	269	26	5	Alabama
	McElroy, Reggie	OT/OG	6-6	270	23	1	West Texas State
56	Mehl, Lance*	LB	6-3	235	25	4	Penn State
77	Neil, Kenny	DE	6-4	244	24	3	Iowa State
62	Pellegrini, Joe	OG/C	6-4	252	26	2	Harvard
79	Powell, Marvin*	OT	6-5	271	28	7	USC
15	Ramsey, Chuck	P	6-2	189	31	7	Wake Forest
28	Ray, Darrol*	S	6-1	206	25	4	Oklahoma
61	Roman, John	OT	6-2	270	31	8	Idaho State
76	Rudolph, Ben	DT/DE	6-5	271	26	3	Long Beach State
10	Ryan, Pat	QB	6-3	205	27	6	Tennessee
74	Salaam, Abdul*	DT	6-3	269	30	8	Kent State
48	Schroy, Ken*	S	6-2	198	30	7	Maryland
82	Shuler, Mickey	TE	6-3	236	27	6	Penn State
87	Sohn, Kurt	KR/WR	5-11	176	26	3	Fordham
21	Springs, Kirk	CB/S	6-0	192	25	3	Miami, Ohio
14	Todd, Richard*	QB	6-2	206	29	8	Alabama
70	Waldemore, Stan*	OG/C/OT	6-4	269	28	6	Nebraska
85	Walker, Wesley*	WR	6-0	179	28	7	California
72	Ward, Chris*	OT	6-3	267	27	6	Ohio State
57	Woodring, John	LB	6-2	230	24	3	Brown

1983 Draft

Round	Name	Pos.	Ht.	Wt.	College
1	O'Brien, Ken	QB	6-4	207	California-Davis
2	Hector, Johnny	RB	5-10	190	Texas A & M
4	Howell, Wes	TE	6-3	212	California
5	Walker, John	DT	6-5	258	Nebraska-Omaha
7	Newbold, Darren	LB	6-2	218	S.W. Missouri State
8	Mullen, Davlin	DB	6-0½	174	Western Kentucky
9	Humphrey, Bobby	WR	5-10	170	New Mexico State
10	Fike, Danny	OT	6-5	268	Florida
11	Harmon, Mike	WR/KR	6-0	200	Mississippi
12	Crum, Stu	K	5-6½	160	Tulsa

Wesley Walker, ace receiver.

AFC Central Division

CINCINNATI BENGALS AFC Central

Address 200, Riverfront Stadium, Cincinnati, Ohio 45202.
Stadium Riverfront Stadium, Cincinnati.
 Capacity 59,754. *Playing Surface* AstroTurf.
Team Colours Orange, Black and White.
Head Coach Forrest Gregg – fourth year.
Championships Conference 1981; Division 1973, '81.
History AFL 1968-69. AFC 1970-

When the Bengals made their AFL debut in 1968, Head Coach and part-owner Paul Brown was already a legend, having directed the Cleveland Browns to seven Championships (four AAFC and three NFL). It was therefore no surprise when, in only their third season, they reached the playoffs, albeit losing to Baltimore. With the platform established, Brown felt able to ease sideways, making way for Homer Rice, and though they won the division in 1973, it was a dispirited organisation which Forrest Gregg took over in 1979. By 1981 however, 'The Iron Man' had them in the Super Bowl, where they were far from disgraced by a 21-26 loss to San Francisco. Indeed, but for a series of crucial errors and a remarkable goal-line stand by the 49ers, they would have won. Last year, again in the playoffs, they fell at the first hurdle to the Jets but, entering 1983, they are surely the most serious threat to the authority of Pittsburgh in the AFC Central.

Offense

All Pro Anthony Munoz dominates the left side of an offensive line which went to the Super Bowl in the 1981 season, but slipped somewhat last year. This is not unusual and they can be expected to return to top standard in 1983, especially if draftee center Dave Rimington is as good as they say.

Running back Pete Johnson (as wide as he is tall) lacks pace but then, so does a JCB (mobile mechanical trench digger), and the problems of tackling either are not dissimilar. His partners, of whom Charles Alexander is the best, contribute little in a rushing offense which is unlikely to improve significantly. By contrast, the passing offense has no problems. Quarterback Ken Anderson is an automatic Pro Bowl selection and throws to a battery of fine wide receivers. Cris Collinsworth heads the Club list, followed by Isaac Curtis and Steve Kreider. Dan Ross is a magnificent pass-receiving tight end and the running backs do their bit in this aerial offense which rates second only to San Diego.

Defense

Last December, a defense which had been under strain was cruelly exposed by San Diego, who drilled in 50 points. The Jets weren't far short with 44 points in the playoffs. The reasons for the apparent decline are difficult to identify. Edwards, Browner and Whitley, pedigree defensive linemen who have done well in the past, are young and healthy. The linebackers though, Jim LeClair excepted, lack the raw-boned aggression of other units around the Conference, and the defensive backs lack pace (and perhaps subtlety). Ken Riley (cornerback) has the brains but, after fourteen seasons, is noticeably slowing up. On the other corner, Louis Breeden is too often caught out of position. Coach Gregg sensibly selected three defensive backs and three linebackers in the College Draft.

Special Teams

Jim Breech pops over the field goals without bother, though Pat McInally's punting average slipped to 38.4 yards. Rodney Tate proved successful returning kicks, and could assume the major role in 1983. Punt returner Mike Fuller had a torrid time with a low average of 5.6 yards per nightmare.

1983 Schedule

4 Sept	LOS ANGELES RAIDERS	1:00
11 Sept	BUFFALO	1:00
15 Sept	at Cleveland	8.30
25 Sept	at Tampa Bay	1:00
2 Oct	BALTIMORE	1:00
10 Oct	PITTSBURGH	9:00
16 Oct	at Denver	2:00
23 Oct	CLEVELAND	1:00
30 Oct	GREEN BAY	4:00
6 Nov	at Houston	12:00
13 Nov	at Kansas City	12:00
20 Nov	HOUSTON	1:00
28 Nov	at Miami	9:00
4 Dec	at Pittsburgh	1:00
11 Dec	DETROIT	1:00
17 Dec	at Minnesota	3:00

Cincinnati Bengals (AFC Central)

No.	Name	Pos.	Ht.	Wt.	Age	NFL Yr.	College
40	Alexander, Charles*	RB	6-1	221	26	5	Louisiana State
14	Anderson, Ken*	QB	6-3	212	34	13	Augustana, Illinois
10	Breech, Jim	K	5-6	161	27	5	California
61	Boyarsky, Jerry	DT	6-3	290	24	3	Pittsburgh
34	Breeden, Louis*	CB	5-11	185	29	6	N. Carolina Central
79	Browner, Ross*	DE	6-3	261	29	6	Notre Dame
74	Bujnoch, Glenn	OG	6-6	265	29	8	Texas A & M
67	Burley, Gary	DE	6-3	274	30	8	Pittsburgh
50	Cameron, Glenn*	LB	6-2	228	30	9	Florida
76	Collins, Glen	DE	6-6	260	24	2	Mississippi State
80	Collinsworth, Cris*	WR	6-5	192	24	3	Florida
85	Curtis, Isaac*	WR	6-1	192	32	11	San Diego State
52	Dinkel, Tom	LB	6-3	237	27	6	Kansas
73	Edwards, Eddie*	DE	6-5	256	29	7	Miami
49	Frazier, Guy	LB	6-2	215	24	3	Wyoming
42	Fuller, Mike	S/PR	5-10	182	30	9	Auburn
45	Griffin, Archie	RB	5-9	184	29	8	Ohio State
44	Griffin, Ray	CB	5-10	186	27	6	Ohio State
66	Hannula, Jim	OT	6-6	251	24	3	N. Illinois

(continued opposite)

Cincinnati Bengals (AFC Central) – *continued*

No.	Name	Pos.	Ht.	Wt.	Age	NFL Yr.	College
53	Harris, Bo*	LB	6-3	226	30	9	Louisiana State
83	Harris, M. L.	TE	6-5	238	29	4	Kansas State
82	Holman, Rodney	TE	6-3	230	23	2	Tulane
27	Hicks, Bryan*	S	6-0	192	26	4	McNeese State
37	Jackson, Robert	S	5-10	184	24	3	Central Michigan
46	Johnson, Pete*	RB	6-0	249	29	7	Ohio State
26	Kemp, Bobby*	DB	6-0	186	24	3	Fullerton
	King, Arthur	DT	6-4	260	23	2	Grambling
86	Kreider, Steve	WR	6-3	192	25	5	Lehigh
62	Lapham, Dave*	OG	6-4	262	31	10	Syracuse
55	LeClair, Jim*	LB	6-3	234	32	12	North Dakota
87	McInally, Pat	P/WR	6-6	212	30	8	Harvard
65	Montoya, Max*	OG	6-5	275	27	5	UCLA
60	Moore, Blake	C	6-5	267	25	4	Wooster
78	Munoz, Anthony*	OT	6-6	278	25	4	USC
68	Obrovac, Mike	OT	6-6	275	27	3	Bowling Green
51	Razzano, Rick	LB	5-11	227	27	4	Virginia Tech
13	Riley, Ken*	CB	6-0	183	36	15	Florida A & M.
89	Ross, Dan*	TE	6-4	235	26	5	Northeastern
72	St. Clair, Mike	DE	6-5	254	29	8	Grambling
15	Schonert, Turk	QB	6-1	185	26	4	Stanford
59	Schuh, Jeff	LB	6-2	228	25	3	Minnesota
25	Simmons, John	CB	5-11	192	24	3	Southern Methodist
56	Simpkins, Ron	LB	6-1	235	25	4	Michigan
23	Tate, Rodney	RB	5-11	190	24	2	Texas
81	Verser, David	WR	6-1	200	25	3	Kansas
63	Wagner, Ray	OT	6-3	290	25	2	Kent State
70	Weaver, Emanuel	DT	6-4	260	22	2	South Carolina
75	Whitley, Wilson*	DT	6-3	265	28	7	Houston
57	Williams, Reggie*	LB	6-0	228	28	8	Dartmouth
77	Wilson, Mike*	OT	6-5	271	28	6	Georgia

Ken Anderson in no mood to mess around.

1983 Draft

Round	Name	Pos.	Ht.	Wt.	College
1	Rimington, Dave	C	6-2	290	Nebraska
2	Horton, Ray	DB	5-10	182	Washington
3	Turner, Jimmy	DB	5-11	190	UCLA
4	Maidlow, Steve	LB	6-1	234	Michigan State
5	Christensen, Jeff	QB	6-2½	202	Eastern Illinois
6	Kinnebrew, Larry	RB	6-1	255	Tennessee State
7	Griffin, James	DB	6-1	190	Mid-Tennessee State
8	Martin, Mike	WR	5-9	180	Illinois
9	Wilson, Stanley	RB	5-9½	208	Oklahoma
10	Krumrie, Tim	DT	6-1½	257	Wisconsin
11	Williams, Gary	WR	6-1	205	Ohio State
12	Young, Andra	LB	6-2	230	Bowling Green

CLEVELAND BROWNS AFC Central

Address Tower B, Cleveland Stadium, Cleveland,
Ohio 44114.
Stadium Cleveland Stadium, Cleveland.
Capacity 80,385. *Playing Surface* Grass.
Team Colours Seal Brown, Orange and White.
Head Coach Sam Rutigliano – sixth year.
Championships AAFC 1946, '47, '48, '49;
NFL 1950, '54, '55, '64. Division 1971, '80.
History AAFC 1946-49. NFL 1950-69. AFC 1970-

There is no other team in Professional Football whose
impact on entering the League can compare with that of
the Browns. They won every Championship in the four
year existence of the AAFC and then, on joining the NFL,
contested the Championship game no fewer than seven
times in eight years, winning three. Their success was due
in no little part to Head Coach Paul Brown (from whom
their name is derived), who is now enshrined in the Pro
Football Hall Of Fame.

Despite the nine-year presence of the NFL's greatest
ever running back, Jim Brown, there would be only one
more Championship (1964). Their best opportunity came
in 1980, when they lost a play-off game to the Raiders on
what many considered to be a coaching error (uncharac-
teristically) by Sam Rutigliano. For 1983 their hopes must
rest on the unlikely event that either Pittsburgh or Cincinnati
will slip up.

Offense

With Joe Delamielleure, Doug Dieken and Tom DeLeone
each approaching the end of an illustrious career, this
once mighty offensive line is beginning to creak and, with
reserve strength rather weak at best, could take a couple
of seasons to repair. Behind them, in the unit which is
supposed to score the points, things were little better.
There is that dreaded problem, uncertainty at quarterback,
where 1980's glamour boy, Brian Sipe, was replaced late in
the season by the inexperienced Paul McDonald. Sipe
must be given every opportunity to re-establish his authority, in the training camp and pre-season games, or he will
surely depart, leaving the Browns in a fix. At wide receiver,
there is now little to choose between Ricky Feacher and
Dave Logan, who are two quality players, given a decent
quarterback service. Tight end Ozzie Newsome is a master
of the art and both Mike Pruitt and Charles White (running
backs) can catch their share of passes. In his main role,
Pruitt ranks with the best, but White remains an enigma.
This former Heisman Trophy winner has yet to complete
the adjustment to the demands of the pro game.

Defense

In 1982, the opposition had no difficulty handling the
defensive line, which is short on tested experience.
Draftee Reggie Camp may find himself pitched in at the
deep end. Behind them though, the linebackers are awesome. Tom Cousineau has taken time to settle in but rookie
Chip Banks is an assassin. Dick Ambrose is the best inside
linebacker never to go to the Pro Bowl, and it will be a
tragedy if Clay Matthews does not recover from a severe
ankle injury. The defensive backs are inexperienced,
except for Clarence Scott (who may retire). With no help
in sight, 1983 could be a long season, as they say.

Special Teams

Kicker Matt Bahr is nothing special, though his fortunes
can be traced to a poor offense, which often comes to a halt
in doubtful field goal range. Steve Cox (punter) is badly let
down by his special team tacklers, who give the punt
returner too much room. Kick and punt returning are poor,
with not one event worth cheering all last season. Dino Hall
and Dwight Walker share jobs, without enthusiasm.

Cleveland Browns (AFC Central)

No.	Name	Pos.	Ht.	Wt.	Age	NFL Yr.	College
80	Adams, Willis	WR/TE	6-2	194	26	5	Houston
52	Ambrose, Dick*	LB	6-0	228	30	9	Virginia
61	Baab, Mike	C	6-4	270	23	2	Texas
9	Bahr, Matt	K	5-10	165	27	5	Penn State
99	Baldwin, Keith	DE	6-4	245	22	2	Texas A & M
56	Banks, Chip*	LB	6-4	244	23	2	USC
91	Bradley, Henry	DT	6-2	260	29	5	Alcorn State
47	Braziel, Larry	CB	6-0	184	26	5	USC
49	Burrell, Clinton*	S	6-1	192	26	4	Louisiana State
50	Cousineau, Tom*	LB	6-2	225	26	2	Ohio State
53	Cowher, Bill	LB	6-3	225	26	3	N. Carolina State
15	Cox, Steve	P	6-4	195	25	3	Arkansas
38	Davis, Johnny	RB	6-1	235	27	6	Alabama
64	Delamielleure, Joe*	OG	6-3	245	32	11	Michigan State
54	DeLeone, Tom*	C	6-2	248	33	12	Ohio State
73	Dieken, Doug*	OT	6-5	252	24	13	Illinois
29	Dixon, Hanford*	CB	5-11	182	24	3	S. Mississippi
83	Feacher, Ricky*	WR	5-10	174	29	8	Mississippi Valley

(continued opposite)

Chip Banks has his beady eyes on the
quarterback (16).

1983 Schedule

Date	Opponent	Time
4 Sept	MINNESOTA	1:00
11 Sept	at Detroit	1:00
15 Sept	CINCINNATI	8.30
25 Sept	at San Diego	1:00
2 Oct	SEATTLE	1:00
9 Oct	NEW YORK JETS	1:00
16 Oct	at Pittsburgh	1:00
23 Oct	at Cincinnati	1:00
30 Oct	HOUSTON	1:00
6 Nov	Green Bay at Milw.	12:00
13 Nov	TAMPA BAY	1:00
20 Nov	at New England	1:00
27 Nov	BALTIMORE	1:00
4 Dec	at Denver	2:00
11 Dec	at Houston	12:00
18 Dec	PITTSBURGH	1:00

No.	Name	Pos.	Ht.	Wt.	Age	NFL Yr.	College
20	Flint, Judson	S/CB	6-0	201	26	4	Memphis State
94	Franks, Elvis	DE	6-4	238	24	4	Morgan State
86	Fulton, Dan	WR	6-2	186	25	4	Nebraska – Omaha
79	Golic, Bob*	DT/LB	6-2	240	25	4	Notre Dame
26	Hall, Dino	KR/RB	5-7	165	27	5	Glassboro State
90	Harris, Marshall*	DE	6-6	261	27	4	Texas Christian
36	Jackson, Billy	S	6-1	202	23	2	North Carolina
68	Jackson, Robert*	G	6-5	260	30	9	Duke
51	Johnson, Eddie	LB	6-1	210	24	3	Louisville
48	Johnson, Lawrence*	CB	5-11	204	25	4	Wisconsin
23	Kafentzis, Mark	S	5-10	185	23	2	Hawaii
85	Logan, Dave*	WR	6-4	216	29	8	Colorado
57	Matthews, Clay*	LB	6-2	230	27	6	USC
16	McDonald, Paul*	QB	6-2	185	25	4	USC
71	Miller, Matt	OT/OG	6-6	270	27	4	Colorado
82	Newsome, Ozzie*	TE	6-2	232	27	6	Alabama
58	Nicholas, Scott	LB	6-3	226	23	2	Miami
43	Pruitt, Mike*	RB	6-0	225	29	8	Purdue
63	Risien, Cody*	OT	6-7	255	26	5	Texas A & M
92	Robinson, Mike*	DE	6-4	260	27	3	Arizona
22	Scott, Clarence*	S	6-0	190	34	13	Kansas State
17	Sipe, Brian	QB	6-1	195	34	10	San Diego State
12	Trocano, Rick	QB	6-0	188	24	3	Pittsburgh
59	Turner, Kevin	LB	6-2	225	25	4	Pacific
42	Walker, Dwight	PR/RB	5-10	185	24	2	Nicholls State
55	Weathers, Curtis	LB	6-5	220	26	5	Mississippi
25	White, Charles*	RB	5-10	198	25	4	USC
81	Whitwell, Mike	WR/S	6-00	175	24	2	Texas A & M

1983 Draft

Round	Name	Pos.	Ht.	Wt.	College
2	Brown, Ron	WR	5-10	180	Arizona State
3	Camp, Reggie	DE	6-4	257	California
5	Contz, Bill	OT	6-5	258	Penn State
6	Strackja, Tim	TE	6-3	212	Wisconsin
6	Puzzuoli, Dave	DE/DT	6-2	244	Pittsburgh
7	Belk, Rocky	WR	5-10	180	Miami, Florida
8	McClearns, Mike	OG	6-4	270	Temple
10	Hopkins, Thomas	OT	6-5½	250	Alabama A & M
11	Green, Boyce	RB	5-11	190	Carson-Newman
11	McAdoo, Howard	LB	6-2	234	Michigan State
12	Farrer, Paul	OT	6-4	255	Boston University

HOUSTON OILERS AFC Central

Address Box 1516, Houston, Texas 77001.
Stadium The Astrodome, Houston.
  Capacity 50,496. *Playing Surface* AstroTurf.
Team Colours Scarlet, Columbia Blue and White.
Head Coach Ed Biles – third year.
Championships AFL 1960, '61.
History AFL 1960-69. AFC 1970-

The Oilers had instant success in the AFL with the first two Championships but their defensive weaknesses were increasingly exploited later in the 1960s, which they ended with a humiliating 56-7 defeat by the Raiders. The situation deteriorated further in the first few years after amalgamation, when they were pulverised by Pittsburgh and Cleveland in the more competitive AFC Central. However, the arrival of Head Coach O. A. 'Bum' Phillips stopped the rot and, after four years, he had them in the playoffs. In addition to his sound defense, he now had the best running back in Football, Earl 'The Hammer' Campbell, on whose back they played post-season Football for three consecutive years. They had terrible luck and more than their fair share of injuries, and by 1980, the rushing offense had become predictable and the defense too had lost its terrors. 'Bum' departed for New Orleans, leaving Ed Biles the job of reconstruction which has, so far, failed to get off the ground.

Offense

The problems of an offensive line, which last year gave neither running room for Earl Campbell nor pass protection for the quarterbacks, can be largely solved by the return of a healthy Mike Munchak (guard) and the successful introduction of the highly rated draftee tackles, Bruce Matthews and Harvey Salem. John Schumacher makes a useful contribution, alongside the experienced Dave Carter, Ed Fisher and Morris Towns, in a unit which is due for a bit of luck. Running back Earl Campbell is the E-Type buffalo, who can take any defense apart and is entitled to the protection afforded the Crown Jewels. Any kind of contribution from Armstrong, Edwards and Allen will be a bonus, in a rushing offense which must surely improve over 1982. Archie Manning is the most experienced of three quarterbacks available and could pose a passing threat which is sorely needed to complement the Campbell rush. Wide receiver Harold Bailey should be ready to produce a genuine pro performance and Mike Renfro is due for a good season. Donnie Craft is an option, floating out from the running back position, but never was there greater need for a big season from the former All Pro, Dave Casper (tight end), who can be unstoppable.

Defense

Andy Dorris, returning from injury, will strengthen a defensive line which generates a good pass rush (31 sacks in 1982). Gregg Bingham and Robert 'Dr. Doom' Brazile, form the hard core of a linebacking quartet which stands little nonsense and has no glaring weaknesses, J. C. Wilson, Vernon Perry and Mike Reinfeldt know the feeling of playing winning football and are battle-hardened. The speedy Willie Tullis will have his chance to stake a place at corner-back, but there will be competition from all of five rookies emerging from the College Draft.

Special Teams

Florian Kempf could develop into a good kicker, given sensible field position for his field goal attempts, and John James (punter) looks comfortable kicking in the Astrodome. Carl Roaches, who returns punts and kicks, had a mediocre season – but look out, he can return them all the way.

Houston Oilers (AFC Central)

No.	Name	Pos.	Ht.	Wt.	Age	NFL Yr.	College
56	Abraham, Robert	LB	6-1	212	23	2	N. Carolina State
31	Allen, Gary	RB	5-10	175	23	2	Hawaii
39	Armstrong, Adger	RB	6-0	222	26	4	Texas A & M
86	Arnold, Walt	TE	6-3	230	25	4	New Mexico
80	Bailey, Harold*	WR	6-2	197	26	3	Oklahoma State
75	Baker, Jesse*	DE	6-5	266	26	5	Jacksonville State
65	Bethea, Elvin	DE	6-2	254	37	16	N. Carolina A & T
65	Bingham, Gregg*	LB	6-1	229	32	11	Purdue
52	Brazile, Robert*	LB	6-4	237	30	9	Jackson State
81	Bryant, Steve	WR	6-2	185	23	2	Purdue
00	Burrough, Ken	WR	6-3	215	35	13	Texas Southern
34	Campbell, Earl*	RB	5-11	237	28	6	Texas
58	Carter, David*	C	6-2	258	29	7	Western Kentucky
87	Casper, Dave*	TE	6-4	249	31	10	Notre Dame
40	Craft, Donnie	RB	6-0	195	23	2	Louisville
66	Davidson, Greg	C	6-2	249	25	4	N. Texas State
69	Dorris, Andy	DE	6-4	262	32	11	New Mexico State
35	Edwards, Stanley*	RB	6-0	208	23	2	Michigan
60	Fisher, Ed*	OG	6-3	260	34	10	Arizona State

(continued opposite)

1983 Schedule

4 Sept	GREEN BAY	12:00
11 Sept	at Los Angeles Raiders	1:00
18 Sept	PITTSBURGH	12.00
25 Sept	at Buffalo	1:00
2 Oct	at Pittsburgh	1:00
9 Oct	DENVER	12:00
16 Oct	at Minnesota	12:00
23 Oct	KANSAS CITY	12:00
30 Oct	at Cleveland	1:00
6 Nov	CINCINNATI	12:00
13 Nov	DETROIT	12:00
20 Nov	at Cincinnati	1:00
27 Nov	at Tampa Bay	1:00
4 Dec	MIAMI	12:00
11 Dec	CLEVELAND	12:00
18 Dec	at Baltimore	2:00

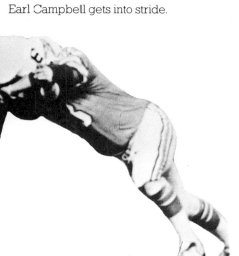

Earl Campbell gets into stride.

Houston Oilers (AFC Central) – *continued*

No.	Name	Pos.	Ht.	Wt.	Age	NFL Yr.	College
36	Hartwig, Carter	S	6-0	205	27	5	USC
84	Holston, Mike	WR	6-3	184	25	3	Morgan State
50	Hunt, Daryl*	LB	6-3	234	26	5	Oklahoma
	Jackson, Robert	LB	6-1	230	28	7	Texas A & M
6	James, John	P	6-3	200	34	12	Florida
22	Kay, Bill*	CB/DB	6-1	190	23	3	Purdue
4	Kempf, Florian	K	5-9	160	27	2	Pennsylvania
71	Kennard, Ken*	DE	6-2	258	28	7	Angelo State
72	Koncar, Mark	OT	6-5	268	30	7	Colorado
10	Luck, Oliver	QB	6-2	190	23	2	West Virginia
8	Manning, Archie*	QB	6-3	200	34	13	Mississippi
63	Munchak, Mike*	OG	6-3	257	23	2	Penn State
14	Nielsen, Gifford	QB	6-4	210	28	6	Brigham Young
32	Perry, Vernon*	S	6-2	210	29	5	Jackson State
21	Randle, Tate	S	6-0	197	24	2	Texas Tech.
37	Reinfeldt, Mike*	S	6-2	196	30	9	Wisconsin-Milwaukee
82	Renfro, Mike*	WR	6-0	184	28	6	Texas Christian
53	Riley, Avon*	LB	6-3	211	24	3	UCLA
85	Roaches, Carl	KR/WR	5-8	165	29	4	Texas A & M
62	Schumacher, John*	OT/OG	6-3	266	27	5	USC
90	Skaugstad, Daryle	DT	6-5	254	26	3	California
83	Smith, Tim	WR	6-2	192	26	4	Nebraska
67	Stensrud, Mike*	DT	6-5	280	27	5	Iowa State
73	Taylor, Malcolm	DE/DT	6-6	250	23	2	Tennessee State
28	Thomaselli, Rich	RB	6-1	196	26	3	W. Virginia Wesleyan
51	Thompson, Ted	LB	6-1	229	30	9	Southern Methodist
76	Towns, Morris*	OT	6-5	251	29	7	Missouri
20	Tullis, Willie*	CB/KR	6-0	190	25	3	Troy State
59	Washington, Ted	LB	6-2	248	35	11	Mississippi Valley
68	Williams, Ralph	OG/OT	6-3	270	25	2	Southern
33	Wilson, J. C.	CB	6-0	178	27	6	Pittsburgh

1983 Draft

Round	Name	Pos.	Ht.	Wt.	College
1	Matthews, Bruce	OG	5-3½	275	USC
2	Salem, Harvey	OT	6-5½	265	California
2	Bostic, Keith	DB	6-0	205	Michigan
3	Joiner, Tim	LB	6-4	221	Louisiana State
3	Dressel, Chris	TE	6-4	232	Stanford
4	Hill, Greg	DB	6-0	185	Oklahoma State
4	McCloskey, Mike	TE	6-5	243	Penn State
5	Moriarty, Larry	RB	6-0	225	Notre Dame
5	Foster, Jerome	DT	6-1	257	Ohio State
6	Haworth, Steve	DB	5-11	184	Oklahoma
7	Walls, Herkie	WR	5-7½	150	Texas
8	Thompson, Robert	LB	6-2½	220	Michigan
9	Potter, Kevin	DB	5-9½	188	Missouri

PITTSBURGH STEELERS AFC Central

Address Three Rivers Stadium, 300 Stadium Circle,
Pittsburgh, Pennsylvania 15212.
Stadium Three Rivers Stadium, Pittsburgh.
Capacity 54,000. *Playing Surface* Tartan Turf.
Team Colours Black and Gold. '
Head Coach Chuck Noll – fourteenth year.
Championships Super Bowl 1974, '75, '78, 79.
Conference 1974, '75, '78, '79.
Division 1972, '74, '75, '76, '77, '78, '79.
History NFL 1933-69. AFC 1970-

All Clubs can refer to their early faltering days, but for the Steelers these days lasted forty-two years. The end of the beginning was in 1969 when owner Art Rooney hired his fourteenth Head Coach, Chuck Noll. His brief was to build a team from the College Draft and he started with 'Mean' Joe Greene, a devastating defensive tackle and around whom was assembled the 'Steel Curtain'. The following year, he took Terry Bradshaw, a young man of raw talent, no nerves and a killer instinct. From the quarterback position, Bradshaw has directed an offense that, at some time or other, has murdered every defense in the League. Since their first Division title in 1972, they have missed the playoffs only twice and in this period have contested the Super Bowl four times without defeat. After a brief pause for Spring cleaning, the Steelers are poised to reassume their dominance of the AFC Central.

Offense
Craig Wolfley and Steve Courson are the established new faces, alongside the veterans Larry Brown and All Pro center Mike Webster, on a no-nonsense offensive line. Ted Petersen is an adequate replacement for Ray Pinney (gone to USFL). In every sense, Terry Bradshaw is one of the finest quarterbacks of all time, and this four-time Super Bowl winner enters 1983 with renewed enthusiasm. There

was a hiccup at wide receiver when the retirement of Lynn Swann was quickly followed by Jim Smith's departure for the USFL. Conceivably, Greg Hawthorne could fill in whilst the rookie, Wayne Capers, learns the system. On the opposite side, John Stallworth, the nine-year veteran, has few equals and will be Bradshaw's prime target, with tight end Bennie Cunningham not far behind. The rushing offense promises to be devastating. Rookie Walter Abercrombie was wisely nursed through last season after an early injury, and the whole of Football is expectantly waiting for the sight of the young genius playing alongside the old master, Franco Harris, who is now only 1,369 yards adrift of Jim Brown's career rushing record. The best guess would have Harris within 400 yards of his goal at the end of 1983.

Defense
Rushing against the 'Steel Curtain', 1980's version, is an unprofitable business. John Goodman is now a regular, alongside Tom Beasley and Gary Dunn, on the front line, which mounts a fearsome rush. The linebackers, with the predatory Jack Lambert directing affairs, rapidly extinguish what little daylight develops. It is the only defense which consistently holds the great Earl Campbell of Houston. The pass defense has improved substantially from 1981's debacle, with the emergence of the lightning fast Dwayne Woodruff at cornerback. Donnie Shell and Mel Blount are reliable veterans, dating back to the successful Super Bowl era. Ron Johnson has served his apprenticeship and now commands the other safety spot.

Special Teams
Gary Anderson missed only two field goals and was a bargain acquisition when discarded by Buffalo. John Goodson punts over 40 yards on average and could well hold off the challenge of Craig Colquitt (returning from injury). Sensibly, Fred Bohannon relieved Abercrombie of his kick return duties and rated a good fourth in the AFC. Ricky Woods was the most successful punt returner, with an excellent 10.9 average (fourth AFC).

Pittsburgh Steelers (AFC Central)

No.	Name	Pos.	Ht.	Wt.	Age	NFL Yr.	College
34	Abercrombie, Walter*	RB	5-11	201	23	2	Baylor
1	Anderson, Gary	K	5-9	156	24	2	Syracuse
65	Beasley, Tom*	DE/DT	6-5	248	29	6	Virginia Tech.
54	Bingham, Craig	LB	6-2	211	23	2	Syracuse
47	Blount, Mel*	CB	6-3	205	35	14	Southern
23	Bohannon, Fred	S	6-0	202	25	2	Mississippi Valley State
71	Boures, Emil	OG/C	6-1	262	23	2	Pittsburgh
12	Bradshaw, Terry*	QB	6-3	215	34	14	Louisiana Tech.
79	Brown, Larry*	OT	6-4	270	34	13	Kansas
56	Cole, Robin*	LB	6-2	220	27	7	New Mexico
5	Colquitt, Craig	P	6-1	182	29	5	Tennessee
77	Courson, Steve*	OG	6-1	260	27	6	South Carolina
89	Cunningham, Bennie*	TE	6-5	260	28	8	Clemson
72	Dallafior, Ken	OT	6-3	268	24	2	Minnesota
45	Davis, Russell	RB	6-1	231	26	4	Michigan

(continued opposite)

1983 Schedule

4 Sept	DENVER	1:00
11 Sept	at Green Bay	12:00
18 Sept	at Houston	12.00
25 Sept	NEW ENGLAND	1:00
2 Oct	HOUSTON	1:00
10 Oct	at Cincinnati	9:00
16 Oct	CLEVELAND	1:00
23 Oct	at Seattle	1:00
30 Oct	TAMPA BAY	1:00
6 Nov	SAN DIEGO	1:00
13 Nov	at Baltimore	2:00
20 Nov	MINNESOTA	1:00
24 Nov	at Detroit	12:30
4 Dec	CINCINNATI	1:00
10 Dec	at New York Jets	12:30
18 Dec	at Cleveland	1:00

Mike Webster (52) brushes aside the defensive tackle and sizes up the linebacker (53).

Pittsburgh Steelers (AFC Central) – continued

No.	Name	Pos.	Ht.	Wt.	Age	Yr.	College
55	Donnalley, Rick	C/OG	6-2	247	24	2	North Carolina
67	Dunn, Gary*	DT	6-3	260	30	7	Miami
48	Fedell, Steve	LB	6-2	238	25	2	Pittsburgh
20	French, Ernie	CB	5-11	188	23	2	Alabama A & M
	Gary, Keith	DE	6-3	257	23	1	Oklahoma
95	Goodman, John*	DE	6-6	250	24	3	Oklahoma
17	Goodson, John	P	6-3	204	23	2	Texas
32	Harris, Franco*	RB	6-2	225	33	12	Penn State
27	Hawthorne, Greg*	WR/RB	6-2	225	26	5	Baylor
53	Hinkle, Bryan	LB	6-1	214	24	2	Oregon
62	Ilkin, Tunch	OT	6-3	253	25	4	Indiana State
29	Johnson, Ron*	S/CB	5-10	200	27	6	East Michigan
90	Kohrs, Bob	DE	6-3	245	24	3	Arizona State
58	Lambert, Jack*	LB	6-4	220	30	10	Kent State
50	Little, David	LB	6-1	220	24	3	Florida
16	Malone, Mark	QB	6-4	223	24	4	Arizona State
57	Merriweather, Mike*	LB	6-2	215	22	2	Pacific
	Meyer, John	OT	6-6	257	24	1	Arizona State
64	Nelson, Ed	DT	6-3	247	23	2	Auburn
	Newton, Tom	RB	6-0	220	29	7	California
66	Peterson, Ted*	OT	6-5	244	28	7	East Illinois
44	Pollard, Frank	RB	5-10	210	26	4	Baylor
87	Rodgers, John	TE	6-2	220	23	2	Louisiana Tech.
36	Ruff, Guy	LB	6-1	215	23	2	Syracuse
31	Shell, Donnie*	S	5-11	190	31	10	South Carolina State
82	Stallworth, John*	WR	6-2	191	31	10	Alabama A & M
18	Stoudt, Cliff	QB	6-4	218	28	7	Youngstown State
85	Sweeney, Calvin	WR	6-2	190	28	4	USC
83	Sydnor, Willie	PR/WR	5-11	170	24	2	Syracuse
51	Toews, Loren*	LB	6-3	220	31	11	California
42	Washington, Anthony	S/CB	6-1	204	25	3	Fresno State
41	Washington, Sam	S/CB	5-8	180	23	2	Mississippi Valley State
52	Webster, Mike*	C	6-1	255	31	10	Wisconsin
93	Willis, Keith	DE/DT	6-1	251	24	2	Northeastern
37	Wilson, Frank	TE/RB	6-2	233	24	2	Rice
73	Wolfley, Craig*	OG	6-1	265	25	4	Syracuse
49	Woodruff, Dwayne*	CB	5-11	198	26	5	Louisville
22	Woods, Rick	KR/S	6-0	196	23	2	Boise State

1983 Draft

Round	Name	Pos.	Ht.	Wt.	College
1	Rivera, Gabriel	DT	6-2	296	Texas Tech.
2	Capers, Wayne	WR	6-2½	190	Kansas
3	Seabaugh, Todd	LB	6-3½	217	San Diego State
4	Metcalf, Bo Scott	DB	5-10	182	Baylor
5	Skanski, Paul	WR	5-11½	190	Washington
5	Garrity, Gregg	WR	5-9½	175	Penn State
6	Williams, Eric	DB	5-11½	180	N. Carolina State
7	Kirchner, Mark	OG	6-3	260	Baylor
8	Odom, Henry	RB	5-9	196	S. Carolina State
8	Dunaway, Craig	TE	6-2	235	Michigan
9	Wingle, Blake	OG	6-2	260	UCLA
10	Straughter, Roosevelt	DB	5-11	190	North-East Louisiana
11	Raugh, Mark	TE	6-3	205	West Virginia
12	Wiley, Roger	RB	5-10	195	Sam Houston State

AFC Western Division

DENVER BRONCOS AFC West

Address 5700, Logan Street, Denver, Colarado 80216.
Stadium Denver Mile High Stadium, Denver.
  Capacity 75,123. *Playing Surface* Grass.
Team Colours Orange, Blue and White.
Head Coach Dan Reeves – third year.
Championships Conference 1977; Division 1977, '78.
History AFL 1960-69. AFC 1970-

For their first twelve years in Football, the Broncos had a thoroughly miserable time. However, their subsequent progress has been that of a gradual and inexorable rise to respectability. They finished the 1970s with three consecutive playoff berths, starting in 1977 with a trip to the Super Bowl where, sadly, they were manhandled by the Cowboys in their least forgiving mood. Undeterred, they have since registered three 10-6 records and in 1981 were kept out of the playoffs only by the tie-breaking system (they were initially tied with Buffalo to whom they had lost in an inter-division game). That they are now to be taken seriously is testimony to the coaching expertise of, first, Red Miller and more recently, Dan Reeves. Dismissing last season (which was unusual to say the least), it is clear that those days of the easy game, one mile high in Denver, are long gone.

Offense

A high position in the College Draft (fourth) was to be the opportunity for repairing some sections of an offensive line, said to be approaching an advanced state of 'maturity', but the departure of number one pick Chris Hinton to Baltimore, in part exchange for John Elway (see later), put paid to that idea. It leaves draftee Mark Cooper as the only new face. The move for quarterback Elway (considered to be of limitless potential) is surprising. It must be with an eye to the future since, initially, he can hardly be expected to be better than the incumbent, Steve DeBerg, who now may not want to stay around. Whoever quarterbacks the team will have the high quality Rick Upchurch and Steve Watson, a dreaded long play threat, as the starting receivers. The new season should also see the emergence of the two 'Ws', Willhite and Winder, as respected running backs competing with Rick Parros and Dave Preston for a place. There is a real future in this section of the offense. Riley Odoms (tight end) certainly represents the past and the search for a replacement must be on.

Defense

The Bronco defense no longer strikes the terror of recent years in the opposition and, though not yet requiring the baling can, has sprung some irritating leaks. What remains of the 'Orange Crush' (defensive line) made only sixteen quarterback sacks yet, with the help of the linebacking quartet, made rushing a high risk business. There is linebacker quality in the All Pros Randy Gradishar, Tom Jackson and Bob Swenson, though the latter is reported to be unsettled and may soon be elsewhere. The return of Steve Foley from injury will strengthen a defensive back four which has lost Aaron Kyle (retired) and badly needs the skills of a revitalised Louis Wright, until recently considered to have no peer. Dennis Smith and Steve Wilson will be pressed by Roger Jackson for a place in the line-up.

Special Teams

Kicker Rich Karlis makes few mistakes and Luke Prestridge (punter) is currently the AFC's best. There is nobody even close to Rick Upchurch on punt returns and the successes of kick returner Wade Manning release Willhite for running back duties.

1983 Schedule

4 Sept	at Pittsburgh	1:00
11 Sept	at Baltimore	4:00
18 Sept	PHILADELPHIA	2.00
25 Sept	LOS ANGELES RAIDERS	2:00
2 Oct	at Chicago	12:00
9 Oct	at Houston	12:00
16 Oct	CINCINNATI	2:00
23 Oct	SAN DIEGO	2:00
30 Oct	KANSAS CITY	2:00
6 Nov	at Seattle	1:00
13 Nov	at Los Angeles Raiders	1:00
20 Nov	SEATTLE	2:00
27 Nov	at San Diego	1:00
4 Dec	CLEVELAND	2:00
11 Dec	BALTIMORE	2:00
18 Dec	at Kansas City	12:00

Denver Broncos (AFC West)

No.	Name	Pos.	Ht.	Wt.	Age	NFL Yr.	College
54	Bishop, Keith	C/G	6-3	260	26	3	Baylor
77	Boyd, Greg	DE	6-6	280	29	6	San Diego State
64	Bryan, Bill*	C	6-2	244	28	7	Duke
58	Busick, Steve	LB	6-4	227	24	3	USC
68	Carter, Rubin*	DT	6-0	253	30	9	Miami
79	Chavous, Barney*	DE	6-3	245	32	11	S. Carolina State
78	Clark, Brian	OT	6-6	260	22	2	Clemson
	Coder, Ron	OG	6-4	260	29	6	East Texas State
59	Comeaux, Darren	LB	6-1	227	23	2	Arizona State
55	Dennison, Rick	LB	6-3	230	25	2	Colorado State
17	DeBerg, Steve*	QB	6-2	205	29	7	San Jose State
85	Egloff, Ron	TE	6-5	227	27	7	Wisconsin
56	Evans, Larry*	LB	6-2	220	30	8	Mississippi College
43	Foley, Steve*	S	6-2	190	29	8	Tulane
62	Glassic, Tom*	OG	6-3	250	29	8	Virginia
53	Gradishar, Randy*	LB	6-2	231	31	10	Ohio State
31	Harden, Mike	S	6-1	190	25	4	Michigan
60	Howard, Paul	OG	63	260	32	10	Brigham Young
28	Jackson, Roger	CB	6-0	186	24	2	Bethune-Cookman
57	Jackson, Tom*	LB	5-11	228	32	11	Louisville

(continued opposite)

Denver Broncos (AFC West) – *continued*

No.	Name	Pos.	Ht.	Wt.	Age	NFL Yr.	College
75	Jones, Rulon*	DE	6-6	260	25	4	Utah
3	Karlis, Rich	K	6fi0	180	24	2	Cincinnati
76	Lanier, Ken*	OT	6-3	269	24	3	Florida State
72	Latimer, Don	DT	6-2	253	28	6	Miami
41	Lytle, Rob	RB	5-11	195	28	7	Michigan
83	Manning, Wade	WR	5-11	190	28	4	Ohio State
66	Manor, Brison	DE	6-4	248	31	7	Arkansas
82	McDaniel, Orlando	WR	6-0	180	22	2	Louisiana State
71	Minor, Claudie*	OT	6-4	275	32	10	San Diego State
88	Odoms, Riley*	TE	6-4	235	33	12	Houston
24	Parros, Rick*	RB	5-11	200	25	3	Utah State
34	Poole, Nathan	RB	5-8	205	26	4	Louisville
46	Preston, Dave*	RB	5-10	195	28	6	Bowling Green
11	Prestridge, Luke	P	6-4	235	26	5	Baylor
50	Ryan, Jim	LB	6-1	212	26	5	William & Mary
49	Smith, Dennis*	S	6-3	200	24	3	USC
70	Studdard, Dave*	OG/OT	6-4	255	27	5	Texas
51	Swenson, Bob*	LB	6-3	225	30	8	California
26	Thomas, J. T.	S	6-2	196	32	10	Florida State
37	Trimble, Steve	CB	5-10	181	25	3	Maryland
67	Uecker, Keith	OT/OG	6-5	260	23	2	Auburn
80	Upchurch, Rick*	WR/PR	5-10	176	31	9	Minnesota
81	Watson, Steve*	WR	6-4	192	26	5	Temple
47	Willhite, Gerald	RB	5-10	200	23	2	San Jose State
45	Wilson, Steve*	CB	5-10	193	26	5	Howard
23	Winder, Sammy	RB	5-11	203	23	2	S. Mississippi
52	Woodard, Ken	LB	6-1	218	23	2	Tuskegee
87	Wright, Jim	TE	6-3	240	27	5	Texas Christian
20	Wright, Louis*	CB	6-2	200	30	9	San Jose State

1983 Draft

Round	Name	Pos.	Ht.	Wt.	College
1	Elway, John	QB	6-3	210	Stamford
2	Cooper, Mark	OT	6-5	258	Miami, Florida
3	Sampson, Clinton	WR	5-11	184	San Diego State
5	Harris, Weedy	LB	6-2	214	Houston
5	Baldwin, Bruce	DB	6-0	200	Harding
6	Heflin, Victor	DB	6-0	185	Delaware State
7	Dupree, Myron	DB	6-0	190	N. Carolina Central
8	Kubiak, Gary	QB	6-0	190	Texas A & M
9	Hawkins, Brian	DE	6-1	190	San Jose State
10	Bowyer, Walt	DE	6-4	230	Arizona State
11	Bailey, Don	C	6-2½	250	Miami, Florida
12	Mecklenberg, Karl	DT	6-4	239	Minnesota

Randy Gradishar in the 'ready' position.

KANSAS CITY CHIEFS AFC Western

Address One Arrowhead Drive, Kansas City, Missouri 64129.
Stadium Arrowhead Stadium, Kansas City.
   Capacity 78,067. *Playing Surface* Tartan Turf.
Team Colours Red and Gold.
Head Coach John Mackovic – first year.
Championships Super Bowl 1969; AFL 1962, '66, '69;
   Division 1971.
History AFL 1960-69. AFC 1970-

The city of Dallas had both its Cowboys (NFL) and Texans (AFL) taking the field in 1960. The Texans were an almost immediate success, winning the AFL Championship in 1962, whilst the Cowboys laboured on, yet with the popular support. In 1963, Lamar Hunt took the Texans to Kansas City where the renamed Chiefs found a permanent home. They took their success with them, earning further AFC titles in 1966 and '69, both occasions leading to the Super Bowl, which they won on their second visit. It was in this period too that there was established probably the most bitter rivalry in Football, with the Raiders.

    The 1970s, however, saw a precipitous decline, reaching an all-time low in 1977 with a 2-12 record. New Head Coach Marv Levy appeared to be succeeding with the slow and painful reconstruction process, yet he was dismissed at the end of 1982. New man John Mackovic (ex-Dallas) will no doubt have a few Landry tricks up his sleeve for the new season.

Offense

Quite simply, the Kansas City offense is nothing like as bad as the statistics would imply. The offensive line is respectable and has a good balance of maturity (Condon and Getty), experience (Herkenhoff and Budde) and youthful promise (Studdard – a rookie in 1982). The problem is one of uncertainty, namely which quarterback to use, Bill Kenney or Steve Fuller. Swapping the two at will, as happened in 1982, made protection a nightmare, hence the 40 quarterback sacks yielded. Conceivably, it could be neither of the two in 1983 since new Coach John Mackovic used his first draft option to take Todd Blackledge. Hopefully for the Chiefs, one of the veterans (4 years each) will stay around to allow for the normal rookie induction period of two to three years. The Football world was stunned by the close-season, accidental death by drowning of Joe Delaney, the Chiefs' thoroughbred running back. The combined efforts of James Hadnot and Billy Jackson cannot possibly make up for the loss of the great man. Henry Marshall is an excellent wide receiver and, in support of J. T. Smith on the opposite sideline, Carlos Carson presents the threat of a long passing target. Anthony Hancock too is itching to have a go in a passing offense which could lead the way back to respectability.

Defense

The defense has quality players spread throughout the unit, with three Pro Bowlers, Art Still (defensive line), Gary Green and Gary Barbaro (defensive backs), and Gary Spani on the verge of selection. The defensive line is sound but has little support in the pass rush from the linebacking quartet. In the latter, teamwork is poor, despite the fact that the four have played together unchanged for two seasons. By contrast, the defensive backs are of high standard as the rearguard of an eleven-man group which rates about halfway in the AFC.

Special Teams

Kicker Nick Lowery is a former All Pro and plays up to that standard. With Jeff Gossett having departed, the search for a punter is on. Anthony Hancock is a speedy kick and punt returner, but his follow-up squad is lax in halting the return runs.

Kansas City Chiefs (AFC West)

No.	Name	Pos.	Ht.	Wt.	Age	NFL Yr.	College
76	Acker, Bill	DT/DE	6-2	255	26	4	Texas
26	Barbaro, Gary*	S	6-4	204	29	8	Nicholls State
85	Beckman, Ed	TE	6-4	237	28	7	Florida State
99	Bell, Mike*	DE	6-4	255	26	4	Colorado State
57	Blanton, Jerry*	LB	6-1	236	26	5	Kentucky
45	Bryant, Trent	CB	5-9	180	24	3	Arkansas
66	Budde, Brad*	OG	6-4	264	25	4	USC
34	Burruss, Lloyd*	S	6-0	201	25	3	Maryland
88	Carson, Carlos	WR	5-10	172	24	4	Louisiana State
20	Cherry, Deron	S	5-11	185	23	3	Rutgers
41	Christopher, Herb	S	5-10	202	29	5	Morris Brown
65	Condon, Tom*	OG	6-3	272	30	10	Boston College
50	Daniels, Calvin	LB	6-3	236	22	2	North Carolina
84	Dixon, Al*	TE	6-5	235	29	7	Iowa State
4	Fuller, Steve	QB	6-4	198	26	5	Clemson
11	Gagliano, Bob	QB	6-3	193	24	3	Utah State
77	Getty, Charlie*	OT	6-4	269	31	10	Penn State

(continued opposite)

Art Still checks the scoreboard.

1983 Schedule

4 Sept	SEATTLE		3:00
12 Sept	SAN DIEGO		8:00
18 Sept	at Washington		1:00
25 Sept	at Miami		1:00
2 Oct	ST. LOUIS		3:00
9 Oct	at Los Angeles Raiders		1:00
16 Oct	NEW YORK GIANTS		3:00
23 Oct	at Houston		12:00
30 Oct	at Denver		2:00
6 Nov	LOS ANGELES RAIDERS		12:00
13 Nov	CINCINNATI		12:00
20 Nov	at Dallas		3:00
27 Nov	at Seattle		1:00
4 Dec	BUFFALO		12:00
11 Dec	at San Diego		1:00
18 Dec	DENVER		12:00

Kansas City Chiefs (AFC West)– continued

No.	Name	Pos.	Ht.	Wt.	Age	NFL Yr.	College
24	Green, Gary*	CB	5-11	184	27	7	Baylor
48	Hadnot, James	RB	6-2	244	26	4	Texas Tech.
82	Hancock, Anthony	KR/WR	6-0	187	23	2	Tennessee
44	Harris, Eric*	CB	6-3	191	28	4	Memphis State
56	Haynes, Louis	LB	6-0	227	23	2	North Texas State
60	Herkenhoff, Matt*	OT	6-4	270	32	8	Minnesota
52	Howard, Thomas*	LB	6-2	215	29	7	Texas Tech.
43	Jackson, Billy*	RB	5-10	223	23	3	Alabama
51	Jackson, Charles*	LB	6-2	220	28	6	Washington
9	Kenney, Bill*	QB	6-4	210	28	5	N. Colorado
55	Klug, Dave	LB	6-4	230	25	3	Concordia
91	Kremer, Ken*	DT	6-4	250	26	5	Ball State
71	Lindstrom, Dave	DE	6-6	257	28	6	Boston University
8	Lowery, Nick	K	6-4	190	27	4	Dartmouth
74	Mangiero, Dino	DE/DT	6-2	265	24	4	Rutgers
89	Marshall, Henry*	WR	6-2	214	29	8	Missouri
	McNorton, Kyle	LB	6-1	220	23	1	Kansas
53	Olenchalk, John	C/LB	6-0	228	28	3	Stanford
61	Parrish, Don	DT	6-2	264	28	6	Pittsburgh
79	Prater, Dean	DE	6-5	245	24	2	Oklahoma State
70	Rourke, Jim	OT	6-5	265	26	4	Boston College
38	Roquemore, Durwood	S	6-1	180	23	2	Texas A & I
81	Scott, Willie	TE	6-4	245	24	3	S. Carolina
73	Simmons, Bob	OG	6-4	260	29	7	Texas
86	Smith, J. T.*	PR/WR	6-2	185	27	6	N. Texas State
59	Spani, Gary*	LB	6-2	230	27	6	Kansas State
69	Steinfeld, Al	C/OT	6-4	256	24	2	C. W. Post
67	Still, Art*	DE	6-8	252	27	6	Kentucky
64	Studdard, Les*	C	6-4	255	24	2	Texas
39	Thompson, Del	RB	6-0	203	22	2	El Paso
	Washington, Tim	CB	5-9	184	23	2	Fresno State
	Washington, Ron	WR	5-9	190	25	2	Arizona State

1983 Draft

Round	Name	Pos.	Ht.	Wt.	College
1	Blackledge, Todd	QB	6-3	220	Penn State
2	Lutz, David	OT	6-5½	272	Georgia Tech.
3	Lewis, Albert	DB	6-2	186	Grambling
4	Wetzel, Ron	TE	6-5½	240	Arizona State
5	Arnold, Jim	P	6-2½	195	Vanderbilt
6	Gardner, Ellis	OT	6-4	258	Georgia Tech.
7	Thomas, Ken	RB/DB	5-9½	195	San Jose State
7	Posey, Darryl	RB	6-0	212	Mississippi College
9	Lingner, Adam	C	6-4	240	Illinois
10	Shumate, Mark	DE/DT	6-4	251	Wisconsin
11	Jackson, DeWayne	DE	6-3½	254	S. Carolina State
12	Jones, Kenny	OT	6-5	259	Tennessee

LOS ANGELES RAIDERS AFC West

Address 332, Center Street, El Segundon, California 90245.
Stadium Los Angeles Memorial Coliseum, Los Angeles.
  Capacity 90,000. *Playing Surface* Grass.
Team Colours Silver and Black.
Head Coach Tom Flores – fifth year.
Championships Super Bowl 1976, '80; AFL 1967;
  Conference 1976, '80; Division 1970, '72, '73, '74, '75, '76.
History AFL 1960-69. AFC 1970-
  (Known as Oakland Raiders until 1982)

For the last twenty years, the Raiders have had the best won-lost record in Football. No fewer than ten times have they contested the Conference Championship game, surprisingly winning only three. These of course led to the Super Bowl, which they have won twice. At the nerve centre throughout this successful period has been Al Davis, first as an outstanding coach and later as senior administrator, and it was his eye for a good deal which brought together a collection of veterans which shocked the League by winning Super Bowl XV. In his time he has hired an endless string of brilliant, charismatic and frustrating players, none more typical than, respectively, Marcus Allen, George Blanda and Daryle 'The Mad Bomber' Lamonica. Under current Head Coach Tom Flores, the tradition will be maintained.

Offense

It is just as well that there is a good deal of experience and confidence on the offensive line, for the number one draftee, Don Mosebar, was found to have back problems which will delay his introduction. It seems likely that the veteran Jim Plunkett will retain his place as the senior quarterback, meaning that the talented Marc Wilson will yet again play a reserve role. Despite his lapses (unaccountable interceptions), Plunkett squeezes the maximum out of a collection of moderate wide receivers to good effect (third in passing, AFC) and the return of a healthy Bob Chandler will be welcomed. But even he is approaching the end of his career and, with Cliff Branch in a similar position, the need for young talent is obvious. Fortunately, Todd Christensen (tight end) can be expected to haul in a hatful of pass receptions (as he did in 1982), thus maintaining the momentum of the offense. Running back Marcus Allen was the 'steal' of the College Draft (third rushing and ninth passing, AFC) and naturally was voted 'Rookie Of The Year'. His partner, Kenny King, is a valuable and elusive alternative but largely (and graciously) functions as a blocker for Allen.

Defense

At the snap of the ball, the Raiders unleash a torrent of bodies and, with Alzado leading the way, registered 38 quarterback sacks in 1982 (NFL best). Dave Browning, returning after injury, will be fighting to get into fit enough trim to join in the fun. The linebackers, Ted 'Mad Stork' Hendricks, Bob Nelson, Rod Martin and Matt Millen, are a wrecking crew with the outstanding Jack Squirek in reserve. The defensive backs are not far short of the best with the brilliance of Lester Hayes (cornerback) and reliability of Burgess Owens and Mike Davis (safeties). However, as Wesley Walker (Jets) demonstrated in the playoffs, Ted Watts has still to work out the subtleties of cornerback play and indeed could be replaced by James Davis, who burst on the scene in late season with two long interception returns.

Special Teams

Chris Bahr is a reliable kicker and occasionally scores from long range. Ray Guy is one of the League's outstanding punters and his attempts are rarely blocked. Greg Pruitt (ex-Cleveland) proved a useful acquisition, sharing the kick returns with Cleo Montgomery and handling the punt returns, though with less success.

Los Angeles Raiders (AFC West)

No.	Name	Pos.	Ht.	Wt.	Age	Yr.	College
32	Allen, Marcus*	RB	6-2	210	23	2	USC
77	Alzado, Lyle*	DE	6-3	250	33	13	Yankton
10	Bahr, Chris	K	5-10	175	30	8	Penn State
56	Barnes, Jeff	LB	6-2	225	28	7	California
80	Barnwell, Malcolm*	WR	5-11	185	25	3	Virgina Union
40	Berns, Rick	RB	6-2	205	27	4	Nebraska
21	Branch, Cliff*	WR	5-11	170	35	12	Colorado
73	Browning, Dave	DE	6-5	245	27	6	Washington
85	Chandler, Bob	WR	6-1	180	34	13	USC
46	Christensen, Todd*	TE/RB	6-3	230	27	5	Brigham Young
50	Dalby, Dave*	C	6-3	250	33	12	UCLA
79	Davis, Bruce*	OT	6-6	280	27	5	UCLA
45	Davis, James	CB	6-0	205	26	2	Southern
36	Davis, Mike*	S	6-3	205	27	6	Colorado
8	Guy, Ray	P	6-3	195	33	11	S. Mississippi
27	Hawkins, Frank	RB	5-9	210	24	3	Reno
57	Hawkins, Mike	LB	6-2	232	27	6	Texas A & I

Ted 'Mad Stork' Hendricks takes off with a fumble recovery against the Chargers.

(continued opposite)

1983 Schedule

4 Sept	at Cincinnati	1:00
11 Sept	HOUSTON	1:00
19 Sept	MIAMI	6.00
25 Sept	at Denver	2:00
2 Oct	at Washington	1:00
9 Oct	KANSAS CITY	1:00
16 Oct	at Seattle	1:00
23 Oct	at Dallas	8:00
30 Oct	SEATTLE	1:00
6 Nov	at Kansas City	12:00
13 Nov	DENVER	1:00
20 Nov	at Buffalo	1:00
27 Nov	NEW YORK GIANTS	1:00
1 Dec	at San Diego	6:00
11 Dec	ST. LOUIS	1:00
18 Dec	SAN DIEGO	1:00

Los Angeles Raiders (AFC West) – continued

No.	Name	Pos.	Ht.	Wt.	Age	NFL Yr.	College
37	Hayes, Lester*	CB	6-0	200	28	7	Texas A & M
83	Hendricks, Ted*	LB	6-7	230	35	15	Miami
48	Hill, Kenny	S	6-0	195	25	3	Yale
42	Jackson, Monte	CB	5-11	195	30	9	San Diego State
31	Jensen, Derrick	RB	6-1	220	27	5	Arlington
90	Jones, Willie	DE	6-4	250	25	5	Florida State
33	King, Kenny*	RB	5-11	205	26	5	Oklahoma
62	Kinlaw, Reggie*	DT	6-2	245	26	4	Oklahoma
70	Lawrence, Henry*	OT	6-4	270	31	10	Florida A & M
75	Long, Howie*	DE	6-5	265	23	3	Villanova
60	Marsh, Curt*	OC	6-5	270	24	3	Washington
53	Martin, Rod*	LB	6-2	215	29	7	USC
65	Marvin, Mickey*	OG	6-4	270	27	7	Tennessee
26	McElroy, Vann	S	6-2	190	23	2	Baylor
23	McKinney, Odis	S	6-2	190	26	6	Colorado
55	Millen, Matt*	LB	6-2	255	25	4	Penn State
28	Montgomery, Cleotha	KR/RB	5-8	185	27	3	Abilene Christian
82	Muhammad, Calvin	WR	5-11	185	24	2	Texas Southern
76	Muransky, Ed	OT	6-7	280	23	2	Michigan
51	Nelson, Bob*	LB	6-4	235	30	7	Nebraska
44	Owens, Burgess*	S	6-2	200	32	11	Miami
54	Peterson, Cal	LB	6-2	220	31	8	UCLA
	Phillips, Irvin	CB	6-1	192	23	3	Arkansas Tech.
16	Plunkett, Jim*	QB	6-2	215	35	13	Stanford
34	Pruitt, Greg	KR/RB	5-10	190	32	11	Oklahoma
84	Ramsey, Derrick	TE	6-5	235	26	6	Kentucky
74	Reece, Archie	DT	6-3	262	27	6	Clemson
68	Robinson, Johnny	DT	6-2	260	24	3	Louisiana Tech.
	Sheppard, Henry	OG	6-6	263	31	8	Southern Methodist
52	Romano, Jim	C	6-3	260	22	2	Penn State
58	Squirek, Jack	LB	6-4	225	24	2	Illinois
66	Sylvester, Steve	OG/C	6-4	260	30	9	Notre Dame
67	Van Divier, Randy	OG	6-5	282	25	3	Washington
99	Vaughan, Reuben	DE	6-2	263	26	4	Colorado
20	Watts, Ted*	CB	6-0	190	24	3	Texas Tech.
38	Willis, Chester	RB	5-11	195	25	3	Auburn
6	Wilson, Marc	QB	6-6	205	26	4	Brigham Young
	Wilson, Tim	RB/TE	6-3	230	28	7	Maryland

1983 Draft

Round	Name	Pos.	Ht.	Wt.	College
1	Mosebar, Don	OT	6-6	275	USC
2	Pickel, Bill	DT	6-5	260	Rutgers
3	Caldwell, Tony	LB	6-1	220	Washington
4	Townsend, Greg	DE	6-2	243	Texas Christian
5	Williams, Dokie	WR	5-10	170	UCLA
7	McCall, Jeff	RB	6-1	227	Clemson
8	Dotterer, Mike	RB	5-11	194	Stanford
9	Jordan, Kent	TE	6-7	240	St. Mary's
12	Lindquist, Scot	QB	6-1½	195	Northern Arizona

SAN DIEGO CHARGERS AFC West

Address San Diego Jack Murphy Stadium, P.O. Box 20666, San Diego, California 92120.

Stadium Jack Murphy Stadium, San Diego. *Capacity* 52,675. *Playing Surface* Grass.

Team Colours Blue, Gold and White.

Head Coach Don Coryell – sixth year.

Championships AFL 1963; Division 1979, '80, '81.

History AFL 1960-69. AFC 1970-
(Known in 1960 only as Los Angeles Chargers)

Throughout their tenure in the AFL and on into the AFC, the Chargers were always respectable and, with the arrival of Head Coach Don Coryell in 1978, they became a genuine threat. But it has been their misfortune to lose the big playoff games, firstly to the Raiders in 1980 and then to Cincinnati, who gained not a little help from their local weather conditions (−35°C compared with Southern California's +27°C). Until recently, the offense had been largely a passing spectacular (The San Diego Air Force) as Dan Fouts serviced the likes of Wes Chandler, Kellen Winslow and Charlie Joiner. However, with the presence of the two running backs, Chuck Muncie and James Brooks, it is now more awesome. Yet defense remains a problem for which there is no quick solution.

Offense

By persisting with three offensive linemen who would qualify for 'Dad's Army', Coach Don Coryell clearly prefers experience to the potential of youth. Wilkerson, White and Washington enter their fourteenth, fifteenth and sixteenth seasons respectively. Still, they do the job, as the NFL's best group of strike players would testify. Quarterback Dan Fouts, re-enlisted for a reported $1,000,000 per season,

was sacked only thirteen times whilst deciding which of several attractive passing options to take. Wide receiver Wes Chandler was the only many to catch passes for over 1000 yards in the strike-shortened season, and these at the breathtaking average of 21.1 yards per catch. The veteran Charlie Joiner is unchallenged, operating on the opposite sideline. Tight end Kellen Winslow, blocking on the line and catching passes wherever it suits him, is the single most potent offensive weapon in the NFL. The rushing offense is only a shade less effective and with Chuck Muncie now rid of his problem of chemical dependancy (the latest cosmetic term for drug taking) the future is secure. James Brooks, equally productive in 1982, should be even better in 1983 and, with John Cappelletti doing relief work, the offensive unit as a whole should retain its number one position.

Defense

The defense is a shambles (third worst in the League) and the acquisition of several experienced players via the transfer market brought about no improvement. Sensibly, they have resorted to the College Draft, taking linebacker Billy Ray Smith (who has the sort of name which sounds just right) with their first option. The defensive line is powerful and certainly not old (all seventh or eighth-year men) but is rather slow. The linebackers are too harrassed to lend a hand and the defensive backs play as if they don't know each other's first names. Reuben Henderson (ex-Chicago) and Ken Greene (ex-St. Louis) are the most recent arrivals in the attempt to effect a solution.

Special Teams

Three years ago kicker Rolf Benirschke overcame serious organic illness and last year represented the AFC in the Pro Bowl. Rookie Maury Buford punted a satisfactory 41.3 yards on average. They take a risk allowing James Brooks to return both kicks and punts and, though he is good, it makes sense to hand over the job to a rookie for 1983.

San Diego Chargers (AFC West)

No.	Name	Pos.	Ht.	Wt.	Age	NFL Yr.	College
91	Ackerman, Richard	DE/DT	6-4	255	24	2	Memphis State
27	Allen, Jeff*	CB	5-11	185	26	4	California-Davis
37	Bauer, Hank	RB	5-11	204	29	7	California Lutheran
42	Bell, Ricky	RB	6-2	220	28	7	USC
6	Benirschke, Rolf	K	6-1	178	28	7	California-Davis
50	Bradley, Carlos	LB	6-0	221	23	3	Wake Forest
21	Brooks, James	RB	5-9	180	24	3	Auburn
61	Brown, Don	OT	6-5	250	24	2	Santa Clara
28	Buchanon, Willie	CB	6-0	185	32	12	San Diego State
7	Buford, Maury	P	6-1	180	23	2	Texas Tech.
25	Cappelletti, John*	RB	6-1	224	31	9	Penn State
89	Chandler, Wes*	WR	5-11	186	27	6	Florida
77	Claphan, Sam	OT	6-6	267	26	3	Oklahoma
82	Duckworth, Bobby	WR	6-3	198	24	2	Arkansas
76	Ferguson, Keith*	DE	6-5	240	24	3	Ohio State
14	Fouts, Dan*	QB	6-3	204	32	11	Oregon
48	Fox, Tim*	S	5-11	190	29	8	Ohio State

(continued opposite)

Dan Fouts awaits the snap from center Don Macek (62).

San Diego Chargers (AFC West) – continued

No.	Name	Pos.	Ht.	Wt.	Age	NFL Yr.	College
75	Gissinger, Drew	OT	6-4	280	24	2	Syracuse
	Goode, Don	LB	6-2	231	32	10	Kansas
	Greene, Ken	S	6-3	205	27	6	Washington State
43	Gregor, Bob	S	6-2	187	26	3	Washington State
	Henderson, Reuben	CB	6-1	200	24	3	San Diego State
88	Holohan, Pete	TE	6-4	226	24	3	Notre Dame
40	Jodat, Jim	RB	5-11	213	29	7	Carthage
79	Johnson, Gary*	DT	6-3	252	30	9	Grambling
18	Joiner, Charlie*	WR	5-11	183	36	15	Grambling
68	Jones, Leroy*	DE	6-8	271	32	8	Norfolk State
74	Kelcher, Louie*	DT	6-5	282	30	9	Southern Methodist
57	King, Linden*	LB	6-4	237	28	6	Colorado State
30	Laird, Bruce*	S	6-1	194	33	12	American International
53	Lewis, David	LB	6-4	240	28	7	USC
64	Loewen, Chuck	OG	6-3	259	26	4	South Dakota
51	Lowe, Woodrow*	LB	6-0	227	29	8	Alabama
11	Luther, Ed	QB	6-2	211	26	4	San Jose State
	Lyles, Warren	DT	6-1	261	24	2	Alabama
62	Macek, Don*	C	6-2	253	29	8	Boston College
60	McKnight, Dennis	OG	6-2	260	23	2	Drake
24	McPherson, Miles	DB	6-0	175	23	2	New Haven College
46	Muncie, Chuck*	RB	6-3	218	30	9	California
	Nelson, Derrie	LB	6-2	225	25	2	Nebraska
52	Preston, Ray	LB	6-0	218	29	8	Syracuse
56	Rush, Bob	C	6-5	264	28	7	Memphis State
87	Scales, Dwight	WR	6-2	185	30	7	Grambling
66	Shields, Billy*	OT	6-8	275	30	9	Georgia Tech.
85	Sievers, Eric	TE	6-4	235	25	3	Maryland
59	Thrift, Cliff*	LB	6-2	232	27	5	E. Central Oklahoma
70	Washington, Russ*	OT	6-7	288	36	16	Missouri
67	White, Ed*	OG	6-2	271	36	15	California
63	Wilkerson, Doug*	OG	6-3	254	36	14	N. Carolina Central
29	Williams, Mike*	CB	5-10	176	29	9	Louisiana State
80	Winslow, Kellen*	TE	6-5	242	25	5	Missouri
90	Woodcock, John	DE	6-3	255	29	7	Hawaii
49	Young, Andre	S	5-11	196	22	2	Louisiana Tech.
99	Young, Wilbur	DT	6-6	290	34	13	William Penn, Iowa

1983 Draft

Round	Name	Pos.	Ht.	Wt.	College
1	Smith, Billy Ray	LB	6-3	237	Arkansas
1	Byrd, Gill	DB	5-9½	187	San Jose State
4	Walters, Danny	DB	6-1	190	Arkansas
7	Elko, Bill	DT	6-4½	270	Louisiana State
8	Jackson, Earnest	RB	5-10	210	Texas A & M
9	Green, Mike	LB	6-0	218	Oklahoma State
10	Mathison, Bruce	DB	6-2	201	Nebraska
11	Kearse, Tim	WR	5-9½	174	San Jose State
12	Blaylock, Billy	DB	6-1	190	Tennessee State
12	Ehin, Chuck	DT/DE	6-3½	255	Brigham Young

SEATTLE SEAHAWKS AFC West

Address 5305, Lake Washington Boulevard, Kirkland,
Washington 98033.

Stadium Kingdome, Seattle.
Capacity 64,757. *Playing Surface* AstroTurf.

Team Colours Blue, Green and Silver.

Head Coach Chuck Knox – first year.

Championships None.

History NFC 1976. AFC 1977-

Together with Tampa Bay, the Seahawks are the most
recent entrants in the NFL, and they play in what is surely
the most beautiful stadium in the League. After the inevitable
opening (2-12) struggle, they rapidly attained respectability
and by 1978 had achieved their first net winning record
(9-7), earning for Head Coach Jack Patera the Coach of
The Year award. After repeating the 9-7 effort in 1979, their
4-12 record in 1980 was a setback and led to a redirection
of emphasis towards defense. They made progress in 1981
but, after a dreadful start to 1982 and amid rumours of
internal strife, Patera was fired. Seahawk fans will be
reassured by the arrival of his replacement, Chuck Knox,
whose Buffalo teams always knew the way into the end zone.

Offense
Coach Knox has begun the rehabilitation process on the
fundamental principle that Football is a rushing game.
Accordingly, Curt Warner of Penn State University was
drafted in the first round to bring potential star quality to
Seattle for the first time in their brief history. At the very
least, his sparkle will deflect defensive attentions away
from his running back partners, including the newly
acquired Cullen Bryant (ex-Rams) and the young David
Hughes, who should respond with improved output. The

passing offense too, now relieved of the responsibility for
almost the total offense, should benefit. Jim Zorn is a mobile
quarterback with an excellent arm and the nerve to use
the 'bomb' pass. His primary targets, Pro Bowler Steve
Largent and the veteran Roger Carr, have proved their
worth over the years and are joined by another exciting
newcomer, Chris Castor. Rookie Pete Metzelaars did an
adequate job in that most demanding of positions, tight
end. He has shown that he can catch passes and will begin
to add his weight (240lb in a 6ft 7in frame) to the offensive
line, which otherwise will have to soldier on for another
year before its turn for reinforcement comes around.

Defense
Defensive problems are less urgent; but for a couple of
loose games in 1982 they would have been up with the
statistical leaders. The defensive line is perhaps light-
weight compared with the monsters around the League,
but has speed and, though youthful, the experience of
having been thrown in at the deep end. All four of Jacob
Green, Robert Hardy, Manu Tuiasosopo and Jeff Bryant
(rookie, 1982), have been first stringers in every game of
their professional careers. Linebacking is sound, with the
ferocious Michael Jackson in the middle, flanked by Keith
Butler and the enormous Bruce Scholtz (6ft 6in and 240lb).
There is quality at defensive back, with safeties Ken Easley
and John Harris (4 interceptions each in 1982) always at the
centre of things.

Special Teams
This is an excellent and important component of the squad.
Norm Johnson (kicker) does everything expected of him
and Jeff West, with help from his special team tacklers,
ensures maximum yield from punts. Paul Johns rates highly
(third, AFC), returning punts and could see more action,
with Horace Ivory and Eric Lane, returning kicks in 1983.

Seattle Seahawks (AFC West)

No.	Name	Pos.	Ht.	Wt.	Age	NFL Yr.	College
12	Adkins, Sam	QB	6-2	214	28	7	Wichita State
63	Anderson, Fred	DE	6-4	245	28	5	Prairie View
76	August, Steve*	OT	6-5	254	28	7	Tulsa
65	Bailey, Edwin*	OG	6-4	265	24	3	S. Carolina State
82	Bell, Mark	DE	6-4	240	26	4	Colorado State
68	Boyd, Dennis*	OT	6-6	255	27	6	Oregon State
22	Brown, Dave*	CB	6-2	190	30	9	Michigan
30	Brown, Theotis	RB	6-3	225	26	5	UCLA
	Bryant, Cullen	RB	6-1	235	32	11	Colorado
77	Bryant, Jeff*	DE	6-5	260	23	2	Clemson
	Bush, Blair	C	6-3	252	26	6	Washington
53	Butler, Keith*	LB	6-4	225	27	6	Memphis State
71	Campbell, Jack	OT	6-5	277	24	2	Utah
87	Carr, Roger	WR	6-2	195	31	10	Louisiana Tech.
83	Doornink, Dan*	RB	6-3	210	27	6	Washington State
25	Dufek, Don	S	6-0	195	29	7	Michigan
66	Dugan, Bill	OG	6-4	271	24	3	Penn State
45	Easley, Ken*	S	6-3	206	24	3	UCLA
64	Essink, Ron	OT	6-6	254	25	4	Grand Valley

(continued opposite)

Ken Easley (45) sharpens up on the
practice field.

1983 Schedule

Date	Opponent	Time
4 Sept	at Kansas City	3:00
11 Sept	at New York Jets	4:00
18 Sept	SAN DIEGO	1:00
25 Sept	WASHINGTON	1:00
2 Oct	at Cleveland	1:00
9 Oct	at San Diego	1:00
16 Oct	LOS ANGELES RAIDERS	1:00
23 Oct	PITTSBURGH	1:00
30 Oct	at Los Angeles Raiders	1:00
6 Nov	DENVER	1:00
13 Nov	at St. Louis	12:00
20 Nov	at Denver	2:00
27 Nov	KANSAS CITY	1:00
4 Dec	DALLAS	1:00
11 Dec	at New York Giants	1:00
18 Dec	NEW ENGLAND	1:00

Seattle Seahawks (AFC West) – *continued*

No.	Name	Pos.	Ht.	Wt.	Age	NFL Yr.	College
50	Flones, Brian	LB	6-1	228	24	3	Washington State
56	Gaines, Greg	LB	6-3	220	24	3	Tennessee
79	Green, Jacob*	DE	6-3	247	26	4	Texas A & M
75	Hardy, Robert*	DT	6-2	250	27	5	Jackson State
44	Harris, John*	S	6-2	200	27	6	Arizona State
46	Hughes, David	RB	6-0	220	24	3	Boise State
32	Ivory, Horace	RB	6-0	198	29	7	Oklahoma
55	Jackson, Michael*	LB	6-1	220	26	5	Washington
85	Johns, Paul*	PR/WR	5-11	170	24	3	Tulsa
27	Johnson, Greggory	CB/S	6-1	188	24	3	Oklahoma
9	Johnson, Norm	K	6-2	193	23	2	UCLA
26	Justin, Kerry	CB/S	5-11	175	28	6	Oregon State
62	Kauahi, Kani	C/OG	6-2	260	23	2	Hawaii
17	Krieg, Dave	QB	6-1	185	24	4	Milton
54	Kuehn, Art	C	6-3	255	30	8	UCLA
37	Lane, Eric	KR/RB	6-0	195	24	3	Brigham Young
80	Largent, Steve*	WR	5-11	184	23	8	Tulsa
48	McAllister, Ken	S/LB	6-5	210	23	2	San Francisco
	McKenzie, Reggie	OG	6-5	242	33	12	Michigan
88	Metzelaars, Pete	TE	6-7	240	23	2	Wabash
72	Nash, Joe	DT	6-3	250	22	2	Boston College
52	Norman, Joe	LB	6-1	220	26	5	Indiana
61	Pratt, Bob*	OG	6-4	250	32	10	N. Carolina
57	Robinson, Shelton	LB	6-2	233	22	2	N. Carolina
81	Sawyer, John	TE	6-2	230	30	8	S. Mississippi
58	Scholtz, Bruce*	LB	6-6	240	24	2	Texas
42	Simpson, Keith*	CB	6-1	195	27	6	Memphis State
47	Smith, Sherman*	RB	6-4	225	28	8	Miami, Ohio
59	Thomas, Rodell	LB	6-2	225	25	3	Alabama State
86	Tice, Mike*	TE	6-7	250	24	3	Maryland
74	Tuiasosopo, Manu*	DT	6-3	252	26	5	UCLA
18	Walker, Byron	WR	6-4	190	23	2	Citadel
8	West, Jeff	P	6-2	220	30	8	Cincinnati
70	White, Mike	DT	6-5	266	26	5	Albany State
54	Williams, Eugene	LB	6-1	220	23	2	Tulsa
51	Yarno, John*	C	6-5	251	28	7	Idaho
10	Zorn, Jim*	QB	6-2	200	30	8	Pomona

1983 Draft

Round	Name	Pos.	Ht.	Wt.	College
1	Warner, Curt	RB	5-11½	200	Penn State
5	Castor, Chris	WR	5-11	165	Duke
6	Gipson, Reginald	RB	6-0½	196	Alabama A & M
7	Merriman, Sam	LB	6-2½	230	Idaho
8	Hernandez, Matt	DT	6-6½	265	Purdue
9	Clasby, Bob	DT	6-5½	264	Notre Dame
10	Speros, Pete	OG	6-2	255	Penn State
11	Mayberry, Bob	OG	6-5	248	Clemson
12	Dow, Don	OT	6-5½	285	Washington

NATIONAL FOOTBALL CONFERENCE

Conference Standings 1982

Washingtons Redskins	8	1	0	190	128
Dallas Cowboys	6	3	0	226	145
Green Bay Packers	5	3	1	226	169
Minnesota Vikings	5	4	0	187	198
Atlanta Falcons	5	4	0	183	199
St. Louis Cardinals	5	4	0	135	170
Tampa Bay Buccaneers	5	4	0	158	178
Detroit Lions	4	5	0	181	176
New Orleans Saints	4	5	0	129	160
New York Giants	4	5	0	163	160
San Francisco 49ers	3	6	0	209	206
Chicago Bears	3	6	0	141	174
Philadelphia Eagles	3	6	0	191	195
Los Angeles Rams	2	7	0	200	250

Teams with identical won-lost records were separated by a specially devised tie-breaker just for the 1982 strike-shortened season.

Playoff Results 1982

1st Round

Dallas Cowboys 30   Tampa Bay Buccaneers 17
Green Bay Packers 41   St. Louis Cardinals 16
Minnesota Vikings 30   Atlanta Falcons 24
Washington Redskins 31   Detroit Lions 7

2nd Round

Dallas Cowboys 37   Green Bay Packers 26
Washington Redskins 21   Minnesota Vikings 7

Championship Game

Washington Redskins 31   Dallas Cowboys 17

NFC Individual Ratings 1982

Passing

		Att.	Comp.	%	Yds.	TD	Lg.	Int.	Rating
Theismann	Washington	252	161	63.9	2033	13	78	9	91.3
White	Dallas	247	156	63.2	2079	16	49	12	91.1
Montana	San Francisco	346	213	61.6	2613	17	55	11	87.9
McMahon	Chicago	210	120	57.1	1501	9	50	7	80.1
Bartkowski	Atlanta	262	166	63.4	1905	8	88	11	78.1
Ferragamo	L.A. Rams	209	118	56.5	1609	9	85	9	77.7
Jaworski	Philadelphia	286	167	58.4	2076	12	57	12	77.5
Kramer	Minnesota	308	176	57.1	2037	15	65	12	77.3
Dickey	Green Bay	218	124	56.9	1790	12	80	14	75.4
Brunner	N.Y. Giants	298	161	54.0	2017	10	47	9	74.1
Stabler	New Orleans	189	117	61.9	1343	6	48	10	71.9
Lomax	St. Louis	205	109	53.2	1367	5	42	6	70.1
Williams	Tampa Bay	258	139	53.9	1704	7	62	9	68.9
Danielson	Detroit	197	100	50.8	1343	10	70	14	60.3

Receiving

		No.	Yds.	Ave.	Lg.	TD
Clark	San Francisco	60	913	15.2	51	5
Wilder	Tampa Bay	53	466	8.8	32	1
Andrews	Atlanta	42	503	12.0	86	2
Tyler	L.A. Rams	38	375	9.9	40	4
Moore	San Francisco	37	405	10.9	55	4

(continued opposite)

(receiving continued)

Tilley	St. Louis	36	465	12.9	34	2
Suhey	Chicago	36	333	9.3	45	0
Lofton	Green Bay	35	696	19.9	80	4
Carmichael	Philadelphia	35	540	15.4	46	4
Hill, T.	Dallas	35	526	15.0	47	1
Monk	Washington	35	447	12.8	43	1
Smith	Philadelphia	34	475	14 0	41	1
Sims	Detroit	34	342	10.1	52	0
Brown	Washington	32	690	21.6	78	8
Green	St. Louis	32	453	14.2	42	3
Payton	Chicago	32	311	9.7	40	0
Guman	L.A. Rams	31	310	10.0	46	0
Brown	Minnesota	31	207	6.7	29	2
Cosbie	Dallas	30	441	14.7	45	4
Groth	New Orleans	30	383	12.8	39	1
Moorehead	Chicago	30	363	12.1	50	5
White, S.	Minnesota	29	503	17.3	65	5
Senser	Minnesota	29	261	9.0	22	1
Giles	Tampa Bay	28	499	17.8	48	3
House	Tampa Bay	28	438	15.6	62	2
Jefferson	Green Bay	27	452	16.7	50	0
Warren	Washington	27	310	11.5	29	0
Mullady	N.Y. Giants	27	287	10.6	32	0
Perkins	N.Y. Giants	26	430	16.5	35	2
Pearson	Dallas	26	382	14.7	48	3

Rushing

		No.	Yds.	Ave.	Lg.	TD
Dorsett	Dallas	177	745	4.2	99	6
Sims	Detroit	172	639	3.7	29	4
Payton	Chicago	148	596	4.0	26	1
Anderson	St. Louis	145	587	4.0	64	3
Andrews	Atlanta	139	573	4.1	19	5
Tyler	L.A. Rams	137	564	4.1	54	9
Riggins	Washington	177	553	3.1	19	3
Rogers, G.	New Orleans	122	535	4.4	38	3
Montgomery	Philadelphia	114	515	4.5	90	7
Brown	Minnesota	120	515	4.3	30	1
Ivery	Green Bay	127	453	3.6	32	9
Woolfolk	N.Y. Giants	112	439	3.9	18	2
Wilson	New Orleans	103	413	4.0	20	3
Wilder	Tampa Bay	83	324	3.9	47	3
Riggs	Atlanta	78	299	3.8	37	5
Moore	San Francisco	85	281	3.3	19	4
Morris	St. Louis	84	274	3.3	11	4
Guman	L.A. Rams	69	266	3.9	15	2

(continued overleaf)

(rushing continued)

Springs	Dallas	59	243	4.1	46	2
Owens	Tampa Bay	76	238	3.1	14	0
Harrington	Philadelphia	56	231	4.1	37	1
Carver	Tampa Bay	70	229	3.3	13	1
Ellis	Green Bay	62	228	3.7	29	1
Suhey	Chicago	70	206	2.9	15	3
Carpenter, R.	N.Y. Giants	67	204	3.0	23	1
Washington	Washington	44	190	4.3	40	1
Mitchell	St. Louis	39	189	4.8	32	1
Ring	San Francisco	48	183	3.8	11	1
Rogers, J.	New Orleans	60	178	3.0	32	2
Rodgers	Green Bay	46	175	3.8	13	1

Kicking (Extra Points & Field Goals)		EP	EP Att.	FG	FG Att.	Pts.
Moseley	Washington	16	19	20	21	76
Capece	Tampa Bay	14	14	18	23	68
Stenerud	Green Bay	25	27	13	18	64
Wersching	San Francisco	23	25	12	17	59
Septien	Dallas	28	28	10	14	58
Danelo	N.Y. Giants	18	18	12	21	54
Luckhurst	Atlanta	21	22	10	14	51
Lansford	L.A. Rams	23	25	9	15	50
Murray	Detroit	16	16	11	12	49
Danmeier	Minnesota	23	23	8	14	47
Franklin	Philadelphia	23	25	6	9	41
Thomas	Chicago	9	9	10	12	39
O'Donoghue	St. Louis	15	16	8	13	39
Roveto	Chicago	10	10	4	13	22
Fritsch	New Orleans	8	9	4	7	20

Kickoff Returns		No.	Yds.	Ave.	Lg.	TD
Hall	Detroit	16	426	26.6	96	1
Nelms	Washington	23	557	24.2	58	0
Redwine	Minnesota	12	286	23.8	76	0
Watts	Chicago	14	330	23.6	36	0
Redden	L.A. Rams	22	502	22.8	85	0
Mitchell	St. Louis	16	364	22.8	33	0
Payton	Minnesota	12	271	22.6	32	0
Henry	Philadelphia	24	541	22.5	44	0
Fellows	Dallas	16	359	22.4	35	0
McLemore	San Francisco	16	353	22.1	45	0
Rodgers	Green Bay	20	436	21.8	76	0
Woolfolk	N.Y. Giants	20	428	21.4	34	0
Lawrence	San Francisco	9	190	21.1	30	0

(continued opposite)

(kickoff returns continued)

		No.	Yds.	Ave.	Lg.	TD
Thompson	New Orleans	10	211	21.1	35	0
Brown	Atlanta	17	340	20.0	33	0
Morton	Tampa Bay	20	359	18.0	26	0
Gentry	Chicago	9	161	17.9	23	0
Martin	Detroit	17	280	16.5	27	0

Punting

		No.	Yds.	Lg.	Ave.	Ret Yds.	Net Ave.
White	Dallas	37	1542	56	41.7	118	37.4
Jennings	N.Y. Giants	49	2096	73	42.8	207	37.3
Birdsong	St. Louis	54	2365	65	43.8	288	36.2
Coleman	Minnesota	58	2384	67	41.1	176	36.0
Erxleben	New Orleans	46	1976	60	43.0	239	35.2
Parsons	Chicago	58	2394	81	41.3	314	34.8
Skladany	Detroit	36	1483	59	41.2	200	34.0
Smigelsky	Atlanta	26	1000	54	38.5	73	33.9
Hayes	Washington	51	1937	58	38.0	106	33.3
Misko	L.A. Rams	45	1961	59	43.6	401	33.0
Runager	Philadelphia	44	1784	53	40.5	316	32.9
Swider	Tampa Bay	39	1620	59	41.5	192	32.7
Stachowicz	Green Bay	42	1687	53	40.2	286	32.4
Miller	San Francisco	44	1671	80	38.0	224	30.8

Punt Returns

		No.	Yds.	Ave.	Lg.	TD
Johnson	Atlanta	24	273	11.4	71	0
Irwin	L.A. Rams	22	242	11.0	63	1
Martin	Detroit	26	275	10.6	58	0
Solomon	San Francisco	13	122	9.4	27	0
Bright	N.Y. Giants	37	325	8.8	33	0
Payton	Minnesota	22	179	8.1	35	0
Nelms	Washington	32	252	7.8	28	0
Fellows	Dallas	25	189	7.6	17	0
Epps	Green Bay	20	150	7.5	35	0
Groth	New Orleans	21	144	6.9	18	0
Bell	Tampa Bay	10	62	6.2	14	0
Mitchell	St. Louis	27	165	6.1	15	0
Hicks	San Francisco	10	54	5.4	13	0
Gentry	Chicago	17	89	5.2	16	0
Henry	Philadelphia	20	103	5.2	11	0

Predictions 1983

East

Dallas Cowboys
Washington Redskins*
New York Giants
Philadelphia Eagles
St. Louis Cardinals

Central

Green Bay Packers
Tampa Bay Buccaneers*
Chicago Bears
Minnesota Vikings
Detroit Lions

West

San Francisco 49ers
Los Angeles Rams
Atlanta Falcons
New Orleans Saints

*Wild Card Teams

After three consecutive losing Championship games in 1980, '81 and '82, the Cowboys are selected to emerge as Conference Champions, before going on to beat San Diego 27-24 to win the Super Bowl.

NFC TEAMS 1983

NFC Eastern Division

DALLAS COWBOYS NFC East

Address 6116, North Central Expressway, Dallas, Texas 75206.

Stadium Texas Stadium, Irving, Texas.
Capacity 65,101. *Playing Surface* Texas Turf.

Team Colours Royal Blue, Metallic Blue and White.

Head Coach Tom Landry – twenty-fourth year.

Championships Super Bowl 1971, '77;
Conference 1970, '71, '75, '77, '78.
Division 1970, '71, '73, '76, '77, '78, '79, '81.

History NFL 1960-69. NFC 1970-

Over the period since their formation in 1960, the very name Dallas Cowboys has become synonymous with consistent excellence and one may assume that they will always and ominously reach the playoffs. Now ranking third in the list of coaches with most wins, behind George Halas and Curly Lambeau, Tom Landry enters his twenty-fourth season and the Cowboy dynasty is without doubt the product of his powers, both of motivation and innovative genius. As a player-coach with the Giants, he introduced the 4-3 defense. Using the particular talents of Roger Staubach, he resurrected the Shotgun Offense and more recently, confused us all with his Flex Defense. Landry and his lads enter the 1983 campaign still smarting from their defeat by Washington in the NFC Championship game, and it will be of no consolation that the victors went on to win the Super Bowl. In the two regular season contests, the sparks will fly.

Offense

The offensive line, as usual, will be excellent. All Pro Herb Scott must regain his place, having recovered from injury, and although there may be positional switches, such as Tom Rafferty from center to guard making way for Robert Shaw, in essence they can perm any five from eight. Despite Gary Hogeboom's commanding display in the Washington playoff game, Danny White (rated second by only a whisker in the NFC) will resume at the controls. At his disposal he has the wide receivers Tony Hill and Drew Pearson, the latter considered still good enough to hold off the challenge of 'Disco Dancing' Butch Johnson, who would be a star with many other clubs. Doug Cosbie (the most productive tight end in the NFC) provides a passing option over the middle. Quicksilver Tony Dorsett, who scored an NFL record 99-yard touchdown in 1982, is the spearhead of the rushing attack with his co-starter, Ron Springs, in the role of lead blocker. Tim Newsome and James Jones wait in reserve to give either man a breather. As a whole, the offense should retain its status as the NFC's best.

Defense

At some time or other, each of Ed 'Too Tall' Jones, John Dutton, Randy White and Harvey Martin, has achieved All Pro selection. Naturally it is the best defensive line in Football, which is just as well, for the linebacking trio of Hegman, Breunig and Brown (who may retire because of neck injury) is less secure. It is reasonable to assert that they have not fully adjusted to the complexities involved in defending against the more varied offenses of the last two or three years. It is also short on speed. By contrast, the defensive backs are excellent and share credit with the defensive line for the Cowboys' remarkable improvement against the pass. Everson Walls has defied his critics by leading the League in interceptions in each of his first two seasons and has established a fine rapport with his safety partner, Michael Downs. Dennis Thurman makes up for lack of speed with savage aggression and though the experienced Benny Barnes may be close to retirement, Dextor Clinkscale is ready to step in.

Special Teams

Septien is an excellent kicker and the former rugby union Springbok, Naas Botha, has arrived to relieve Danny White of the punting job. Ron Fellows doubles as kick and punt returner though the real burning speed comes from Rod Hill, who may play a greater part in 1983.

Dallas Cowboys (NFC East)

No.	Name	Pos.	Ht.	Wt.	Age	NFL Yr.	College
62	Baldinger, Brian	C/OG	6-4	255	24	2	Duke
31	Barnes, Benny*	S	6-1	203	32	12	Stanford
76	Bethea, Larry	DE	6-5	249	27	6	Michigan State
	Botha, Naas	P					
53	Breunig, Bob*	LB	6-2	223	30	9	Arizona State
59	Brown, Guy*	LB	6-4	228	28	7	Houston
18	Carano, Glenn	QB	6-3	198	27	7	Nevada, Las Vegas
47	Clinkscale, Dextor	S	5-11	189	25	3	S. Carolina State
61	Cooper, Jim*	OT	6-5	263	27	7	Temple
84	Cosbie, Doug*	TE	6-6	226	27	5	Santa Clara

Tony Dorsett takes the outside route.

In the team lists the asterisks (*) denote prospective starters.

(continued opposite)

1983 Schedule

5 Sept	at Washington	9:00
11 Sept	at St. Louis	12:00
18 Sept	NEW YORK GIANTS	3.00
25 Sept	NEW ORLEANS	12:00
2 Oct	at Minnesota	12:00
9 Oct	TAMPA BAY	3:00
16 Oct	at Philadelphia	4:00
23 Oct	LOS ANGELES RAIDERS	8:00
30 Oct	at New York Giants	1:00
6 Nov	PHILADELPHIA	12:00
13 Nov	at San Diego	1:00
20 Nov	KANSAS CITY	3:00
24 Nov	St LOUIS	3:00
4 Dec	at Seattle	1:00
11 Dec	WASHINGTON	3:00
19 Dec	at San Francisco	6:00

Dallas Cowboys (NFC East) – *continued*

No.	Name	Pos.	Ht.	Wt.	Age	NFL Yr.	College
51	Dickerson, Anthony	LB	6-2	222	26	4	Southern Methodist
83	Donley, Doug	WR	6-0	175	24	3	Ohio State
67	Donovan, Pat*	OT	6-4	259	30	9	Stanford
33	Dorsett, Tony*	RB	5-11	185	29	7	Pittsburgh
26	Downs, Michael*	S	6-3	198	24	3	Rice
89	Dupree, Billy Joe	TE	6-4	228	33	11	Michigan State
78	Dutton, John*	DT	6-7	263	32	10	Nebraska
	Eliopulos, Jim	LB	6-2	224	24	1	Wyoming
27	Fellows, Ron	CB	6-0	170	24	3	Missouri
58	Hegman, Mike*	LB	6-1	225	30	8	Tennessee State
25	Hill, Rod	CB/PR	6-0	182	24	2	Kentucky State
80	Hill, Tony*	WR	6-2	206	27	7	Stanford
14	Hogeboom, Gary	QB	6-4	200	25	4	Central Michigan
34	Hunter, Monty	S	6-0	201	24	2	Salem
86	Johnson, Butch	WR	6-1	180	29	8	Cal-Riverside
72	Jones, Ed*	DE	6-9	272	32	8	Tennessee State
23	Jones, James	RB	5-10	196	24	4	Mississippi State
57	King, Angelo	LB	6-1	220	25	3	S. Carolina State
79	Martin, Harvey*	DE	6-5	252	32	11	East Texas State
49	McClean, Scott	LB	6-4	231	22	2	Florida State
44	Newhouse, Robert	RB	5-10	220	33	12	Houston
30	Newsome, Tim	RB	6-1	232	25	4	Winston-Salem
88	Pearson, Drew*	WR	6-0	190	32	11	Tulsa
22	Peoples, George	RB	6-0	202	22	2	Auburn
65	Petersen, Kurt*	OG	6-4	266	26	4	Missouri
75	Pozderac, Phil	OT	6-9	260	23	2	Notre Dame
64	Rafferty, Tom*	C/G	6-3	258	29	8	Penn State
70	Richards, Howard	OG	6-6	248	24	3	Missouri
50	Rohrer, Jeff	LB	6-3	228	25	2	Yale
68	Scott, Herb*	OG	6-2	258	30	9	Virginia Union
1	Septien, Rafael	K	5-9	174	29	7	Southwest Louisiana
52	Shaw, Robert	C	6-4	260	27	5	Tennessee
60	Smerek, Don	DT	6-7	256	26	3	Nevada-Reno
55	Spradlin, Danny	LB	6-1	221	24	3	Tennessee
20	Springs, Ron*	RB	6-1	216	26	5	Ohio State
32	Thurman, Dennis*	CB	5-11	178	27	6	USC
63	Titensor, Glen	OG	6-4	257	25	3	Brigham Young
24	Walls, Everson*	CB	6-1	189	23	3	Grambling
11	White, Danny*	QB/P	6-2	196	31	8	Arizona State
54	White, Randy*	DT	6-4	250	30	9	Maryland
15	Wright, Brad	QB	6-2	209	24	2	New Mexico
73	Wright, Steve	OT	6-5	250	24	3	Northern Iowa

1983 Draft

Round	Name	Pos.	Ht.	Wt.	College
1	Jeffcoat, Jim	DE/DT	6-5	263	Arizona State
2	Walter, Mike	DE	6-3	228	Oregon
3	Caldwell, Bryan	DE	6-4	252	Arizona State
4	Faulkner, Chris	TE	6-4	231	Florida
5	McSwain, Chuck	RB	5-11	195	Clemson
7	Schultz, Chris	OT	6-8	261	Arizona
8	Ricks, Lawrence	RB	5-9	194	Michigan
9	Gross, Al	S	6-3	190	Arizona
11	Taylor, Dan	OT	6-4	262	Idaho State
12	Bouier, Lorenzo	RB	6-0	200	Maine

NEW YORK GIANTS NFC East

Address Giants Stadium, East Rutherford, New Jersey 07073.
Stadium Giants Stadium, East Rutherford.
  Capacity 76,891. *Playing Surface* AstroTurf.
Team Colours Blue, Red and White.
Head Coach Bill Parcells – first year.
Championships NFL 1927, '34, '38, '56.
History NFL 1925-69. NFC 1970-

Four outright titles represent poor reward for a Club which has contested the Championship Game thirteen times and played its full part in the establishment of the NFL by hanging on through the grim years of the late twenties and early thirties. Not since 1956 have they tasted success, despite an abundance of great players such as Andy Robustelli, Frank Gifford and Alex Webster. Former assistant coaches too have left to discover success elsewhere. Vince Lombardi went to Green Bay and ironically, when Tom Landry returns, it is only to pick up regular wins with his Cowboys. There were definite signs that the Giants were back when, in the 1981 playoffs, they narrowly lost to the 49ers who went on to win the Super Bowl. In 1982 there were several narrow defeats in games when victory in only one would have taken them to the post-season tournament. Former Head Coach Ray Perkins has gone to Alabama, leaving the responsibility for continued recovery on the shoulders of new man Bill Parcells.

Offense
There is little wrong with an offensive line which gave up only 17 quarterback sacks (third best in NFC) and the low rating for rushing offense could well have arisen from problems elsewhere (see running backs). Certainly, Bill Parcells was not panicked into seeking new talent from the College Draft. Having returned after resolving his contractual disagreements with the club, running back Rob Carpenter is expected to be the power that he was when he arrived from Houston in 1981. He is the ideal foil for the classy Butch Woolfolk, who had to bear the brunt of last year's rushing offense, and with Joe Morris as an option, they should rise above their ranking (thirteenth NFC) of 1982. Either Scott Brunner or Phil Simms (injured all last year) can do an effective job at quarterback, though their receivers are less than spectacular. However Floyd Eddings, who may initially have to play in a reserve role behind Perkins and Gray, gave indications of long play potential in 1982. The current tight ends are ordinary and, not surprisingly, Jamie Williams and Malcolm Scott were drafted in to challenge Mullady and Shirk.

Defense
The defense is sound, rating fifth (NFC) against both rushing and passing in yards yielded per attempt. The three-man line is settled and is reinforced by draftee Leonard Marshall, who more than compensates for the loss of a disgruntled Gary Jeter to the Rams. Brad Van Pelt, Brian Kelley, Harry Carson and Lawrence Taylor ('The Crunch Bunch'), form an awesome linebacking quartet, probably the NFC's best. The defensive backs too have improved with the emergence of All Pro Mark Haynes as a dominating figure at cornerback. Draftee Terry Kinard, rated the best safety in the colleges, will be on hand to maintain the quality, should either Bill Currier or Beasley Reece falter.

Special Teams
Kicker Joe Danelo had a below par season and may be replaced, but punter Dave Jennings quite properly gained All Pro status. Danny Pittman will take over as kick returner and Leon Bright seems sure to break for a long one, returning punts.

New York Giants (NFC East)

No.	Name	Pos.	Ht.	Wt.	Age	NFL Yr.	College
67	Ard, Billy*	OG	6-3	250	24	3	Wake Forest
74	Baldinger, Richard	OT	6-4	272	23	2	Wake Forest
60	Benson, Brad*	OT	6-3	258	27	6	Penn State
45	Bright, Leon	KR/RB	5-9	192	28	3	Florida State
12	Brunner, Scott	QB	6-5	200	26	4	Delaware
64	Burt, Jim	DT	6-1	255	24	3	Miami
22	Carpenter, Brian	DB	5-10	166	22	2	Michigan
26	Carpenter, Rob*	RB	6-1	230	28	7	Miami, Ohio
53	Carson, Harry*	LB	6-2	235	29	8	S. Carolina State
31	Chatman, Cliff	RB	6-2	225	24	2	Central State
29	Currier, Bill*	S	6-0	195	28	7	South Carolina
18	Danelo, Joe	K	5-9	166	29	9	Washington State
46	Dennis, Mike	CB	5-10	190	25	4	Wyoming
88	Eddings, Floyd	WR	5-11	177	24	2	California
37	Flowers, Larry	S	6-1	190	25	3	Texas Tech.
66	Foote, Chris	C	6-3	247	26	4	USC
83	Gray, Earnest*	WR	6-3	195	26	5	Memphis State
79	Hardison, Dee	DE	6-4	269	27	6	North Carolina
36	Haynes, Mark*	CB	5-11	185	24	4	Colorado

(continued opposite)

New York Giants (NFC East) – *continued*

Nc.	Name	Pos.	Ht.	Wt.	Age	NFL Yr.	College
27	Heater, Larry	RB	5-11	205	25	4	Arizona
61	Hughes, Ernie	C	6-3	265	28	5	Notre Dame
57	Hunt, Byron	LB	6-4	230	24	3	Southern Methodist
24	Jackson, Terry*	CB	5-11	197	27	6	San Diego State
13	Jennings Dave	P	6-4	205	31	10	St. Lawrence
55	Kelley, Brian*	LB	6-4	222	31	11	California Lutheran
72	King, Gordon*	OT	6-6	275	27	6	Stanford
51	Marion, Fred	LB	6-3	228	32	7	Florida A & M
75	Martin, George	DE	6-4	245	30	9	Oregon
69	Matthews, Bill	LB	6-2	235	27	5	South Dakota State
39	Mayock, Mike	S	6-1	195	25	2	Boston College
76	McGriff, Curtis*	DE	6-5	265	25	4	Alabama
52	McLaughlin, Joe	LB	6-1	235	26	5	Massachusetts
85	Mistler, John	WR	6-2	186	24	3	Arizona State
20	Morris, Joe	RB	5-7	190	22	2	Syracuse
81	Mullady, Tom*	TE	6-3	232	26	5	Southwestern (Memphis)
77	Neill, Bill*	DT	6-4	255	24	3	Pittsburgh
86	Perkins, Johnny*	WR	6-2	205	30	7	Abilene Christian
82	Pittman, Danny	WR	6-2	205	25	4	Wyoming
28	Reece, Beasley*	S	6-1	195	29	8	North Texas State
8	Reed, Mark	QB	6-3	195	24	2	Moorhead
17	Rutledge, Jeff	QB	6-2	187	26	5	Alabama
78	Sally, Jerome	DT	6-3	253	24	2	Missouri
44	Shaw, Pete	S	5-10	183	29	7	Northwestern
87	Shirk, Gary	TE	6-1	220	33	8	Morehead State
11	Simms, Phil*	QB	6-3	216	26	5	Morehead State
65	Tautolo, John	OG	6-3	260	24	2	UCLA
56	Taylor, Lawrence*	LB	6-3	237	24	3	North Carolina
68	Turner, J. T.*	OG	6-3	250	30	7	Duke
59	Umphrey, Rich*	C	6-3	255	24	2	Colorado
10	Van Pelt, Brad*	LB	6-5	235	32	11	Michigan State
58	Whittington, Mike	LB	6-2	220	25	4	Notre Dame
25	Woolfolk, Butch*	RB	6-1	207	23	2	Michigan

1983 Draft

Round	Name	Pos.	Ht.	Wt.	College
1	Kinard, Terry	DB	6-0½	190	Clemson
2	Marshall, Leonard*	DT	6-2½	274	Louisiana State
3	Williams, Jamie	TE	6-3½	240	Nebraska
3	Nelson, Karl	OT	6-6	280	Iowa State
5	Scott, Malcolm	TE	6-4	238	Louisiana State
6	Patterson, Darrell	LB	6-2½	228	Texas Christian
6	Belcher, Kevin	OG	6-2	250	Texas, El Paso
7	Williams, Perry	DB	6-1½	190	N. Carolina State
8	Headon, Andy	LB	6-4	222	Clemson
9	Haji-Sheikh, Ali	K	6-0	170	Michigan
11	Jenkins, Lee	DB	5-10	172	Tennessee
11	Pierson, Clenzie	DE/DT	6-6	254	Rice
12	Jones, Robbie	LB	6-3	235	Alabama
12	Magwood, Frank	WR	5-11½	187	Clemson
12	Tuggle, John	RB	5-11½	212	California

1983 Schedule

Date		Time
4 Sept	LOS ANGELES RAMS	1:00
11 Sept	at Atlanta	1:00
18 Sept	at Dallas	3.00
26 Sept	GREEN BAY	9:00
2 Oct	SAN DIEGO	4:00
9 Oct	PHILADELPHIA	4:00
16 Oct	at Kansas City	3:00
24 Oct	at St. Louis	8:00
30 Oct	DALLAS	1:00
7 Nov	at Detroit	9:00
13 Nov	WASHINGTON	4:00
20 Nov	at Philadelphia	1:00
27 Nov	at Los Angeles Raiders	1:00
4 Dec	St. LOUIS	1:00
11 Dec	SEATTLE	1:00
17 Dec	at Washington	12:30

Harry Carson in classic linebacker stance (reproduced by kind permission of the New York Giants).

125

PHILADELPHIA EAGLES NFC East

Address Philadelphia Veterans Stadium, Broad St. and Pattison Ave., Philadelphia, Pa. 19148.

Stadium Philadelphia Veterans Stadium, Philadelphia. *Capacity* 72,204. *Playing Surface* Grass.

Team Colours Kelly Green, White and Silver.

Head Coach Marion Campbell – first year.

Championships NFL 1948, '49, '60; Conference 1980; Division 1980.

History NFL 1933-69. NFC 1970-

Another of the NFL's senior Clubs, the Eagles entered the League in 1933 when the Frankford Yellowjackets franchise was transferred to Philadelphia. They spent the first ten years usually in bottom place before making a gradual rise and, after a loss to Chicago in 1947, won Championships in 1948, '49 and later in 1960. Then came another barren period in a division dominated by Cleveland. The arrival of Head Coach Dick Vermeil signalled a return to respectability and in his third season (1978) they were back in the playoffs. They lost to Atlanta but for the next three seasons, each time reaching the playoffs, were never to be beaten easily. Their losses both in the 1980 Super Bowl to Oakland and the 1981 Wild Card game to New York, were the result of mistakes, uncharacteristic of a team coached by Vermeil, an acknowledged workaholic. They were next to bottom in the NFC in 1982 and a 'burnt out' Vermeil opted for a television job, making way for new man Marion Campbell.

Offense

The offensive line can call on the vast experience of Stan Walters, Guy Morriss and Jerry Sisemore, whilst Steve Kenney and Ron Baker have learned the ropes. Yet an uncomfortable 31 quarterback sacks yielded must be accounted for, and it could well be that one or two of the veterans are feeling the pace. Frank Giddens, a second year man, is likely to see more playing time at the expense of Sisemore. Quarterback Ron 'The Polish Rifle' Jaworski is still struggling to regain his 1980 form, even with the options presented by a sound corps of pass receivers. Harold Carmichael rates with the best and, statistically, Ron Smith is not far behind with the potential of a young Mike Quick as yet untapped. John Spagnola (tight end) is coming off his best year and the remarkable Wilbert Montgomery (running back) is an ever present danger, drifting into unmarked positions. Naturally, in his main role (rushing) he led the Eagles with a 4.5 yard average (NFC best), not forgetting his 90-yard touchdown against Houston. With the arrival of draftee Michael Haddix, the prospects for the rushing offense become really exciting.

Defense

The defensive line, in which Pro Bowler Dennis Harrison is outstanding, gives up little against the rush but, despite registering 30 quarterback sacks (only three behind Dallas, the NFC leaders), the loss of Charlie Johnson to Minnesota had its effect. Opposing quarterbacks were able to pass against even this secondary defense (linebackers and defensive backs), which has few obvious weaknesses. The linebacking quartet underwent major reorganisation in 1982 with no apparent loss in effectiveness; indeed Jerry Robinson seems even more aggressive playing in a central position. The defensive backs too are sound, Herman Edwards and Roynell Young making 5 and 4 interceptions respectively. Draftee Wes Hopkins will find it difficult to displace either of the two safeties, Brenard Wilson and Randy Logan.

Special Teams

Tony Franklin is erratic and kicks barefooted, even in a cold Philadelphia December. He is retained, probably for the magnificent effort he occasionally pulls out of the bag. Max Runager punts a respectable distance, but not always with the accuracy demanded by modern tactics (aiming for the sideline). Wally Henry has been released, leaving both the kick and punt return assignments available to anyone with a death wish.

Philadelphia Eagles (NFC East)

No.	Name	Pos.	Ht.	Wt.	Age	NFL Yr.	College
96	Armstrong, Harvey	DT	6-2	255	23	2	Southern Methodist
63	Baker, Ron*	OG	6-4	250	28	5	Oklahoma State
27	Blackmore, Richard	CB	5-10	174	27	4	Mississippi State
98	Brown, Greg	DE	6-5	240	26	3	Kansas State
	Calhoun, Don	RB	6-0	212	31	10	Kansas State
37	Campfield, Billy	KR/RB	6-0	205	27	5	Kansas
17	Carmichael, Harold*	WR	6-8	225	33	12	Southern
71	Clarke, Ken*	DT	6-2	255	27	5	Syracuse
57	Curcio, Mike	LB	6-1	237	26	2	Temple
25	Devaughn, Dennis	S	5-10	175	22	2	Bishop
46	Edwards, Herman*	CB	6-0	190	29	6	San Diego State
24	Ellis, Ray	DB	6-1	192	24	3	Ohio State
1	Franklin, Tony	K	5-8	182	26	4	Texas A & M
	Fritzsche, Jim	OT	6-8	265	22	1	Purdue
79	Giddens, Frank	OT	6-7	300	24	3	New Mexico

(continued opposite)

Philadelphia Eagles (NFC East) – *continued*

No.	Name	Pos.	Ht.	Wt.	Age	NFL Yr.	College
58	Griggs, Anthony	LB	6-3	220	23	2	Ohio State
78	Hairston, Carl*	DE	6-3	260	30	7	Maryland State
35	Harrington, Perry*	RB	5-11	210	25	3	Jackson State
68	Harrison, Dennis*	DE	6-8	275	27	5	Vanderbilt
85	Hoover, Melvin	PR/WR	6-0	185	24	2	Arizona State
7	Jaworski, Ron*	QB	6-2	196	32	9	Youngstown
	Jenkins, Ken	RB	5-9	183	24	1	Bucknell
84	Kab, Vyto	TE	6-5	255	23	2	Penn State
73	Kenney, Steve*	OG	6-4	262	27	3	Clemson
55	Lemaster, Frank*	LB	6-2	238	31	10	Kentucky
41	Logan, Randy*	S	6-1	195	32	10	Michigan
45	Mansfield, Von	DB	5-11	185	23	2	Wisconsin
64	Miraldi, Dean	OG	6-5	254	25	3	Utah
99	Mitchell, Leonard	DE	6-7	272	24	3	Houston
31	Montgomery, Wilbert*	RB	5-10	195	28	6	Abilene Christian
50	Morriss, Guy*	C	6-4	255	32	10	Texas Christian
34	Oliver, Hubert	RB	5-10	212	25	3	Arizona
6	Pastorini, Dan	QB	6-3	205	34	13	Santa Clara
62	Perot, Petey	OG	6-2	261	26	4	Northwest Louisiana
9	Pisarcik, Joe	QB	6-4	220	31	6	New Mexico State
	Porter, Rick	RB	5-10	190	23	2	Slippery Rock State
82	Quick, Mike	WR	6-2	190	24	2	North Carolina State
56	Robinson, Jerry*	LB	6-2	218	26	4	UCLA
4	Runager, Max	P	6-1	189	27	4	South Carolina
87	Sampleton, Lawrence	TE	6-5	233	23	2	Texas
21	Sciarra, John	S	5-11	185	29	5	UCLA
76	Sisemore, Jerry*	OT	6-4	265	32	10	Texas
61	Slater, Mark	C	6-2	257	28	5	Minnesota
81	Smith, Ron*	WR	6-0	185	26	5	San Diego State
88	Spagnola, John*	TE	6-4	240	26	4	Yale
54	Valentine, Zack*	LB	6-2	220	26	5	East Carolina
42	Wagner, Steve	LB	6-2	208	29	7	Wisconsin
75	Walters, Stan*	OT	6-6	275	35	11	Syracuse
51	Wilkes, Reggie*	LB	6-4	230	27	5	Georgia Tech.
22	Wilson, Brenard*	S	6-0	175	28	4	Vanderbilt
89	Woodruff, Tony	WR	6-0	175	24	2	Fresno State
43	Young, Roynell*	CB	6-1	181	25	3	Alcorn State

1983 Draft

Round	Name	Pos.	Ht.	Wt.	College
1	Haddix, Michael	RB	6-1	227	Mississippi State
2	Hopkins, Wes	DB	6-0	205	Southern Methodist
2	Schulz, Jody	LB	6-3	238	East Carolina
3	Young, Glen	WR	6-2	196	Mississippi State
4	Williams, Mike	RB	6-1	212	Mississippi College
5	Darby, Byron	LB	6-3	244	USC
6	Oatis, Victor	WR	5-11	174	Northwestern Louisiana
7	Edgar, Anthony	RB	5-9	175	Hawaii
7	Schultheis, Jon	OG	6-2	265	Princeton
8	Kraynak, Rich	LB	6-0½	217	Pittsburgh
9	Pelzer, Rich	OT	6-5	280	Rhode Island
10	Strauthers, Thomas	DE	6-3½	255	Jackson State
11	Sebahar, Steve	C	6-3½	248	Washington State
12	Mangrum, David	QB	6-4	200	Baylor

1983 Schedule

4 Sept	at San Francisco	1:00
11 Sept	WASHINGTON	1:00
18 Sept	at Denver	2.00
25 Sept	St. LOUIS	1:00
2 Oct	at Atlanta	1:00
9 Oct	at New York Giants	4:00
16 Oct	DALLAS	4:00
23 Oct	CHICAGO	1:00
30 Oct	BALTIMORE	1:00
6 Nov	at Dallas	12.00
13 Nov	at Chicago	12.00
20 Nov	NEW YORK GIANTS	1:00
27 Nov	at Washington	1:00
4 Dec	LOS ANGELES RAMS	1:00
11 Dec	NEW ORLEANS	1:00
18 Dec	at St. Louis	12:00

Tony Franklin 'foots' an extra point.

127

NFC Eastern Division

St. LOUIS CARDINALS NFC East

Address 200, Stadium Plaza, St. Louis, Missouri 63102.
Stadium Busch Memorial Stadium, St. Louis.
  Capacity 51,392. *Playing Surface* AstroTurf.
Team Colours Cardinal Red, White and Black.
Head Coach Jim Hanifan – fourth year.
Championships NFL 1925, '47; Division 1974, '75.
History NFL 1921-69. NFC 1970-
  (Until 1960 known as Chicago Cardinals)

The Cardinals, then based in Chicago, were founder members of the NFL in 1921. They had the best record in the League in 1925 though this 'Championship' was rather hollow, arising as it did from technical violations by the Pottsville Maroons. It was to be 1947, after years of disappointment and failure, before their first title was unequivocally earned. They moved to St. Louis in 1960 and took their luck, such as it was, with them. There was a flurry of excitement in 1974 and '75 when, under Don Coryell, they won their division but on each occasion fell at the first hurdle. Since then there has been little of note except the odd win over Dallas, always an achievement.

There are, however, some signs of encouragement in that last year's 5-4 record was good enough to put them in the playoffs. They can look forward to 1983 with experienced veterans (Jim Hart and Pat Tilley), talented youth (Neil Lomax and E. J. Junior) and the excellent coaching of Jim Hanifan.

Offense

For the first time in years, the Cardinals have the makings of an offensive line. Dan Dierdorf (288lb) is the anchor at center, Joe Bostic and Terry Stieve are unchallenged in the guard positions and the whole is kept intact by two monster tackles, Luis Sharpe and James 'Tootie' Robbins, both of them rookies in 1982. For four of these years, Ottis Anderson (running back) has broken all Cardinal records and flirted with the NFL rushing title, but always having to settle for silver or bronze. Now, behind a predictably secure offensive line, he could well deliver the goods. However, his supporting cast of runners is rather thin. Wayne Morris is unlikely to improve and 'Stump' Mitchell is at best a stop-gap. Quarterback Neil Lomax was a flame thrower in college and, after two learning years in partnership with the veteran Jim Hart, should be ready to cut loose with the pros. Hart, one of only eight quarterbacks to have passed for over 30,000 yards, is retained, just in case. The reliable Pat Tilley holds down one receiver position and he is partnered by the remarkably versatile Roy Green. Hired as a defensive back, Green used to practise pass receiving just for a laugh and when given his chance against Dallas, in 1981, caught a 60-yard pass on his very first play. That same season, he became the only man for 25 years to score with a touchdown pass reception and make an interception in the same game (Washington).

Defense

The defense as a whole is not bad (halfway in the NFC) but is apparently a major priority area for 1983, since Hanifan used his first five draft options for defensive players. Ramsey Dardar and Mark Duda could help a defensive line which had difficulty nailing the quarterbacks in 1982. Craig Puki arrives from San Francisco to challenge for the middle linebacker position, flanked by Charlie Baker and the extremely talented E. J. Junior. The incumbents at defensive back, noticeably short on individual glamour, will be pressed by draftees Leonard Smith and Cedric Mack, drafted first and second respectively.

Special Teams

Carl Birdsong registered the highest average punting distance in the NFC and Neil O'Donoghue can punch the field goals over if the offense can give him sensible field position. Reserve running back 'Stump' Mitchell handles, or rather legs, the kick returns adequately, but is less successful returning punts.

St. Louis Cardinals (NFC East)

No.	Name	Pos.	Ht.	Wt.	Age	NFL Yr.	College
58	Ahrens, Dave*	LB	6-3	230	24	3	Wisconsin
51	Allerman, Kurt	LB	6-2	222	28	7	Penn State
32	Anderson, Ottis*	RB	6-2	220	26	5	Miami
	Audick, Dan	OT	6-3	253	28	6	Hawaii
52	Baker, Charlie*	LB	6-2	218	25	4	New Mexico
41	Bedford, Vance	CB	6-0	170	25	2	Texas
46	Bessillieu, Don	S	6-1	200	27	5	Georgia Tech.
18	Birdsong, Carl	P	6-0	192	24	3	Southwest Oklahoma
71	Bostic, Joe*	OG	6-3	268	26	5	Clemson
69	Brown, Rush*	DT	6-2	257	29	4	Ball State
64	Clark, Randy	C/OG	6-3	254	26	4	N. Illinois
60	Cotton, Barney	OG	6-5	265	26	5	Nebraska
73	Dawson, Mike*	DT	6-4	275	29	8	Arizona
72	Dierdorf, Dan*	C/OT	6-3	288	34	12	Michigan

(continued opposite)

1983 Schedule

4 Sept	at New Orleans	12:00
11 Sept	DALLAS	12:00
18 Sept	SAN FRANCISCO	12.00
25 Sept	at Philadelphia	1:00
2 Oct	at Kansas City	3:00
9 Oct	WASHINGTON	12:00
16 Oct	at Tampa Bay	1:00
24 Oct	NEW YORK GIANTS	8:00
30 Oct	MINNESOTA	12:00
6 Nov	at Washington	4.00
13 Nov	SEATTLE	12:00
20 Nov	SAN DIEGO	12:00
24 Nov	at Dallas	3:00
4 Dec	at New York Giants	1:00
11 Dec	at Los Angeles Raiders	1:00
18 Dec	PHILADELPHIA	12:00

Ottis Anderson slides around left end.

St. Louis Cardinals (NFC East) – *continued*

No.	Name	Pos.	Ht.	Wt.	Age	NFL Yr.	College
31	Ferrell, Earl	RB	6-0	215	23	2	E. Tennessee State
65	Galloway, David	DT/DE	6-3	283	24	2	Florida
57	Gillen, John	LB	6-3	228	24	3	Illinois
81	Green, Roy*	WR/DB	6-0	195	26	5	Henderson State
75	Greer, Curtis*	DE	6-4	258	25	4	Michigan
35	Griffin, Jeff*	CB	6-0	185	25	3	Utah
78	Grooms, Elois*	DE	6-4	250	30	9	Tennessee Tech.
39	Harrell, Willard	RB	5-8	192	30	9	Pacific
17	Hart, Jim	QB	6-1	210	39	18	Southern Illinois
54	Junior, E. J.*	LB	6-3	235	23	3	Alabama
89	Lafleur, Greg	TE	6-4	236	24	3	Louisiana State
16	Lisch, Rusty	QB	6-3	215	26	4	Notre Dame
15	Lomax, Neil*	QB	6-3	214	24	3	Portland State
40	Love, Randy	RB	6-1	205	26	5	Houston
80	Marsh, Doug*	TE	6-3	238	25	4	Michigan
76	Mays, Stafford	DE	6-2	250	25	4	Washington
87	McGill, Eddie	TE	6-6	225	23	2	Western Carolina
30	Mitchell, Stump	KR/RB	5-9	188	24	3	Citadel
24	Morris, Wayne*	FB	6-0	203	29	8	Southern Methodist
38	Nelson, Lee*	S	5-10	185	29	8	Florida State
11	O'Donoghue, Neil	K	6-6	210	30	7	Auburn
23	Perrin, Benny*	S	6-2	175	23	2	Alabama
70	Plunkett, Art	OT	6-7	262	24	3	Nevada, Las Vegas
50	Puki, Craig	LB	6-1	231	26	4	Tennessee
63	Robbins, James 'Tootie'*	OT	6-5	278	25	2	East Carolina
74	Sebro, Bob	OG/OT	6-4	255	24	2	Colorado
53	Shaffer, Craig	LB	6-0	230	24	2	Indiana State
67	Sharpe, Luis*	OT	6-4	260	23	2	UCLA
84	Shumann, Mike	WR	6-0	175	27	6	Florida State
	Smith, Wayne	CB	6-0	170	26	4	Purdue
21	Stief, Dave	S	6-3	195	27	6	Portland State
68	Stieve, Terry*	OG	6-2	265	29	7	Wisconsin
82	Thompson, Ken	WR	6-2	170	24	2	Utah State
79	Thornton, Bruce	DT	6-5	262	25	5	Illinois
83	Tilley, Pat*	WR	5-10	175	30	8	Louisiana Tech.
84	Whitely, Eddy	TE	6-3	228	25	2	Kansas State
42	Williams, Herb*	CB/S	6-0	200	25	4	Southern

1983 Draft

Round	Name	Pos.	Ht.	Wt.	College
1	Smith, Leonard	DB	5-10½	198	McNeese State
2	Mack, Cedric	DB	5-10½	183	Baylor
3	Dardar, Ramsey	DT	6-1½	250	Louisiana State
4	Duda, Mark	DT	6-2½	265	Maryland
4	Washington, Lionel	DB	5-11	180	Tulane
5	Bird, Steve	WR	5-10	174	Eastern Kentucky
6	Schmitt, George	DB	5-11	188	Delaware
7	Scott, Carlos	C	6-2½	290	Texas, El Paso
8	Harris, Bob	DB	6-2	210	Auburn
9	Brown, Otis	RB	5-11	198	Jackson State
11	Williams, Aaron	WR	5-11	165	Washington
12	Lane, James	LB	6-1	225	Alabama State

WASHINGTON REDSKINS NFC Eastern

Address Redskins Park, P.O. Box 17247,
Dulles International Airport, Washington, D.C., 20041.
Stadium Robert F. Kennedy Stadium, Washington.
Capacity 55,045. *Playing Surface* Grass.
Team Colours Burgundy and Gold.
Head Coach Joe Gibbs – third year.
Championships Super Bowl 1982; NFL 1937, '42;
Conference 1972, '82; Division 1972.
History NFL 1932-69. NFC 1970-
(Until 1937 known as Boston Braves)

In 1937 after five years in Boston, the Redskins moved to Washington D.C., where they promptly rewarded their new fans with the NFL Championship. They repeated in 1942 and, with quarterback Sammy Baugh at the controls, these were indeed 'The Glory Years'. However, by the time of Baugh's retirement in 1952, they were into decline and the sixties were worse. Vince Lombardi restored respectability in 1969 when, for the first time in eleven years, they had a net winning record. It was a foundation on which George Allen would build with his 'Over The Hill Gang' (he preferred seasoned veterans to young players). They lost in Super Bowl VII to Miami but during Allen's tenure (1971-77) went to the playoffs five times. After a dreadful start under Joe Gibbs in 1981 (losing the first five games) they recovered to end with an 8-8 record. With last year's magnificent victory in Super Bowl XVII they are about to discover how it feels to be the coconut on its shy.

Offense

The potential of the offensive line is frightening and it is unknown for a unit containing so little experience to handle defensive lines in a way they did against the Cowboys. Joe Jacoby, Russ Grimm and Mark May will be entering only their third seasons and Jeff Bostic his fourth. John Riggins prospered on their emerging dominance as he steadily warmed up during the regular season before exploding in the playoffs (660 rushing yards in four games). His partner, Joe Washington, provides an added dimension as one of several receivers who thrived on Joe Theismann's application of Coach Gibbs's complicated passing formula. Charlie Brown developed as a genuine big play receiver whilst Art Monk confirmed his reputation with thirty-five receptions. Monk, returning from injury, will have to work to replace the diminutive Alvin Garrett, who stepped in for the playoffs and caught five touchdown passes.

Defense

In 1982, the defense yielded the fewest points (128) in the whole NFL (Miami gave up 131) and again, three of the four starters on the defensive line, Darryl Grant, Matt Mendenhall and Dexter Manley, will be entering their third seasons in 1983. Furthermore, it is a well-balanced defense (fourth and third against the rush and pass respectively). The linebackers, Monte Coleman, Neal Olkewicz and Rich Milot, arent' exactly household names, but are highly mobile and ferocious in the tackle. Gibbs has sufficient confidence to use his most important draft options for elsewhere. Of the defensive backs, Jeris White is suspect, noticeably lacking speed (he was beaten badly several times in the playoffs). It is also fair to state that Tony Peters was flattered by his Pro Bowl selection. Yet Mark Murphy led the team in solo tackles and the rookie, Vernon Dean, was a revelation. Sensibly, Darrell Green (described as a blur over forty yards) was selected in round one of the draft.

Special Teams

Mark Moseley has nerves of steel and missed only one field goal in the regular season. The punter, Jeff Hayes, is less effective and could be replaced. Mike Nelms is above average returning punts but is the NFL's premier kick returner, always likely to go 'all the way'.

Washington Redskins (NFC East)

No.	Name	Pos.	Ht.	Wt.	Age	NFL Yr.	College
53	Bostic, Jeff*	C	6-2	246	24	4	Clemson
69	Brooks, Perry*	DT	6-3	260	28	6	Southern
87	Brown, Charlie*	WR	5-10	179	26	3	S. Carolina State
65	Butz, Dave*	DT	6-7	295	33	11	Purdue
82	Caster, Rich	TE	6-5	230	34	14	Jackson State
35	Claitt, Rickey	RB	5-10	206	26	4	Bethune-Cookman
51	Coleman, Monte	LB	6-2	230	25	5	Central Arkansas
54	Cronan, Peter	LB	6-2	238	28	6	Boston College
32	Dean, Vernon*	CB	5-11	178	24	2	San Diego State
86	Didier, Clint	TE	6-5	240	24	2	Portland State
59	Dusek, Brad	LB	6-2	223	32	10	Texas A & M
89	Garrett, Alvin	KR/WR	5-7	178	27	4	Angelo State
30	Giaquinto, Nick	RB	5-11	204	28	4	Connecticut
77	Grant, Darryl	DT	6-1	230	23	3	Rice
68	Grimm, Russ*	OG/C	6-3	250	24	3	Pittsburgh

(continued opposite)

1983 Schedule

5 Sept	DALLAS	9:00
11 Sept	at Philadelphia	1:00
18 Sept	KANSAS CITY	1.00
25 Sept	at Seattle	1:00
2 Oct	LOS ANGELES RAIDERS	1:00
9 Oct	at St. Louis	12:00
17 Oct	at Green Bay	8:00
23 Oct	DETROIT	1:00
31 Oct	at San Diego	6:00
6 Nov	St. Louis	4.00
13 Nov	at New York Giants	4:00
20 Nov	at Los Angeles Rams	1:00
27 Nov	PHILADELPHIA	1:00
4 Dec	ATLANTA	1:00
11 Dec	at Dallas	3:00
17 Dec	NEW YORK GIANTS	12:30

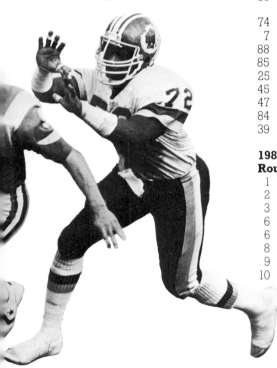

Dexter Manley (72) about to give Jeff Kemp a 'gentle' pat on the back.

Washington Redskins (NFC East) – continued

No.	Name	Pos.	Ht.	Wt.	Age	NFL Yr.	College
38	Harmon, Clarence	RB	5-11	209	27	7	Mississippi State
5	Hayes, Jeff	P	5-11	175	24	2	North Carolina
8	Holly, Bob	QB	6-2	195	23	2	Princeton
40	Jackson, Wilbur	RB	6-1	219	31	9	Alabama
66	Jacoby, Joe*	OT	6-7	282	34	3	Louisville
22	Jordan, Curtis	CB/S	6-2	205	29	7	Texas Tech.
55	Kaufman, Mel*	LB	6-2	214	25	3	Cal Poly Slo
50	Kubin, Larry	LB	6-2	234	24	2	Penn State
62	Laster, Don	OT	6-5	285	24	2	Tennessee State
79	Liebenstein, Todd	DE	6-6	245	23	2	Nevada, Las Vegas
56	Lowry, Quentin	LB	6-2	225	25	3	Youngstown State
72	Manley, Dexter*	DE	6-3	240	24	3	Oklahoma State
73	May, Mark*	OG	6-6	270	23	3	Pittsburgh
46	McDaniel, Lecharls	CB/S	5-9	169	24	3	Cal Poly Slo
78	McGee, Tony	DE	6-4	250	34	13	Bishop
76	Mendenhall, Matt*	DE	6-6	253	26	3	Brigham Young
57	Milot, Rich*	LB	6-4	230	26	4	Penn State
81	Monk, Art*	WR	6-3	209	25	4	Syracuse
3	Moseley, Mark	K	6-0	205	35	12	Stephen F. Austin
29	Murphy, Mark*	S	6-4	210	28	7	Colgate
21	Nelms, Mike	KR/S	6-1	185	28	4	Baylor
75	Ogrin, Pat	DE	6-5	265	25	3	Wyoming
52	Olkewicz, Neal*	LB	6-0	227	26	5	Maryland
17	Owen, Tom	QB	6-1	194	30	10	Wichita State
23	Peters, Tony*	S	6-1	177	30	9	Oklahoma
44	Riggins, John*	RB	6-2	230	34	12	Kansas
64	Saul, Ron	OG	6-3	254	35	14	Michigan State
80	Seay, Virgil	WR	5-8	170	25	3	Troy State
	Smigelsky, Dave	P	5-11	180	24	2	Virginia Tech.
74	Starke, George*	OT	6-5	250	35	11	Columbia
7	Theismann, Joe*	QB	6-0	195	33	10	Notre Dame
88	Walker, Rick	TE	6-4	235	28	7	UCLA
85	Warren, Don*	TE	6-4	236	27	5	San Diego State
25	Washington, Joe*	RB	5-10	179	29	7	Oklahoma
45	White, Jeris*	CB	5-10	188	30	10	Hawaii
47	Williams, Greg	S	5-11	185	24	2	Mississippi State
84	Williams, Mike	TE	6-4	245	24	2	Alabama A & M
39	Wonsley, Otis	RB	5-10	214	26	3	Alcorn State

1983 Draft

Round	Name	Pos.	Ht.	Wt.	College
1	Green, Darrell	DB	5-8½	172	Texas A & I
2	Williams, Richard	RB	6-0	209	Memphis State
3	Mann, Charles	DE	6-5½	233	Nevada Reno
6	Winckler, Bob	OG	6-2½	290	Wisconsin
6	Laufenberg, Babe	QB	6-2	190	Indiana
8	Hallstrom Todd	OT	6-6	255	Minnesota
9	Gilbert, Marcus	RB	5-9½	185	Texas Christian
10	Candy, Geff	LB	6-2	228	Baylor

NFC Central Division

CHICAGO BEARS NFC Central

Address 250, North Washington, Lake Forest, Illinois 60045.
Stadium Soldier Field, Chicago.
Capacity 65,077. *Playing Surface* AstroTurf.
Team Colours Burnt Orange, Navy Blue and White.
Head Coach Mike Ditka – second year.
Championships NFL 1921, '32, '33, '40, '41, '43, '46, '63.
History NFL 1921-69. NFC 1970-
(Known as Chicago Staleys for 1921 only)

The same George Halas who took part in the original 1920 meeting at the Hupmobile Agency still presides over the Bears in their sixty-fourth year in the NFL. A League-leading twenty former players, including Halas, are enshrined in the Hall Of Fame, and with eight Championships they rate second only to Green Bay. Yet, despite having their fair share of star players, there has been no success of any kind since 1963. Gale Sayers (running back) and Dick Butkus (linebacker) during the sixties maintained the star tradition established by 'Red' Grange, 'Bronko' Nagurski, Sid Luckman and even Halas himself. Walter Payton carries on in the same vein but that winning team formula has continued to elude successive Head Coaches. The latest, second year man, Mike Ditka, has chosen to rebuild around quarterback Jim McMahon, whose style and composure in his rookie year offered real signs of encouragement.

Offense

In 1982, there were several critical injuries to the offensive line and, not surprisingly, the walking wounded were dreadful. The quarterback was sacked thirty-three times (NFC worst) and running backs were obliged to make their own daylight. However, given any luck and soundness in returnees Ted Albrecht, Dennis Lick and Revie Sorey, the line could be respectable, and Jimbo Covert needs only to confirm his college rating to arouse memories of old. Rookie quarterback Jim McMahon exceeded all expectations and rapidly established himself as a genuine long passing threat. He extracted the maximum out of Moorehead, Margerum and Baschnagel, whilst the running backs, Walter Payton and Matt Suhey combined for a useful 640 yards. The prospects for the big play become really exciting with the acquisition of draftee Willie Gault, a sprinter of Olympic calibre. It is a rejuvenated Payton who anticipates improved blocking assistance in his quest for Jim Brown's all-time rushing record. He seems certain to register yet another 1000-yard season which, with Matt Suhey's usual contribution and the foil of a genuine passing alternative, will present problems for the opposition.

Defense

There are quality individuals in each phase of defense, in Dan Hampton (defensive line), Mike Singletary (linebacker) and Gary Fencik (safety). Overall then, it is acceptable, particularly against the rush (second NFC), but too often their commitment to nailing the quarterback (blitzing) left the defensive backs unaided and vulnerable. In one game, Vince Ferragamo (Rams) cut loose for 509 passing yards, which may lead to the adoption of the safer zone defense in 1983. Also, there are questions to be asked of the two cornerbacks, Schmidt and Frazier. Thus Mike Richardson (defensive back) was drafted in the second round.

Special Teams

Bob Thomas, the kicker, proved a point at Detroit and was welcomed back by the Bears who had released him prior to the season. Bob Parsons is a perfectly adequate punter but, ironically, may be released purely because his salary as a twelve-year veteran ($150,000 and automatic under the new player contract) may be considered too high – he would play for less but is not allowed to. Ricky Watts has breakaway speed as a kick returner though Dennis Gentry and Jeff Fisher are sub par returning the punts.

1983 Schedule		
4 Sept	ATLANTA	12:00
11 Sept	TAMPA BAY	12:00
18 Sept	at New Orleans	12.00
25 Sept	at Baltimore	2:00
2 Oct	DENVER	12:00
9 Oct	MINNESOTA	12:00
16 Oct	at Detroit	1:00
23 Oct	at Philadelphia	1:00
30 Oct	DETROIT	12:00
6 Nov	at Los Angeles Rams	1.00
13 Nov	PHILADELPHIA	12:00
20 Nov	at Tampa Bay	1:00
27 Nov	SAN FRANCISCO	12:00
4 Dec	at Green Bay	12:00
11 Dec	at Minnesota	12:00
18 Dec	GREEN BAY	12:00

Chicago Bears (NFC Central)

No.	Name	Pos.	Ht.	Wt.	Age	NFL Yr.	College
64	Albrecht, Ted	OT/OG	6-4	250	28	6	California
7	Avellini, Bob	QB	6-2	210	29	9	Maryland
84	Baschnagel, Brian*	WR	6-0	184	29	8	Ohio State
79	Becker, Kurt	OG	6-5	251	22	2	Michigan
25	Bell, Todd	S	6-0	207	24	3	Ohio State
54	Cabral, Brian	LB	6-1	224	27	5	Colorado
59	Campbell, Gary*	LB	6-1	220	31	7	Colorado
57	Chesley, Al	LB	6-3	240	25	5	Pittsburgh
10	Clifford, Tim	QB	6-1	207	25	3	Indiana
72	Doerger, Jerry	OT	6-5	255	22	2	Wisconsin
81	Earl, Robin	TE	6-5	240	28	7	Washington
8	Evans, Vince	QB	6-2	212	28	7	USC
45	Fencik, Gary*	S	6-1	197	29	8	Yale
24	Fisher, Jeff	DB/PR	5-10	188	25	3	USC
21	Frazier, Leslie*	DB	6-0	189	24	3	Alcorn State
	Frederick, Andy	OT	6-6	265	29	7	New Mexico

(continued opposite)

Chicago Bears (NFC Central) – *continued*

No.	Name	Pos.	Ht.	Wt.	Age	NFL Yr.	College
29	Gentry, Dennis	RB	5-8	173	23	2	Baylor
99	Hampton, Dan*	DT	6-5	255	26	5	Arkansas
35	Harper, Roland	RB	5-11	210	30	8	Louisiana Tech.
71	Hartnett, Perry*	OT	6-5	285	22	2	Southern Methodist
90	Harris, Al*	DE	6-5	240	26	5	Arizona State
73	Hartenstine, Mike*	DE	6-3	243	30	9	Penn State
51	Herron, Bruce	LB	6-2	220	29	6	New Mexico
63	Hilgenberg, Jay	C	6-3	250	24	3	Iowa
57	Huther, Bruce	LB	6-1	220	29	7	New Hampshire
65	Jackson, Noah*	G	6-2	265	32	9	Tampa
62	Jiggets, Dan	OT	6-5	270	29	8	Harvard
70	Lick, Dennis	OT	6-3	265	29	8	Wisconsin
82	Margerum, Ken*	WR	5-10	170	24	3	Stanford
37	McClendon, Willie	RB	6-1	205	25	5	Georgia
67	McKinnely, Phil*	OT	6-4	250	29	8	UCLA
9	McMahon, Jim*	QB	6-0	180	23	2	Brigham Young
76	McMichael, Steve	DT/DE	6-1	245	25	4	Texas
87	Moorehead, Emery*	TE	6-2	210	29	7	Colorado
58	Muckensturm, Jerry	LB	6-4	220	29	8	Arkansas State
52	Neal, Dan*	C	6-4	255	33	11	Kentucky
68	Osborne, Jim*	DT	6-3	245	33	12	Southern
86	Parsons, Bob	P	6-5	225	33	12	Penn State
34	Payton, Walter*	RB	5-10	202	29	9	Jackson State
	Saldi, Jay	TE	6-3	223	28	8	S. Carolina
44	Schmidt, Terry*	CB	6-0	177	31	10	Ball State
89	Scott, James	WR	6-1	190	31	6	Henderson
50	Singletary, Mike*	LB	5-11	230	24	3	Baylor
69	Sorey, Revie	G	6-2	260	29	9	Illinois
26	Suhey, Matt*	RB	5-11	217	25	4	Penn State
16	Thomas, Bob	K	5-10	175	31	9	Notre Dame
33	Thomas, Calvin	RB	5-11	220	23	2	Illinois
78	Van Horne, Keith*	OT	6-6	265	25	3	USC
75	Waechter, Henry	DT	6-5	270	23	2	Nebraska
23	Walterscheid, Len*	S	5-11	190	28	7	Southern Utah State
80	Watts, Rickey	WR	6-1	203	26	5	Tulsa
88	Williams, Brooks	TE	6-4	226	28	6	N. Carolina
43	Williams, Walt	CB	6-1	185	29	7	New Mexico State
55	Wilson, Otis*	LB	6-2	222	25	4	Louisville

1983 Draft

Round	Name	Pos.	Ht.	Wt.	College
1	Covert, Jimbo	OT	6-4	280	Pittsburgh
1	Gault, Willie	WR	6-0	178	Tennessee
2	Richardson, Mike	DB	5-11	190	Arizona State
3	Duerson, Dave	DB	6-0½	205	Notre Dame
4	Dunsmore, Pat	TE	6-2	228	Drake
8	Dent, Richard	DE	6-4	236	Tennessee State
8	Bortz, Mark	DT	6-5	266	Iowa
9	Fada, Rob	OG	6-1½	257	Pittsburgh
9	Zavagnin, Mark	LB	6-2	226	Notre Dame
10	Hutchison, Anthony	RB	5-9	179	Texas Tech.
11	Worthy, Gary	RB	5-11	190	Wilmington
12	Williams, Oliver	WR	6-2	184	Illinois

Gary Fencik, Chicago's All Pro safety.

DETROIT LIONS NFC Central

Address Pontiac Silverdrome, 1200 Featherstone Road,
Box 4200, Pontiac, Michigan 48057.
Stadium Pontiac Silverdome, Pontiac.
Capacity 80,638. *Playing Surface* AstroTurf.
Team Colours Honolulu Blue and Silver.
Head Coach Monte Clark – sixth year.
Championships NFL 1935, '52, '53, '57.
History NFL 1930-69. NFC 1970-
(Until 1934 known as Portsmouth Spartans)

The city of Detroit can truly claim to have been in on the ground floor when, in 1920, Professional Football was organised. The Heralds were followed by the Panthers who gave way to the Wolverines, but it was when the Spartans moved in for the 1934 season that the franchise became firmly established. They were a powerhouse in the fifties but since then, with only two playoff appearances (1970 and 1982) times have been lean. Always they have played second fiddle in the 'Black and Blue' division, to Green Bay in the sixties and to Minnesota in the seventies. The efforts of Alex Karras (defensive lineman), Lem Barney (defensive back) and the incomparable Charlie Sanders (tight end), went for nought. There were signs of re-emergence in 1981 but these gradually dissipated in 1982, culminating in a lamentable playoff performance against the Redskins. Yet the talent is there, and in Billy Sims they have one of the best half-dozen running backs in Football. With a few changes in the playbook, Monte Clark's Lions could well pose a serious threat to the Packers, who start the season as division favourites.

Offense

If the offensive line can settle down and forget what were significant internal wranglings of 1982, they could be very good indeed. They have experience, an average age of only twenty-five years and are injury free. They are joined by draftee Rich Strenger, a 6ft 7in monster tackle. Sadly, a disgruntled Russ Bolinger, displaced half way through last season, and who could have provided much needed reserve support, has gone to the Rams and Karl Baldischwiler, for identical reasons, is also likely to pack his bags. Those who stay have the responsibility (some would say good fortune) to block for running back Billy Sims. He is joined by draftee James Jones, the top-rated heavyweight running back in college. Together with Dexter Bussey, the experienced ten-year veteran in the background, they could rapidly re-establish the feared Lion rushing offense. It seems likely that quarterback Eric Hipple will get the nod at the expense of Gary Danielson, who may also wish to depart, leaving only Mike Machurek as reserve. Unless Mark Nichols can return after injury, the veterans Leonard Thompson and Fred Scott will be the starting wide receivers, with the ever dependable David Hill (tight end) operating in the middle where the going gets tough.

Defense

The four man line is awesome. Indeed, Bubba Baker, a three-time Pro Bowler and twice the NFL sack leader, cannot find a place – he too wants to leave. Ever mindful of their reputation, the Lions drafted Mike Cofer, just in case. The linebackers too are only a shade less fearsome and, with a healthy Jimmy Williams ready to return, the loss of Stan White to the USFL will not be felt. There are problems in the back four, riddled by the Jets and Redskins in 1982. Clark may well pick up a veteran in exchange for Baker.

Special Teams

With Eddie Murray (kicker) and Tom Skladany (punter) the Lions have the NFC's best kicking combination. Again, Alvin Hall and Robbie Martin are equal to the best in returning kicks and punts respectively.

Detroit Lions (NFC Central)

No.	Name	Pos.	Ht.	Wt.	Age	NFL Yr.	College
60	Baker, Al*	DE	6-6	250	30	10	UCLA
76	Baldischwiler, Karl	OT	6-5	265	27	6	Oklahoma
54	Barnes, Roosevelt	LB	6-2	215	23	2	Purdue
24	Bussey, Dexter*	RB	6-1	210	31	10	Arlington
31	Callicut, Ken	RB/DB	6-0	190	28	6	Clemson
53	Cobb, Garry*	LB	6-2	220	26	5	USC
16	Danielson, Gary*	QB	6-2	195	31	7	Purdue
72	Dieterich, Chris*	OT	6-3	269	25	4	N. Carolina State
58	Doig, Steve	LB	6-3	240	23	2	New Hampshire
70	Dorney, Keith*	OT	6-5	265	25	5	Penn State
61	Elias, Homer*	OG	6-3	255	28	6	Tennessee State
78	English, Doug*	DT	6-5	255	30	7	Texas
	Fanning, Mike	DT	6-6	255	30	9	Notre Dame
57	Fantetti, Ken*	LB	6-2	230	26	5	Wyoming
65	Fowler, Amos*	C	6-3	250	27	6	S. Mississippi
79	Gay, Bill*	DE/DT	6-3	250	28	6	USC
33	Graham, William*	S	5-11	188	22	2	Texas
26	Gray, Hector	DB	6-1	197	26	3	Florida State

(continued opposite)

Detroit Lions (NFC Central) – *continued*

No.	Name	Pos.	Ht.	Wt.	Age	NFL Yr.	College
67	Greco, Don*	OG	6-2	256	24	2	Western Illinois
62	Green, Curtis	DE	6-3	256	26	3	Alabama State
35	Hall, Alvin*	S	5-10	193	25	3	Miami, Ohio
51	Harrell, James	LB	6-2	215	26	5	Florida
81	Hill, David*	TE	6-2	230	29	8	Texas A & I
17	Hipple, Eric	QB	6-1	196	25	4	Utah State
32	Kane, Rick	RB	6-0	200	28	7	San Jose State
25	King, Horace	RB	5-10	210	30	9	Georgia
43	Latimer, Al*	CB	5-11	172	25	3	Clemson
47	Lee, Edward	WR	6-0	185	22	2	S. Carolina State
64	Lee, Larry	OG/C	6-2	274	23	3	UCLA
14	Machurek, Mike	QB	6-0	202	23	2	Idaho State
83	Martin, Robbie	KR/WR	5-8	179	24	3	Cal Poly Slo
29	McNorton, Bruce	CB	5-11	172	23	2	Georgetown, Kentucky
63	Moss, Martin	DT/DE	6-4	250	23	2	UCLA
3	Murray, Eddie	K	5-9	164	27	4	Tulane
86	Nichols, Mark*	WR	6-2	213	23	3	San Jose State
80	Norris, Ulysses	TE	6-4	230	26	5	Georgia
89	Porter, Tracy	WR	6-1	196	24	3	Louisiana State
75	Pureifory, Dave*	DE	6-1	255	34	12	Eastern Michigan
84	Rubick, Rob	TE	6-2	225	22	2	Grand Valley State
87	Scott, Fred*	WR	6-2	175	31	10	Amherst
20	Sims, Billy*	RB	6-0	212	27	4	Oklahoma
1	Skladany, Tom	P	6-0	195	28	5	Ohio State
50	Tautolo, Terry	LB	6-2	235	29	8	UCLA
39	Thompson, Leonard	WR	5-11	190	31	9	Oklahoma State
38	Thompson, Vince	RB	6-0	230	26	3	Villanova
55	Turnure, Tom	C	6-3	243	26	4	Washington
34	Wagoner, Dan	DB	5-10	175	22	2	Kansas
27	Watkins, Bobby*	CB	5-11	184	23	2	South West Texas St.
59	Williams, Jimmy*	LB	6-3	221	22	2	Nebraska

1983 Draft

Round	Name	Pos.	Ht.	Wt.	College
1	Jones, James	RB	6-2	236	Florida
2	Strenger, Rich	OT	6-7	270	Michigan
3	Cofer, Mike	DE	6-4½	235	Tennessee
4	Curley, August	LB	6-3	230	USC
5	Johnson, Demetrious	DB	5-11	191	Missouri
5	Mott, Steve	C	6-2	255	Alabama
7	Black, Mike	P	6-1	190	Arizona State
8	Stapleton, Bill	DE	5-11	187	Washington
9	Supplemental Draft Pick				
10	Laube, Dave	OG	6-2	260	Penn State
11	Tate, Ben	RB	6-0	230	N. Carolina State
12	Lane, Jim	C	6-3	243	Idaho State

Doug English (78) rounds the corner.

GREEN BAY PACKERS NFC Central

Address 1265, Lombardi Avenue, Green Bay,
Wisconsin 54303.

Stadium Lambeau Field, Green Bay and Milwaukee
County Stadium, Milwaukee.
Capacity (Lambeau Field) 56,189, (Milwaukee County)
55,958. *Playing Surface* Grass.

Team Colours Green and Gold.

Head Coach Bart Starr – ninth year.

Championships Super Bowl 1966, '67.
NFL 1929, '30, '31, '36, '39, '44, '61, '62, '65, '66, '67.
Division 1972.

History NFL 1921-69. NFC 1970-

Sixty-three years after their formation as the works teams of the Acme Packing Company, Green Bay Packers can claim to be the most successful team in Football, with eleven Championships including the first two Super Bowls. But for the last fifteen of these years, they have been haunted by the memories of two great dynasties, under Lambeau in the thirties and Lombardi in the sixties. Under Head Coach and former quarterback hero Bart Starr, the 'Green And Gold' have had to live with the jeers (not in Green Bay but around the League) and it was only the man's personal magnetism and the esteem in which he is held that kept him in a job. This faith appeared justified when in 1981 they narrowly missed the playoffs and was confirmed by last year's third place finish in the conference. Never was true Packer grit more in evidence than in their game against the Rams, when they overcame a 23-point deficit. Their fans have every reason for believing that 'The Pack Is Back'.

Offense

The offensive line is average at best and draftee David Drechsler could step into a starting role. They had difficulty blasting the holes for the running backs and the quarterback was sacked thirty-two times, though in fairness nine were against Detroit in one bad game and Lynn Dickey is not the most mobile of players. Given any kind of protection, he can unleash the most devastating passing offense in the NFC. James Lofton is a superb athlete with magnificent hands and blistering pace. He teams up with John Jefferson, whom many would regard his equal and who has settled down after leaving San Diego. With the defense doubly covering these two, tight end Paul Coffman gains extra freedom to roam in the medium range. Were this not enough, last year's rookie, Phil Epps, registered the highest average yardage per reception (22.6) and he is joined by rookie Mike Miller, reputed to be the fastest man in America over forty yards. The rushing offense hardly needs to be better than par, which just about sums it up. Eddie Lee Ivery knows the way into the end zone (nine touchdowns) but Gerry Ellis has still to fulfil his promise and there is little experienced reserve strength.

Defense

The pass rush is weak (only twenty sacks) and yet, as a whole, the defense ranks second in the NFC against both the pass and the rush in yards yielded per attempt. It is a measure of their strength at linebacker that Rich Wingo cannot displace Randy Scott, and means that Starr can use his draft options for elsewhere. The defensive backs are excellent and all four will enter 1983, unchallenged for his position. Still, Tim Lewis was too good to miss when it came round to the Packers' turn in the draft, but even he will have to beat out Estus Hood for a place when the defensive backs expand to five on obvious passing downs.

Special Teams

Jan Stenerud, third in the all-time list of kickers, may retire, making way for Eddie Garcia. Ray Stachowicz, the punter, performs adequately. Del Rodgers and Phil Epps make few mistakes, returning kicks and punts respectively.

Green Bay Packers (NFC Central)

No.	Name	Pos.	Ht.	Wt.	Age	NFL Yr.	College
59	Anderson, John*	LB	6-3	221	27	6	Michigan
73	Braggs, Byron	DE/DT	6-4	290	23	3	Alabama
93	Brown, Robert	LB	6-2	238	22	2	Virginia Tech.
77	Butler, Mike*	DE	6-5	265	29	7	Kansas
19	Campbell, Rich	QB	6-4	224	24	3	California
88	Cassidy, Ron	WR	6-0	185	26	5	Utah State
34	Clark, Allan	RB	5-10	186	26	4	Northern Arizona
82	Coffman, Paul*	TE	6-3	218	27	6	Kansas State
52	Cumby, George*	LB	6-0	215	27	4	Oklahoma
12	Dickey, Lynn*	QB	6-4	210	33	12	Kansas State
53	Douglass, Mike*	LB	6-0	224	28	6	San Diego
31	Ellis, Gerry*	RB	5-11	216	25	4	Missouri
85	Epps, Philip	WR	5-10	165	23	2	Texas Christian
79	Fields, Angelo	OT	6-6	319	25	4	Michigan State
57	Gofourth, Derrel*	OG	6-3	260	28	7	Oklahoma State
24	Gray, Johnnie*	S	5-11	185	29	8	Fullerton

(continued opposite)

1983 Schedule

4 Sept	at Houston	12:00
11 Sept	PITTSBURGH	12:00
18 Sept	LOS ANGELES RAMS at Milw.	12.00
26 Sept	at New York Giants	9:00
2 Oct	TAMPA BAY	12:00
9 Oct	at Detroit	1:00
17 Oct	WASHINGTON	8:00
23 Oct	MINNESOTA	12:00
30 Oct	at Cincinnati	4:00
6 Nov	CLEVELAND at Milw.	12.00
13 Nov	at Minnesota	12:00
20 Nov	DETROIT at Milw.	12:00
27 Nov	at Atlanta	4:00
4 Dec	CHICAGO	12:00
12 Dec	at Tampa Bay	9:00
18 Dec	at Chicago	12:00

James Lofton (80) evades the flying tackle.

Green Bay Packers (NFC Central) – continued

No.	Name	Pos.	Ht.	Wt.	Age	NFL Yr.	College
65	Hallstrom, Ron	OG	6-6	286	23	2	Iowa
69	Harris, Leotis*	OG	6-1	267	28	6	Arkansas
23	Harvey, Maurice*	S	5-10	190	27	5	Ball State
38	Hood, Estus	DB	5-11	180	27	6	Illinois State
25	Huckleby, Harlan	RB	6-1	199	25	4	Michigan
74	Huffman, Tim	OG/OT	6-5	277	24	3	Notre Dame
40	Ivery, Eddie Lee*	RB	6-0	210	26	4	Georgia Tech.
83	Jefferson, John*	WR	6-1	198	27	6	Arizona State
90	Johnson, Ezra*	DE	6-4	240	27	7	Morris Brown
21	Jolly, Mike	S	6-3	185	25	3	Michigan
63	Jones, Terry*	DT	6-2	259	26	6	Alabama
64	Kitson, Syd	OG	6-4	252	24	4	Wake Forest
68	Koch, Greg*	OT	6-4	265	28	7	Arkansas
60	Laslavic, Jim	LB	6-2	229	31	10	Penn State
22	Lee, Mark*	CB	5-11	187	25	4	Washington
56	Lewis, Cliff	LB	6-1	226	23	3	S. Mississippi
81	Lewis, Gary	TE	6-5	234	24	3	Arlington
80	Lofton, James*	WR	6-3	187	27	6	Stanford
54	McCarren, Larry*	C	6-3	248	31	11	Illinois
29	McCoy, Mike*	CB	5-11	183	30	8	Colorado
39	Meade, Mike	RB	5-11	228	23	2	Penn State
78	Merrill, Casey	DE	6-4	255	26	5	California, Davis
62	Merrill, Mark	LB	6-4	240	23	5	Minnesota
37	Murphy, Mark	S	6-2	199	25	3	West Liberty
94	Parlavecchio, Chet	LB	6-2	225	23	2	Penn State
51	Prather, Guy	LB	6-2	230	25	3	Grambling
35	Rodgers, Del	KR/RB	5-10	197	23	2	Utah
58	Rubens, Larry	C	6-1	253	24	2	Montana State
55	Scott, Randy	LB	6-1	220	24	3	Alabama
16	Stachowicz, Ray	P	5-11	185	24	3	Michigan State
10	Stenerud, Jan	K	6-2	190	39	17	Montana State
76	Stokes, Tim*	OT	6-2	232	33	10	Oregon
67	Swanke, Karl	OT/C	6-6	251	25	4	Boston College
75	Turner, Richard	OT	6-2	260	24	3	Oklahoma
30	Whitaker, Bill	DB	6-0	182	23	3	Missouri
17	Whitehurst, Dave	QB	6-2	204	28	7	Furman
50	Wingo, Rich*	LB	6-1	230	27	4	Alabama

1983 Draft

Round	Name	Pos.	Ht.	Wt.	College
1	Lewis, Tim	DB	5-11½	190	Pittsburgh
2	Drechsler, David	OG	6-4	248	North Carolina
4	Miller, Mike	WR	5-11	182	Tennessee
5	Thomas, Bryan	RB	5-9½	189	Pittsburgh
6	Sams, Ron	OG	6-2	265	Pittsburgh
7	Clark, Jessie	RB	6-0	230	Arkansas
8	Briscoe, Carlton	DB	5-11	180	McNeese State
9	Ham, Robin	C	6-3	252	West Texas State
10	Williams, Bryon	WR	6-1	174	Texas, Arlington
10	Thomas, Jimmy	DB	5-11	185	Indiana
11	Scribner, Bucky	P	6-0	210	Kansas
12	Harvey, John	DT	6-3	235	USC

MINNESOTA VIKINGS NFC Central

Address 9520, Viking Drive, Eden Prairie,
   Minnesota 55344.
Stadium Hubert H. Humphrey Metrodome, Minneapolis.
   Capacity 62,212. Playing Surface Super Turf.
Team Colours Purple, White and Gold.
Head Coach Bud Grant – seventeenth year.
Championships NFL 1969; Conference 1973, '74, '76.
   Division 1970, '71, '73, '74, '75, '76, '77, '78, '80.
History NFL 1961-69. NFC 1970-

If success is to be measured by post-season participation, the Vikings must surely rank alongside the Rams and even the mighty Cowboys in the NFC. In twelve out of the last fifteen years, eleven as Division Champions, they have reached the playoffs. Yet each time all the power of the regular season juggernaut has evaporated in the heat of the big game. Four times with the infamous 'Purple Gang' of defensive linemen Carl Eller, Alan Page, Jim Marshall and Gary Larsen, they have swept to the Super Bowl, only to grub out a mere 34 points in total and in none did they threaten to win. The old problems returned in last year's playoff game against the Redskins, when several relatively simple potential touchdown passes were dropped in the end zone. However Head Coach Bud Grant who, like Tom Landry of Dallas, rarely smiles, is undeterred and enters his seventeenth season in Minnesota, looking for division title number twelve.

Offense

The offensive line is not noted for its flamboyance and does not dominate in any particular phase of the game, yet it contains a good deal of Football experience and is never beaten badly. It enables quarterback Tommy Kramer to direct an offense which still relies heavily on the passing game (third NFC). With Ahmad Rashad having retired, Sammy White assumes seniority in one wide receiver spot whilst Terry LeCount and Sam McCullum will share the other. Joe Senser (tight end) adds his weight to the offensive line before filtering into the open to provide a third target. But the momentum of the offense is maintained by Ted Brown (running back), who caught the most passes of all (thirty-one). The rushing game could well be on the way to shedding the problems which, in recent years, have been chronic. Ted Brown now averages 4.3 yards per carry and last year's rookie, Darrin Nelson, appears to have settled for playing in Minnesota (he didn't want to) and will be better for having spent a learning year. The reliable Tony Galbreath will be around to block for the speedsters.

Defense

The line was improved enormously by the arrival of Pro Bowler Charlie Johnson from Philadelphia and the dramatic emergence of Doug Martin, who led the NFL with eleven solo quarterback sacks and was accorded All Pro status in some quarters. There is ample depth at linebacker but, with the exception of Matt Blair, a shortage of outstanding talent, and it is difficult to imagine the arrival of rookie Lee Ashley improving matters. The same is true at defensive back, where only Willie Teal shows signs of being on the upgrade. Again, it would be asking a lot of rookie safety Joey Browner to make significant impact.

Special Teams

Rick Danmeier is not a long specialist but has the nerve to step up and kick vital late field goals and Greg Coleman is a sound punter. Rookie Joey Browner will see action, returning both kicks and punts, following the retirement of Eddie Payton (no doubt fed up with being quoted as brother of Chicago's illustrious Walter).

Minnesota Vikings (NFC Central)

No.	Name	Pos.	Ht.	Wt.	Age	NFL Yr.	College
69	Basten, Bob	OT	6-5	255	23	2	St. John's University
21	Bess, Rufus	CB	5-9	180	26	5	S. Carolina State
59	Blair, Matt*	LB	6-5	229	31	10	Iowa State
62	Boyd, Brent	OG	6-3	260	26	4	UCLA
23	Brown, Ted*	RB	5-10	198	26	5	N. Carolina State
82	Bruer, Bob	TE	6-5	235	30	5	Mankato State
8	Coleman, Greg	P	6-0	178	28	7	Florida A & M
7	Danmeier, Rick	K	6-0	183	31	6	Sioux Falls
12	Dils, Steve	QB	6-1	190	27	5	Stanford
73	Elshire, Neil	DE	6-6	250	25	3	Oregon
32	Galbreath, Tony*	RB	6-0	230	29	8	Missouri
61	Hamilton, Wes*	OG	6-3	255	30	8	Tulsa
45	Hannon, Tom*	S	5-11	193	28	7	Michigan State
36	Harrell, Sam	RB	6-2	213	26	3	East Carolina
75	Holloway, Randy	DE	6-5	245	28	6	Pittsburgh
51	Hough, Jim*	OG	6-2	267	27	6	Utah State
24	Howard, Bryan	S	6-1	200	24	2	Tennessee State
56	Huffman, Dave	C	6-6	255	26	5	Notre Dame
76	Irwin, Tim*	OT	6-6	275	26	3	Tennessee

(continued opposite)

1983 Schedule

4 Sept	at Cleveland	1:00
8 Sept	SAN FRANCISCO	7.30
18 Sept	at Tampa Bay	4.00
25 Sept	DETROIT	12:00
2 Oct	DALLAS	12:00
9 Oct	at Chicago	12:00
16 Oct	HOUSTON	12:00
23 Oct	at Green Bay	12:00
30 Oct	at St. Louis	12:00
6 Nov	TAMPA BAY	12.00
13 Nov	GREEN BAY	12.00
20 Nov	at Pittsburgh	1:00
27 Nov	at New Orleans	12:00
5 Dec	at Detroit	9:00
11 Dec	CHICAGO	12:00
17 Dec	CINCINNATI	3:00

Joe Senser (81) beats Clarence Scott for the touchdown.

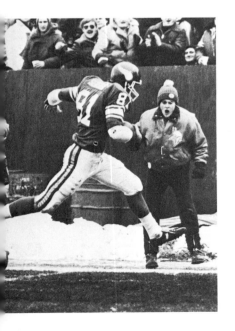

Minnesota Vikings (NFC Central) – *continued*

No.	Name	Pos.	Ht.	Wt.	Age	NFL Yr.	College
65	Johnson, Charlie*	DT	6-3	262	31	7	Colorado
52	Johnson, Dennis*	LB	6-3	230	25	4	USC
53	Johnson, Henry	LB	6-2	235	25	4	Georgia Tech.
83	Jordan, Steve	TE	6-4	228	22	2	Brown
25	Knoff, Kurt	S	6-2	188	29	8	Kansas
9	Kramer, Tommy*	QB	6-1	199	28	7	Rice
80	LeCount, Terry*	WR	5-10	172	27	6	Florida
87	Lewis, Leo	WR	5-8	170	27	3	Missouri
79	Martin, Doug*	DE	6-3	258	26	4	Washington
84	McCullum, Sam	WR	6-2	190	30	10	Montana State
88	McDole, Mardye	WR	5-11	195	24	3	Mississippi State
54	McNeill, Fred*	LB	6-2	229	31	10	UCLA
77	Mullaney, Mark*	DE	6-6	242	30	9	Colorado State
20	Nelson, Darrin	RB	5-8	181	24	2	Stanford
49	Nord, Keith	S	6-0	197	26	5	St. Cloud State
22	Redwine, Jarvis	RB	5-10	198	26	3	Nebraska
78	Riley, Steve*	OT	6-6	253	30	10	USC
68	Rouse, Curtis	OG	6-2	304	23	2	Chattanooga
57	Sendlein, Robin	LB	6-3	224	24	3	Texas
81	Senser, Joe*	TE	6-4	238	27	4	West Chester State
50	Siemon, Jeff	LB	6-3	237	33	12	Stanford
71	Stephanos, Bill	OT	6-4	262	26	1	Boston College
55	Studwell, Scott*	LB	6-2	224	29	7	Illinois
29	Swain, John*	CB	6-1	195	24	3	Miami
67	Swilley, Dennis*	C	6-3	241	28	7	Texas A & M
66	Tausch, Terry	OT	6-4	278	24	2	Texas
37	Teal, Willie*	CB	5-10	195	25	4	Louisiana State
27	Turner, John*	S	6-0	199	26	6	Miami
72	White, James	DT	6-3	263	29	8	Oklahoma State
85	White, Sammy*	WR	5-11	189	29	8	Grambling
11	Wilson, Wade	QB	6-3	212	24	3	East Texas State
91	Yakavonis, Ray	DE	6-4	243	26	3	East Stroudsberg State
34	Young, Rickey	RB	6-2	195	29	9	Jackson State

1983 Draft

Round	Name	Pos.	Ht.	Wt.	College
1	Browner, Joey	DB	6-2	208	USC
3	Ashley, Walker Lee	LB	5-11½	230	Penn State
5	Stewart, Mark	LB	6-2½	230	Washington
6	Jones, Mike	WR	5-11½	176	Tennessee State
7	Lee, Carl	DB	5-11	180	Marshall
8	Brown, Norris	TE	6-3	220	Georgia
9	Achter, Rod	WR	6-1	190	Toledo
10	Brown, Melvin	DB	5-10½	177	Mississippi
10	Tate, Walker	C	6-4	247	Tennessee State
12	Turner, Maurice	RB	5-11	205	Utah State

TAMPA BAY BUCCANEERS NFC Central

Address One Buccaneer Place, Tampa, Florida 33607.
Stadium Tampa Stadium, Tampa.
  Capacity 72,128. *Playing Surface* Grass.
Team Colours Florida Orange, White and Red.
Head Coach John McKay – eighth year.
Championships Division 1979, '81.
History AFC 1976. NFC 1977-

Together with Seattle, the Buccaneers are the most recent entrants into the NFL (1976). After a depressing but predictable start (0-14), there were to be two learning campaigns (2-12 and 5-11) before, in 1979, they staggered us all by winning their Division. They went even further, beating Philadelphia before losing narrowly (0-9) to the Rams in a bitterly fought contest which would have taken them to Super Bowl XIV. Their 1980 season might be considered a pause for reflection before, in 1981, they did it again with their second Division title. This however merely earned them the right to be routed, as they were (0-38) by the Cowboys in vintage form. Again they fell to Dallas (17-30) in the 1982 playoffs, but the warning to all is clear. Coach John McKay now has the meat to which the spices of choice draft selections will add flavour.

Offense

The offensive line combines the experience of Dave Reavis, who has been with the Bucs since their formation, and the youthful potential of Ray Snell and Sean Farrell, both former first round draft selections. In terms of quarterback protection, they rate first in the NFC (only eleven sacks), but still do not explode the offensive holes for the running backs. In recognition of this, Randy Grimes (center) and Kelly Thomas (tackle) were drafted first and third respectively. However, running backs James Wilder, Mel Carver and James Owens face another hard year in the trenches. By contrast, the passing offense can be a spectacular sight and with Doug Williams primed and ready to fire, they strike without warning. Kevin House received much closer defensive attention following his phenomenal 1981 performance, and his output dropped accordingly. It was almost exactly matched by the combined efforts of Gordon Jones and Theo Bell operating down the other sideline. The real bonus (and surprise) came from James Wilder, flaring out from the running back position, whose fifty-three receptions placed him second in the Conference. Jimmie Giles (tight end) was his reliable self, completing a receiving corps which could present problems if Doug Williams can add finesse to the power of his pass.

Defense

This is the real Tampa Bay strongpoint and overall they rate number one in the NFC. Lee Roy Selmon, Dave Logan and Dave Stalls, are a fearsome front three but, when joined in the rush by Hugh Green, they are virtually impassable. Originally an All American defensive lineman, Green was drafted specifically for conversion to linebacker by the shrewd McKay. He has delivered the goods, leading the team in solo tackles and being selected for the Pro Bowl in only his second year. It is almost certainly the front seven (defensive line and linebackers) which must take credit for an asphyxiating pass defense which gave up a full twenty yards fewer per game than the next best (Giants). The back four need the infusion of talent which comes with Jeremiah Castille, taken second in the draft.

Special Teams

The kicker, Bill Capece, had a surprisingly good year (second NFC) and Larry Swider maintained a good average (41.5 yards) punting but unfortunately was let down by the chasing mob, who occasionally allowed the punt returner to slip by.

Tampa Bay Buccaneers (NFC Central)

No.	Name	Pos.	Ht.	Wt.	Age	NFL Yr.	College
30	Barrett, Dave	RB	6-0	230	23	2	Houston
82	Bell, Jerry	TE	6-5	230	24	2	Arizona State
83	Bell, Theo	WR	5-11	180	29	7	Arizona
52	Brantley, Scott	LB	6-1	230	25	4	Florida
34	Brown, Cedric*	S	6-2	205	29	7	Kent State
78	Cannon, John	DE	6-5	250	23	2	William & Mary
3	Capece, Bill	K	5-7	170	24	3	Florida State
87	Carter, Gerald	WR	6-1	185	26	4	Texas A & M
28	Carver, Mel*	RB	5-11	210	24	2	Nevada, Las Vegas
20	Colzie, Neal*	S	6-2	200	30	9	Ohio State
33	Cotney, Mark	S	6-0	205	31	8	Cameron State
58	Davis, Jeff	LB	6-0	225	23	2	Clemson
	Dykes, Donald	CB	5-11	184	28	4	South-eastern Louisiana
62	Farrell, Sean*	OG	6-2	255	23	2	Penn State
88	Giles, Jimmie*	TE	6-3	245	28	7	Alcorn State
11	Golsteyn, Gerry	QB	6-4	210	29	5	Northern Illinois
53	Green, Hugh*	LB	6-2	225	24	3	Pittsburgh

(continued opposite)

Doug Williams, Tampa Bay's rifleman.

1983 Schedule

4 Sept	DETROIT	1:00
8 Sept	at Chicago	12:00
18 Sept	MINNESOTA	4:00
25 Sept	CINCINNATI	1:00
2 Oct	at Green Bay	12:00
9 Oct	at Dallas	3:00
16 Oct	St. LOUIS	1:00
23 Oct	NEW ORLEANS	4:00
30 Oct	at Pittsburgh	1:00
6 Nov	at Minnesota	12:00
13 Nov	at Cleveland	1:00
20 Nov	CHICAGO	1:00
27 Nov	HOUSTON	1:00
4 Dec	at San Francisco	1:00
12 Dec	GREEN BAY	9:00
18 Dec	at Detroit	4:00

Tampa Bay Buccaneers (NFC Central) – *continued*

No.	Name	Pos.	Ht.	Wt.	Age	NFL Yr.	College
73	Hannah, Charley*	OT	6-6	265	28	7	Alabama
59	Hawkins, Andy*	LB	6-2	230	25	4	Texas A & M
21	Holt, John	CB	5-11	180	24	3	West Texas State
89	House, Kevin*	WR	6-1	175	25	4	Southern Illinois
56	Johnson, Cecil*	LB	6-2	235	28	7	Pittsburgh
84	Jones, Gordon*	WR	6-0	190	26	5	Pittsburgh
57	Leonard, Jim	C/CG/OT	6-3	250	25	4	Santa Clara
76	Logan, David*	DT	6-2	250	26	5	Pittsburgh
39	Middleton, Terdell	RB	6-0	195	28	7	Memphis State
24	Morris, Thomas	DB	5-10	175	23	2	Michigan State
1	Morton, Michael	KR/WR	5-6	170	23	2	Nevada, Las Vegas
35	Moser, Rick	RB	6-0	210	26	6	Rhode Island
51	Nafziger, Dana	LB	6-1	225	29	6	Cal Poly Slo
86	Obradovich, Jim	TE	6-2	230	30	9	USC
	O'Steen, Dwayne	DB	6-1	195	28	6	San Jose State
26	Owens, James	RB	5-11	190	28	5	UCLA
	Powell, Carl	WR	6-0	182	25	2	Jackson State
15	Quinn, Jeff	QB	6-3	206	25	2	Nebraska
15	Reavis, Dave*	OT	6-5	265	33	9	Arkansas
66	Reece, Booker	DE	6-6	260	23	2	Bethune-Cookman
61	Roberts, Greg	OG	6-3	260	26	5	Oklahoma
74	Sanders, Gene	OT	6-3	270	26	5	Texas A & M
63	Selmon, Lee Roy*	DE	6-3	250	28	8	Oklahoma
22	Smith, Johnny Ray	S/CB	5-9	175	25	2	Lamar
72	Snell, Ray*	OG	6-3	260	25	4	Wisconsin
65	Stalls, Dave*	DE	6-4	260	27	7	Northern Colorado
9	Swider, Larry	P	6-2	195	28	5	Pittsburgh
41	Thomas, Norris*	CB	5-11	185	29	7	Southern Mississippi
	Thompson, Jack	QB	6-3	217	27	5	Washington State
81	Tyler, Andre	WR	6-0	185	24	2	Stanford
40	Washington, Mike*	CB	6-2	200	30	8	Alabama
90	White, Brad	DT	6-2	250	24	3	Tennessee
32	Wilder, James*	RB	6-2	220	25	3	Missouri
12	Williams, Doug*	QB	6-4	215	28	6	Grambling
50	Wilson, Steve*	C	6-3	265	29	8	Georgia
54	Wood, Richard*	LB	6-2	230	30	9	USC
68	Yarno, George	OG	6-2	255	25	5	Washington State

1983 Draft

Round	Name	Pos.	Ht.	Wt.	College
2	Grimes, Randy	C	6-3	260	Baylor
3	Castille, Jeremiah	LB	5-9½	178	Alabama
4	Thomas, Kelly	OT	6-5	265	USC
5	Chickillo, Tony	DT	6-3	249	Miami, Florida
6	Branton, Rheugene	WR	6-3½	212	Texas Southern
6	Kaplan, Ken	OT/OG	6-4	258	New Hampshire
7	Ledbetter, Weldon	RB	6-0	216	Oklahoma
8	Samuelson, John	LB	6-3	205	Azusa Pacific
9	Arbubakrr, Hassan	DT	6-3½	248	Texas Tech.
10	Durham, Darius	WR	6-1½	190	San Diego State
11	Witte, Mark	TE	6-3	220	North Texas State
12	Higginbotham, John	DT	6-2	270	North East Oklahoma

ATLANTA FALCONS NFC West

Address Suwanee Road at 1-85, Suwanee, Georgia 30174.
Stadium Atlanta-Fulton County Stadium.
  Capacity 60,748. *Playing Surface* Grass.
Team Colours Red, Black, White and Silver.
Head Coach Dan Henning – first year.
Championships Division 1980.
History NFL 1966-69. NFC 1970-

Purely in terms of their won-lost record, Atlanta's story is one of mediocrity punctuated by the odd foray into the playoffs. On the first two occasions they lost to the Cowboys, 20-27 in 1978 and 27-30 in 1980, and yet each time they could so easily have won, as also was the case in their 1982 loss, 24-30 to Minnesota. Despite clear weaknesses in defense, they were expected to be a contender in the eighties but, even with an abundance of talent elsewhere, they have lost vital games when it came to the crunch. The problem was diagnosed as one of coaching and accordingly, Leeman Bennett had to make way for Dan Henning. With San Francisco still reeling from a disastrous 1982, the Saints not quite ready to challenge and the Rams with some problems to solve, 1983 offers their best opportunity to date.

Offense
All three of Jeff Van Note, Mike Kenn and R. C. Thielemann, are Pro Bowlers and form the heart of an offensive line which rates highly in the Conference. Last season, quarterback Steve Bartkowski had perhaps that fraction longer time to look for receivers, and both his pass completion percentage and yards per attempt went up.' Under Bennett, they were clearly shifting from the hitherto ambitious and effective long passing game, opting for the safer medium range offense – Jenkins and Jackson had only one touchdown each. Yet Dan Henning, who has arrived from Washington, may well loose the shackles and, in tight end Junior Miller, he has the perfect foil for his speedsters. As usual, William Andrews at running back was the multiple threat, rating fifth and third in rushing and passing respectively, in the NFC. He will benefit from the slashing runs of last year's rookie, Gerald Riggs, who will fulfil his college promise and, together with Lynn Cain, makes up a frightening threesome.

Defense
The top-rated rookies, Mike Pitts and Andrew Provence, could go some way towards improving a defensive line which is weak (only eighteen sacks in 1982) and always requires the services of linebacker Joel Williams in the attempt to generate a pass rush. Kuykendall, Richardson and Curry, together with Williams, form an excellent quartet which in effect, holds the defense together. With the exception of Bobby Butler, there is an absence of speed at defensive back and even the talented Butler still has to master the subtleties of cornerback play. Rookie safety James Britt could step into the starting lineup.

Special Teams
Mick Luckhurst (one of two Englishmen in the NFL) is unchallenged at kicker and has ridden the storm of some dreadfully bad luck when attempting field goals at vital moments. George Roberts at punter is no better than ordinary. There is a touch of sparkle in Billy 'White Shoes' Johnson, who returns the punts, but Reggie Brown is well below average as a kick returner.

1983 Schedule

Date	Opponent	Time
4 Sept	at Chicago	12:00
11 Sept	NEW YORK GIANTS	1.00
18 Sept	at Detroit	1.00
25 Sept	at San Francisco	1:00
2 Oct	PHILADELPHIA	1:00
9 Oct	NEW ORLEANS	1:00
16 Oct	at Los Angeles Rams	1:00
23 Oct	at New York Jets	1:00
30 Oct	NEW ENGLAND	1:00
6 Nov	at New Orleans	12.00
14 Nov	LOS ANGELES RAMS	9:00
20 Nov	SAN FRANCISCO	4:00
27 Nov	GREEN BAY	4:00
4 Dec	at Washington	1:00
10 Dec	at Miami	4:00
18 Dec	BUFFALO	1:00

Atlanta Falcons (NFC West

No.	Name	Pos.	Ht.	Wt.	Age	NFL Yr.	College
31	Andrews, William*	RB	6-0	200	27	5	Auburn
82	Bailey, Stacey	WR	6-0	162	23	2	San Jose State
10	Bartkowski, Steve*	QB	6-4	213	30	9	California
99	Brown, Clay	TE	6-2	223	24	2	Brigham Young
46	Brown, Reggie	RB/KR	5-11	210	23	2	Oregon
66	Bryant, Warren*	OT	6-6	270	27	7	Kentucky
23	Butler, Bobby*	CB	5-11	170	24	3	Florida State
21	Cain, Lynn*	RB	6-1	205	27	5	USC
89	Curran, Willie	WR/KR	5-10	175	23	2	UCLA
50	Curry, Buddy*	LB	6-3	221	25	4	North Carolina
59	Davis, Paul	LB	6-1	215	25	3	North Carolina
	De Bruijn, Case	P	6-0	176	23	2	Idaho State
34	Gaison, Blane	S	6-0	185	25	3	Hawaii
36	Glazebook, Bob*	S	6-1	200	27	6	Fresno State
83	Hodge, Floyd	WR	6-0	195	24	2	Utah
64	Howell, Pat*	G	6-5	253	26	5	USC
85	Jackson, Alfred*	WR	5-11	176	27	6	Texas
84	Jenkins, Alfred*	WR	5-10	172	31	9	Morris Brown
81	Johnson, Billy	WR/PR	5-9	170	31	7	Widener
37	Johnson, Kenny*	CB	5-10	176	25	4	Mississippi State
20	Jones, Earl	CB	6-0	178	26	4	Norfolk State

(continued opposite)

Atlanta Falcons (NFC West) – *continued*

No.	Name	Pos.	Ht.	Wt.	Age	NFL Yr.	College
78	Kenn, Mike*	T	6-6	257	27	6	Michigan
14	Komlo, Jeff	QB	6-2	200	27	5	Delaware
54	Kuykendall, Fulton*	LB	6-5	225	30	9	UCLA
51	Laughlin, Jim	LB	6-0	212	25	4	Ohio State
18	Luckhurst, Mick	K	6-0	180	25	3	California
75	Merrow, Jeff*	DE	6-4	255	30	9	West Virginia
87	Mikeska, Russ	TE	6-3	225	27	5	Texas A & M
80	Miller, Junior*	TE	6-4	235	25	4	Nebraska
15	Morosk, Mike	QB	6-4	200	25	5	California, Davis
53	Musser, Neal	LB	6-2	218	26	2	North Carolina State
71	Perko, Mike	DT	6-2	241	26	2	Utah State
27	Pridemore, Tom*	S	5-10	186	27	6	West Virginia
56	Richardson, Al*	LB	6-2	206	25	4	Georgia Tech
42	Riggs, Gerald	RB	6-1	230	22	2	Arizona State
12	Roberts, George	P	6-0	186	29	6	Virginia Tech
33	Robinson, Bo	RB	6-2	225	27	5	West Texas State
77	Rogers, Doug	DE	6-4	255	23	2	Stanford
67	Sanders, Eric	T	6-6	255	24	3	Nevada, Reno
70	Scott, Dave	G	6-4	265	29	8	Kansas
61	Scully, John	C	6-5	255	25	3	Notre Dame
65	Smith, Don*	DT	6-5	248	26	5	Miami
47	Spivey, Mike	DB	6-0	198	29	7	Colorado
25	Strong, Ray	RB	5-9	184	27	6	Nevada, Las Vegas
68	Thielemann, R. C.*	G	6-4	247	27	7	Arkansas
57	Van Note, Jeff*	C	6-2	247	37	15	Kentucky
52	White, Lyman	LB	6-0	217	24	3	Louisiana State
58	Williams, Joel*	LB	6-0	215	26	5	Wisconsin, La Crosse
79	Yeates, Jeff*	DE	6-3	248	32	12	Boston College
63	Zele, Mike	DT	6-3	236	27	5	Kent State

Mick Luckhurst pops one over.

1983 Draft

Round	Name	Pos.	Ht.	Wt.	College
1	Pitts, Mike	DE	6-4	260	Alabama
2	Britt, James	DB	5-11	188	Louisiana State
3	Provence, Andrew	DT/DE	6-3	247	South Carolina
4	Harper, John	LB	6-1	234	Southern Illinois
5	Miller, Brett	OT	6-6	265	Iowa
7	Turk, Jeff	DB	6-0	180	Boise State
8	Rade, John	LB	6-2	215	Boise State
10	Giacomarro, Ralph	P	6-1	195	Penn State
11	Salley, John	DB	5-11	190	Wyoming
12	Matthews, Allama	TE	6-2	225	Vanderbilt

LOS ANGELES RAMS NFC West

Address 2327, West Lincoln Avenue, Anaheim, California 92801.

Stadium Anaheim Stadium, Anaheim.
Capacity 69,007. *Playing Surface* Grass.

Team Colours Royal Blue, Gold and White.

Head Coach John Robinson – first year.

Championships NFL 1945, '51; Conference 1979. Division 1973, '74, '75, '76, '77, '78, '79.

History NFL 1937-69. NFC 1970-
(Known as Cleveland Rams until 1946)

Only two Championships in thirty-eight seasons does not even begin to represent the true picture of the Rams, this enigma of the NFL. Van Brocklin, Waterfield, Hirsch and Fears of the fifties, gave way to Arnett, Bass, Olsen and David 'The Deacon' Jones in the sixties. Through the seventies and on into the eighties, they regularly provided half a dozen players for the Pro Bowl. Yet despite all these, and seven consecutive Division titles beginning in 1973, and a place in the playoffs in 1980, the boardroom has remained empty of trophies for over thirty years. In 1982, they frittered away leads of 23, 14, 21 and 14 points respectively in four games, when victory in just two could have taken them to the playoffs. In fairness they suffered a succession of crippling injuries which decimated even this squad, always knee deep in talent. Still, Head Coach Ray Malavasi, a perfect gentleman, had to make way for John Robinson, who will hope to transfer his success with the University of Southern California to the professional game.

Offense

After a 1981 season littered with injuries, the Rams offensive line returned in fine style to yield only fifteen quarterback sacks (second to Tampa Bay). The quintent of Pankey, Hill,

Smith, Harrah and Slater, is probably the best in Football and they are supported by Russ Bolinger (ex-Detroit) in reserve. Vince Ferragamo, who took over at quarterback when Bert Jones was injured, certainly has the arm, but there still remain doubts about his ability to read defenses. Jones' retirement leaves only the untried Jeff Kemp and novice Clete Casper in reserve. The surprising trade of Wendell Tyler to San Francisco would cripple most clubs and yet, as usual, the Rams will simply dip into the pool. Farmer, Miller, Dennard and Barber (tight end) will maintain the pace in pass receiving and Guman, at running back, will benefit from his new senior status. He is joined by a potential superstar in rookie Eric Dickerson, the top rated running back in the College Draft. Barry Redden too should develop after a learning rookie year in 1982.

Defense

It was in defense that the injuries were felt and it is reported that all will return sound of limb. There will be some shuffling around on the defensive line to make room for Gary Jeter (ex-Giants), who is sorely needed after the trade of Mike Fanning to Detroit. Larry Brooks could return to give reserve strength. The linebackers will be good if Mel Owens and Jim Collins progress as expected – Jim Youngblood is always excellent. The defensive backs, on paper, are the NFL's strongest but, having had to cover for weak linebacking in 1982, ended the season in a state of shock. Even Nolan Cromwell, who has been known to make interceptions one-handed, came under criticism.

Special Teams

Mike Lansford kept his head kicking the field goals and John Misko obtains excellent distance with his punts. Both are likely to improve after serving their rookie years. LeRoy Irvin is a potential game breaker returning the punts and Barry Redden averaged 22.6 yards, including an 85-yarder against the Raiders, returning kicks.

Los Angeles Rams (NFC West)

No.	Name	Pos.	Ht.	Wt.	Age	NFL Yr.	College
35	Alexander, Robert	RB	6-0	185	25	2	West Virginia
52	Andrews, George*	LB	6-3	221	27	5	Nebraska
62	Bain, Bill	OG	6-4	285	31	8	USC
86	Barber, Mike*	TE	6-3	225	30	7	Louisiana Tech.
96	Barnett, Doug	DE	6-3	250	23	2	Azusa Pacific
81	Battle, Ron	TE	6-3	225	24	3	N. Texas State
51	Bechtold, Bill	C	6-4	255	24	2	Oklahoma
	Bolinger, Russ	OC	6-5	255	28	7	Long Beach State
90	Brooks, Larry*	DT	6-3	255	33	12	Virginia State
54	Carson, Howard	LB	6-2	230	26	3	Howard Payne
50	Collins, Jim*	LB	6-2	230	25	3	Syracuse
42	Collins, Kirk	DB	5-11	183	25	3	Baylor
21	Cromwell, Nolan*	S	6-1	200	28	7	Kansas
70	DeJurnett, Charles	DT	6-4	260	31	7	San Jose State
88	Dennard, Preston*	WR	6-1	183	27	6	New Mexico
71	Doss, Reggie*	DE	6-4	263	26	6	Hampton Institute
55	Ekern, Carl	LB	6-3	222	29	7	San Jose State
84	Farmer, George	WR	5-10	175	24	2	Southern

(continued opposite)

Nolan Cromwell (21) snares an interception.

Los Angeles Rams (NFC West) – *continued*

No.	Name	Pos.	Ht.	Wt.	Age	NFL Yr.	College
15	Ferragamo, Vince*	QB	6-3	212	29	6	Nebraska
44	Guman, Mike*	RB	6-2	218	25	4	Penn State
60	Harrah, Dennis*	OG	6-5	255	30	9	Miami
87	Hill, Drew	WR	5-9	170	26	5	Georgia Tech.
72	Hill, Kent*	OG	6-5	260	26	5	Georgia Tech.
47	Irvin, LeRoy	PR/CB	5-11	184	25	4	Kansas
	Jeter, Gary*	DE	6-4	260	28	7	USC
20	Johnson, Johnnie*	S	6-1	183	26	4	Texas
24	Jones, A. J.	RB	6-1	202	24	2	Texas
9	Kemp, Jeff	QB	6-0	201	24	3	Dartmouth
68	Kersten, Wally	OT	6-5	270	23	2	Minnesota
4	Lansford, Mike	K	6-0	183	25	2	Washington
67	Lapka, Myron	DT	6-4	260	27	3	USC
59	Lilja, George	C	6-4	250	25	2	Michigan
83	Locklin, Kerry	TE	6-3	217	23	2	New Mexico State
69	Meisner, Greg	DE	6-3	253	24	3	Pittsburgh
82	Miller, Willie*	WR	5-9	173	35	8	Colorado State
6	Misko, John	P	6-5	207	28	2	Oregon State
58	Owens, Mel	LB	6-2	224	24	3	Michigan
75	Pankey, Irv*	OT	6-4	267	25	4	Penn State
49	Perry, Rod*	CB	5-9	185	29	9	Colorado
30	Redden, Barry	KR/RB	5-10	205	23	2	Richmond
57	Reilly, Mike	LB	6-4	217	24	2	Oklahoma
78	Slater, Jackie*	OT	6-4	271	29	8	Jackson State
56	Smith, Doug*	C	6-3	253	26	6	Bowling Green
23	Smith, Lucious	CB	5-10	190	26	4	Fullerton
37	Sully, Ivory	S	6-0	201	26	5	Delaware
33	Thomas, Jewerl	FB	5-10	228	25	4	San Jose State
27	Thomas, Pat*	CB	5-9	190	28	8	Texas A & M
	Thompson, John	TE	6-3	228	26	4	Utah State
66	Williams, Eric	LB	6-2	235	28	7	USC
73	Yary, Ron	OT	6-6	255	37	16	USC
85	Youngblood, Jack*	DE	6-4	242	33	13	Florida
53	Youngblood, Jim*	LB	6-3	231	33	11	Tennessee Tech.

1983 Draft

Round	Name	Pos.	Ht.	Wt.	College
1	Dickerson, Eric*	RB	6-2	214	Southern Methodist
2	Ellard, Henry	WR	5-10	174	Fresno State
2	Wilcher, Mike	LB	6-2½	230	North Carolina
4	Nelson, Chuck	K	5-11	180	Washington
4	Newsome, Vince	DB	5-11½	190	Washington
4	Reed, Doug	DE/DT	6-2	250	San Diego State
5	Grant, Otis	WR	6-2	207	Michigan State
6	Kowalski, Gary	OT	6-5½	250	Boston College
7	Simmons, Jeff	WR	6-2	190	USC
8	West, Troy	DB	5-10½	205	USC
9	Belcher, Jack	C	6-4	265	Boston College
11	Triplett, Danny	LB	6-2	224	Clemson
12	Casper, Clete	QB	6-3	192	Washington State

NEW ORLEANS SAINTS NFC West

Address 944, St. Charles Avenue, New Orleans, Louisiana 70130.
Stadium Louisiana Superdome, New Orleans.
Capacity 71,330. *Playing Surface* AstroTurf.
Team Colours Old Gold, Black and White.
Head Coach O. A. 'Bum' Philips – third year.
Championships None.
History NFL 1967-69. NFC 1970-

For the Saints, who joined in 1967, life in the NFL has been a struggle. They have won games at the miserable average of four per season, and only once, in 1979, have they broken even at 8-8. In 1980 it was to be the penultimate week of the season before they earned their first win, a 21-20 squeaker over the Jets, and not surprisingly their impatient fans renamed them 'The New Orleans Aints'. However, the arrival of new Head Coach O. A. 'Bum' Phillips in 1981 could well mark the beginning of a new era. He used his number one position in the College Draft to select George Rogers, and was fully vindicated when this powerful running back won the League rushing title with most yards gained. In other dealings, this master of the horse trade has brought in Leon Gray (ex-Houston), Dennis Winston (ex-Steelers) and Ken 'The Snake' Stabler (ex-Raiders and Houston), to help his young men through their early years. The best estimate puts the Saints only one season away from posing a serious threat.

Offense
The arrival of Leon Gray and rookie guard Steve Korte should give body to an offensive line which must dominate if the strike players are to be effective. Even the rookie tight end, John Tice, seems likely to be used primarily in blocking assignments. Quarterbacking could be a problem if the highly rated, but as yet untried, Dave Wilson has not responded to surgery. Ken Stabler is vastly experienced but no longer has the powerful arm (or the mobility) to develop the talents of Lindsay Scott, Jeff Groth and Eugene Goodlow, recently arrived from Canada with a tremendous reputation. Once more the prime offensive responsibility will fall to George Rogers, one of the top half-dozen running backs in the NFL, alongside whom Wayne Wilson will provide both rushing support and a pass receiving option.

Defense
Slowly, the defense is firming up and now rates as the division best (though defensively this is a weak division). Bruce Clark and Jim Wilks led the charge which produced thirty-one quarterback sacks and has sound reserve strength in Frank Warren. At linebacker, Dennis 'Dirt' Winston brought all his Steeler experience and aggression with him and Rickey Jackson, a rookie in 1982, exceeded all expectations. The four defensive backs work well as a unit, with Russell Gary outstanding.

Special Teams
Morten 'Thunderboot' Andersen has unlimited potential as he showed when returning after injury in his rookie year (1982). Russell Erxleben maintains a high 43-yard punting average through his special team tacklers are less effective in nailing the punt receiver. Kick and punt returning will need some attention, since Aundra Thompson and Jeff Groth, respectively, are well down the lists. Wayne Wilson is an excellent kick returner but as running back is too valuable to risk in this suicidal business.

1983 Schedule

Date	Opponent	Time
4 Sept	St. LOUIS	12:00
11 Sept	at Los Angeles Rams	1.00
18 Sept	CHICAGO	12:00
25 Sept	at Dallas	12:00
2 Oct	MIAMI	3:00
9 Oct	at Atlanta	1:00
16 Oct	SAN FRANCISCO	12:00
23 Oct	at Tampa Bay	4:00
30 Oct	at Buffalo	1:00
6 Nov	ATLANTA	12.00
13 Nov	at San Francisco	1:00
21 Nov	NEW YORK JETS	8:00
27 Nov	MINNESOTA	12:00
4 Dec	at New England	1:00
11 Dec	at Philadelphia	1:00
18 Dec	LOS ANGELES RAMS	12:00

New Orleans Saints (NFC West)

No.	Name	Pos.	Ht.	Wt.	Age	NFL Yr.	College
7	Andersen, Morten	K	6-2	190	23	2	Michigan State
50	Bordelon, Ken	LB	6-4	226	29	7	Louisiana State
85	Brenner, Hoby*	TE	6-4	240	24	3	USC
67	Brock, Stan*	OT	6-6	275	25	4	Colorado
75	Clark, Bruce*	DE	6-2	260	26	2	Penn State
78	Clark, Kelvin	OG	6-3	245	27	5	Nebraska
83	Duckett, Kenny	WR	6-0	187	23	2	Wake Forest
63	Edelman, Brad*	C	6-6	255	22	2	Missouri
99	Elliot, Tony	DT/DE	6-2	247	24	2	North Texas State
14	Erxleben, Russell	P	6-4	219	26	4	Texas
46	Gajan, Hokie	RB	5-11	215	23	2	Louisiana State
20	Gary, Russell*	S	5-11	195	24	3	Nebraska
	Goodlow, Eugene	WR	6-2	190	24	1	Kansas State
33	Gray, Kevin	DB	5-11	179	25	2	Eastern Illinois
72	Gray, Leon*	OT	6-3	258	31	11	Jackson State
86	Groth, Jeff*	WR	5-10	172	26	5	Bowling Green
87	Hardy, Larry	TE	6-3	230	27	6	Jackson State
62	Hill, John*	C	6-2	246	33	12	Lehigh
28	Hurley, Bill	S	6-2	205	26	3	Syracuse
57	Jackson, Rickey*	LB	6-2	230	25	3	Pittsburgh

(continued opposite)

New Orleans Saints (NFC West) – *continued*

No.	Name	Pos.	Ht.	Wt.	Age	NFL Yr.	College
52	Kovach, Jim	LB	6-2	225	27	5	Kentucky
21	Krimm, John	S	6-2	190	23	2	Notre Dame
64	Lafary, Dave	OT	6-7	280	28	7	Purdue
	Lewis, Marvin	RB	6-3	208	23	2	Tulane
29	Lewis, Rodney	CB	5-11	190	24	2	Nebraska
84	Mauti, Rich	WR	6-0	190	29	6	Penn State
19	Merkens, Guido	WR	6-1	195	28	6	Sam Houston State
74	Moore, Derland*	DT	6-4	253	31	11	Oklahoma
37	Myers, Tom	S	6-0	180	32	12	Syracuse
55	Nairne, Rob*	LB	6-4	227	29	7	Oregon State
66	Oubre, Louis*	OG	6-4	262	25	2	Oklahoma
51	Paul, Whitney	LB	6-3	220	27	8	Colorado
53	Pelluer, Scott	LB	6-2	215	24	3	Washington State
76	Pietrzak, Jim	C	6-5	260	30	9	East Michigan
25	Poe, Johnnie*	CB	6-1	182	24	3	Missouri
58	Redd, Glen*	LB	6-1	225	25	3	Brigham Young
38	Rogers, George*	RB	6-1	224	24	3	South Carolina
41	Rogers, Jimmy	RB	5-10	190	28	4	Oklahoma
80	Scott, Lindsay*	WR	6-1	190	22	2	Georgia
54	Simonini, Ed	LB	6-0	206	29	8	Texas A & M
79	Slaughter, Chuck	OT	6-5	260	24	2	South Carolina
16	Stabler, Ken*	QB	6-3	210	38	14	Alabama
89	Thompson, Aundra	WR	6-1	186	30	7	East Texas State
42	Tyler, Toussaint	RB	6-2	220	24	3	Washington
73	Warren, Frank	DE	6-4	275	23	3	Auburn
49	Wattelet, Frank*	S	6-0	185	24	3	Kansas
44	Waymer, Dave*	CB	6-1	195	25	4	Notre Dame
94	Wilks, Jim*	DT/DE	6-4	252	25	3	San Diego State
18	Wilson, Dave	QB	6-3	195	24	3	Illinois
30	Wilson, Wayne*	RB	6-3	208	25	5	Shepherd
56	Winston, Dennis*	LB	6-0	228	27	7	Arkansas

1983 Draft

Round	Name	Pos.	Ht.	Wt.	College
2	Korte, Steve	OG	6-2	267	Arkansas
3	Tice, John	TE	6-5	242	Maryland
3	Austin, Cliff	RB	6-0	195	Clemson
4	Lewis, Gary	DT	6-3	255	Oklahoma State

George Rogers makes for daylight.

SAN FRANCISCO 49ers NFC West

Address 711, Nevada Street, Redwood City, California 94061.
Stadium Candlestick Park, San Francisco. *Capacity* 61,185. *Playing Surface* Grass.
Team Colours Forty Niner Gold and Scarlet.
Head Coach Bill Walsh – fifth year.
Championships Super Bowl 1981; Conference 1981. Division 1970, '71, '72, '81.
History AAFC 1946-49. NFL 1950-69. NFC 1970-

The 49ers have always been in the forefront of the NFL with outstanding players and innovative coaches. In the fifties, Joe Perry and Hugh 'The King' McElhenny ran riot but never quite enough to master the 'Black and Blue' division. For a time in the sixties, Red Hickey's Shotgun Offense led the opposition a merry dance and later, quarterback John Brodie used the 'T' formation to devastating effect. Throughout the seventies, despite regularly parading six Pro Bowlers, they remained empty handed. Success finally came in 1981 when they thrashed Dallas 45-14 in the regular season, confirmed the form, albeit narrowly, in the NFC Championship game and comfortably beat the Bengals in Super Bowl XVI. 1982 was a disaster, culminating in a loss to the Rams (always a bitter pill to swallow) and it is apparently a reluctant Bill Walsh who has stayed on to attempt the comeback.

Offense

A pre-season injury to starting All Pro guard Randy Cross would be felt all year as the offensive line failed to reproduce its 1981 dominance, and even though they yielded only twenty quarterback sacks, this was probably more a measure of Joe Montana's elusiveness than the protection he received. Yet again, their rushing attack was abysmal (last in NFC) and just as did Earl Cooper before him,

rookie running back Jeff Moore found it easier to catch passes than to grind out the yards on the ground. Wendell Tyler, obtained from the Rams, should change all this. He will bring durability, elusiveness and blazing speed, in addition to providing an extra target for Montana's bewildering array of passes. Montana, who bravely plays with recurrent arm problems, confirmed his status as one of the best quarterbacks and there could be no greater praise than his comparison with the AFC's bomb thrower *extraordinaire*, Dan Fouts. Pure pass receiving is not a problem and in Dwight Clark, they have the NFC's most productive target. Freddie Solomon and Renaldo Nehemiah (the former hurdler) will compete for the other starting position, whilst Charle Young and Russ Francis will share at tight end.

Defense

With Archie Reese gone to the Raiders, Dwaine Board out for the season and both Fred Dean and Lawrence Pillers playing with injuries, the pass rush was non-existent (only fifteen sacks – NFC worst). Dan Bunz missed the whole season and Craig Puki went to St Louis, leaving a responsibility which the linebackers could not shoulder. The effect was felt in the defensive back four, where Pro Bowlers Ronnie Lott and Dwight Hicks were made to look ordinary. Blanchard Montgomery (linebacker) and Tom Holmoe (defensive back) were drafted to provide depth for a unit which, with only the slightest luck in injury rehabilitation, must surely make significant improvement.

Special Teams

The reliable Ray Wersching does everything required of him kicking field goals, but over a season, the cumulative effect of Jim Miller's low 38-yard punting average is felt. Dana McLemore graduated to both kick and punt return duties, taking the weight off 'Famous' Amos Lawrence and Freddie Solomon respectively. He will hope to repeat his 93-yard touchdown punt return of 1982.

1983 Schedule		
4 Sept	PHILADELPHIA	1:00
8 Sept	at Minnesota	7.30
18 Sept	at St. Louis	12.00
25 Sept	ATLANTA	1:00
2 Oct	at New England	1:00
9 Oct	LOS ANGELES RAMS	1:00
16 Oct	at New Orleans	12:00
23 Oct	at Los Angeles Rams	1:00
30 Oct	NEW YORK JETS	1:00
6 Nov	MIAMI	1.00
13 Nov	NEW ORLEANS	1:00
20 Nov	at Atlanta	4:00
27 Nov	at Chicago	12:00
4 Dec	TAMPA BAY	1:00
11 Dec	at Buffalo	1:00
19 Dec	DALLAS	6:00

San Francisco 49ers (NFC West)

No.	Name	Pos.	Ht.	Wt.	Age	NFL Yr.	College
68	Ayers, John*	OG	6-5	260	30	7	West Texas State
63	Beeson, Terry	LB	6-3	235	27	7	Kansas
7	Benjamin, Guy	QB	6-3	210	28	6	Stanford
76	Board, Dwaine*	DE	6-4	250	26	5	N. Carolina A & T
72	Bungarda, Ken	OT	6-6	270	26	2	Missouri
57	Bunz, Dan*	LB	6-4	225	27	6	Long Beach
60	Choma, John	OT/OG/C	6-6	261	28	3	Virginia
15	Clark, Bryan	QB	6-2	196	23	2	Michigan State
87	Clark, Dwight*	WR	6-4	210	26	5	Clemson
90	Clark, Mike	DE	6-4	240	24	3	Florida
47	Collier, Tim	CB	6-0	176	29	8	East Texas State
	Collins, George	OG/OT	6-2	265	27	6	Georgia
49	Cooper, Earl	RB	6-2	227	25	4	Rice
51	Cross, Randy*	OG	6-3	250	29	8	UCLA

(continued opposite)

San Francisco 49ers (NFC West) – *continued*

No.	Name	Pos.	Ht.	Wt.	Age	NFL Yr.	College
74	Dean, Fred	DE	6-2	236	31	9	Louisiana Tech
62	Downing, Walt	OC/C	6-3	254	27	6	Michigan
71	Fahnhorst, Keith*	OT	6-6	263	31	10	Minnesota
54	Ferrari, Ron	LB	6-0	212	24	2	Illinois
81	Francis, Russ	TE	6-6	242	30	8	Oregon
24	Gervais, Rick	CB/S	5-11	190	23	3	Stanford
59	Harper, Willie*	LB	6-2	215	33	10	Nebraska
75	Harty, John	DT/DE	6-4	253	24	3	Iowa
22	Hicks, Dwight*	S	6-1	189	27	5	Michigan
55	Horn, Bob	LB	6-4	230	29	8	Oregon State
	Jones, Cody	DT	6-5	255	32	9	San Jose State
50	Judie, Ed	LB	6-2	231	24	2	Arizona
66	Kennedy, Allan	OT	6-7	275	25	3	Washington State
67	Kugler, Pete*	DT	6-4	255	24	3	Penn State
20	Lawrence, Amos	RB	5-10	179	25	3	North Carolina
52	Leopold, Bobby	LB	6-1	215	25	4	Notre Dame
42	Lott, Ronnie*	CB	6-0	199	24	3	USC
78	Mason, Lindsey*	OT	6-5	275	28	5	Kansas
53	McColl, Milt	LB	6-6	220	24	3	Stanford
43	McLemore, Dana	KR/DB	5-10	183	23	2	Hawaii
3	Miller, Jim	P	5-11	183	26	4	Mississippi
16	Montana, Joe*	QB	6-2	200	27	5	Notre Dame
25	Moore, Jeff*	RB	6-0	195	27	4	Jackson State
83	Nehemiah, Renaldo	WR	6-1	177	24	2	Maryland
	Perry, Leon	RB	5-11	224	26	4	Mississippi
65	Pillers, Lawrence	DT	6-4	260	30	8	Alcorn State
56	Quillan, Fred*	C	6-5	260	27	6	Oregon
80	Ramson, Eason	TE	6-2	234	27	5	Washington State
64	Reynolds, Jack*	LB	6-1	232	35	14	Tennessee
30	Ring, Bill	RB	5-10	215	26	3	Brigham Young
88	Soloman, Freddie*	WR	5-11	185	30	9	Tampa
72	Stover, Jeff	DE/DT	6-5	275	25	2	Oregon
79	Stuckey, Jim*	DE	6-4	251	25	4	Clemson
58	Turner, Keena*	LB	6-2	219	24	4	Purdue
	Tyler, Wendell*	RB	5-10	198	28	6	UCLA
14	Wersching, Ray	K	5-11	210	33	11	California
45	Williams, Newton	RB	5-10	204	24	2	Arizona State
27	Williamson, Carlton*	S	6-0	204	25	3	Pittsburgh
85	Wilson, Mike	WR	6-3	210	24	3	Washington State
21	Wright, Eric*	CB	6-1	180	24	3	Missouri
86	Young, Charle*	TE	6-4	232	32	11	USC

A little sleight of hand by Joe Montana.

1983 Draft

Round	Name	Pos.	Ht.	Wt.	College
2	Craig, Roger	RB	6-0½	220	Nebraska
3	Montgomery, Blanchard	LB	6-2½	238	UCLA
4	Holmoe, Tom	DB	6-1½	190	Brigham Young
5	Gray, Riki	LB	6-1	227	USC
7	Moten, Gary	LB	6-1½	214	Southern Methodist
8	Mularkey, Mike	TE	6-3	245	Florida
10	Merrell, Jeff	DT	6-3	260	Nebraska
11	Sapolu, Jesse	C	6-3	260	Hawaii

149

SCHEDULE FOR 1983

1983 National Football League Schedule
(All times local)

Sunday, September 4 (First Weekend)

1.	Atlanta at Chicago	12:00
2.	Baltimore at New England	1:00
3.	Denver at Pittsburgh	1:00
4.	Detroit at Tampa Bay	1:00
5.	Green Bay at Houston	12:00
6.	Los Angeles Raiders at Cincinnati	1:00
7.	Los Angeles Rams at New York Giants	1:00
8.	Miami at Buffalo	1:00
9.	Minnesota at Cleveland	1:00
10.	New York Jets at San Diego	1:00
11.	Philadelphia at San Francisco	1:00
12.	St. Louis at New Orleans	12:00
13.	Seattle at Kansas City	3:00

Monday, September 5

14.	Dallas at Washington	9:00

Thursday, September 8 (Second Weekend)

15.	San Francisco at Minnesota	7:30

Sunday, September 11

16.	Buffalo at Cincinnati	1:00
17.	Cleveland at Detroit	1:00
18.	Dallas at St. Louis	12:00
19.	Denver at Baltimore	4:00
20.	Houston at Los Angeles Raiders	1:00
21.	New England at Miami	4:00
22.	New Orleans at Los Angeles Rams	1:00
23.	New York Giants at Atlanta	1:00
24.	Pittsburgh at Green Bay	12:00
25.	Seattle at New York Jets	4:00
26.	Tampa Bay at Chicago	12:00
27.	Washington at Philadelphia	1:00

Monday, September 12

28.	San Diego at Kansas City	8:00

Thursday, September 15 (Third Weekend)

29.	Cincinnati at Cleveland	8:30

Sunday, September 18

30.	Atlanta at Detroit	1:00
31.	Baltimore at Buffalo	1:00
32.	Chicago at New Orleans	12:00
33.	Kansas City at Washington	1:00
34.	Los Angeles Rams vs. Green Bay at Milw.	12:00
35.	Minnesota at Tampa Bay	4:00
36.	New York Giants at Dallas	3:00
37.	New York Jets at New England	1:00
38.	Philadelphia at Denver	2:00
39.	Pittsburgh at Houston	12:00
40.	San Diego at Seattle	1:00
41.	San Francisco at St. Louis	12:00

Monday, September 19

42.	Miami at Los Angeles Raiders	6:00

Sunday, September 25 (Fourth Weekend)

43.	Atlanta at San Francisco	1:00
44.	Chicago at Baltimore	2:00
45.	Cincinnati at Tampa Bay	1:00
46.	Cleveland at San Diego	1:00
47.	Detroit at Minnesota	12:00
48.	Houston at Buffalo	1:00
49.	Kansas City at Miami	1:00
50.	Los Angeles Raiders at Denver	2:00
51.	Los Angeles Rams at New York Jets	4:00
52.	New England at Pittsburgh	1:00
53.	New Orleans at Dallas	12:00
54.	St. Louis at Philadelphia	1:00
55.	Washington at Seattle	1:00

Monday, September 26

56.	Green Bay at New York Giants	9:00

Sunday, October 2 (Fifth Weekend)

57.	Baltimore at Cincinnati	1:00
58.	Dallas at Minnesota	12:00
59.	Denver at Chicago	12:00
60.	Detroit at Los Angeles Rams	1:00
61.	Houston at Pittsburgh	1:00
62.	Los Angeles Raiders at Washington	1:00
63.	Miami at New Orleans	3:00
64.	Philadelphia at Atlanta	1:00
65.	St. Louis at Kansas City	3:00
66.	San Diego at New York Giants	4:00
67.	San Francisco at New England	1:00
68.	Seattle at Cleveland	1:00
69.	Tampa Bay at Green Bay	12:00

Monday, October 3

70.	New York Jets at Buffalo	9:00

Sunday, October 9 (Sixth Weekend)

71.	Buffalo at Miami	1:00
72.	Denver at Houston	12:00

(continued opposite)

73.	Green Bay at Detroit	1:00
74.	Kansas City at Los Angeles Raiders	1:00
75.	Los Angeles Rams at San Francisco	1:00
76.	Minnesota at Chicago	12:00
77.	New England at Baltimore	2:00
78.	New Orleans at Atlanta	1:00
79.	New York Jets at Cleveland	1:00
80.	Philadelphia at New York Giants	4:00
81.	Seattle at San Diego	1:00
82.	Tampa Bay at Dallas	3:00
83.	Washington at St. Louis	12:00

Monday, October 10
84.	Pittsburgh at Cincinnati	9:00

Sunday, October 16 (Seventh Weekend)
85.	Atlanta at Los Angeles Rams	1:00
86.	Buffalo at Baltimore	2:00
87.	Chicago at Detroit	1:00
88.	Cincinnati at Denver	2:00
89.	Cleveland at Pittsburgh	1:00
90.	Dallas at Philadelphia	4:00
91.	Houston at Minnesota	12:00
92.	Los Angeles Raiders at Seattle	1:00
93.	Miami at New York Jets	1:00
94.	New York Giants at Kansas City	3:00
95.	St. Louis at Tampa Bay	1:00
96.	San Diego at New England	1:00
97.	San Francisco at New Orleans	12:00

Monday, October 17
98.	Washington at Green Bay	8:00

Sunday, October 23 (Eighth Weekend)
99.	Atlanta at New York Jets	1:00
100.	Chicago at Philadelphia	1:00
101.	Cleveland at Cincinnati	1:00
102.	Detroit at Washington	1:00
103.	Kansas City at Houston	12:00
104.	Los Angeles Raiders at Dallas	8:00
105.	Miami at Baltimore	2:00
106.	Minnesota at Green Bay	12:00
107.	New England at Buffalo	1:00
108.	New Orleans at Tampa Bay	4:00
109.	Pittsburgh at Seattle	1:00
110.	San Diego at Denver	2:00
111.	San Francisco at Los Angeles Rams	1:00

Monday, October 24
112.	New York Giants at St. Louis	8:00

Sunday, October 30 (Ninth Weekend)
113.	Baltimore at Philadelphia	1:00
114.	Dallas at New York Giants	1:00
115.	Detroit at Chicago	12:00
116.	Green Bay at Cincinnati	4:00
117.	Houston at Cleveland	1:00
118.	Kansas City at Denver	2:00

119.	Los Angeles Rams at Miami	1:00
120.	Minnesota at St. Louis	12:00
121.	New England at Atlanta	1:00
122.	New Orleans at Buffalo	1:00
123.	New York Jets at San Francisco	1:00
124.	Seattle at Los Angeles Raiders	1:00
125.	Tampa Bay at Pittsburgh	1:00

Monday, October 31
126.	Washington at San Diego	6:00

Sunday, November 6 (Tenth Weekend)
127.	Atlanta at New Orleans	12:00
128.	Baltimore at New York Jets	4:00
129.	Buffalo at New England	1:00
130.	Chicago at Los Angeles Rams	1:00
131.	Cincinnati at Houston	12:00
132.	Cleveland vs. Green Bay at Milwaukee	12:00
133.	Denver at Seattle	1:00
134.	Los Angeles Raiders at Kansas City	12:00
135.	Miami at San Francisco	1:00
136.	Philadelphia at Dallas	12:00
137.	St. Louis at Washington	4:00
138.	San Diego at Pittsburgh	1:00
139.	Tampa Bay at Minnesota	12:00

Monday, November 7
140.	New York Giants at Detroit	9:00

Sunday, November 13 (Eleventh Weekend)
141.	Buffalo at New York Jets	1:00
142.	Cincinnati at Kansas City	12:00
143.	Dallas at San Diego	1:00
144.	Denver at Los Angeles Raiders	1:00
145.	Detroit at Houston	12:00
146.	Green Bay at Minnesota	12:00
147.	Miami at New England	1:00
148.	New Orleans at San Francisco	1:00
149.	Philadelphia at Chicago	12:00
150.	Pittsburgh at Baltimore	2:00
151.	Seattle at St. Louis	12:00
152.	Tampa Bay at Cleveland	1:00
153.	Washington at New York Giants	4:00

Monday, November 14
154.	Los Angeles Rams at Atlanta	9:00

Sunday, November 20 (Twelfth Weekend)
155.	Baltimore at Miami	1:00
156.	Chicago at Tampa Bay	1:00
157.	Cleveland at New England	1:00
158.	Detroit vs. Green Bay at Milwaukee	12:00
159.	Houston at Cincinnati	1:00
160.	Los Angeles Raiders at Buffalo	1:00
161.	Kansas City at Dallas	3:00
162.	Minnesota at Pittsburgh	1:00
163.	New York Giants at Philadelphia	1:00
164.	San Diego at St. Louis	12:00

165.	San Francisco at Atlanta	4:00
166.	Seattle at Denver	2:00
167.	Washington at Los Angeles Rams	1:00

Monday, November 21

| 168. | New York Jets at New Orleans | 8:00 |

**Thursday, November 24
(Thirteenth Weekend)**
(Thanksgiving Day)

| 169. | Pittsburgh at Detroit | 12:30 |
| 170. | St. Louis at Dallas | 3:00 |

Sunday, November 27

171.	Baltimore at Cleveland	1:00
172.	Buffalo at Los Angeles Rams	1:00
173.	Denver at San Diego	1:00
174.	Green Bay at Atlanta	4:00
175.	Houston at Tampa Bay	1:00
176.	Kansas City at Seattle	1:00
177.	Minnesota at New Orleans	12:00
178.	New England at New York Jets	1:00
179.	New York Giants at Los Angeles Raiders	1:00
180.	Philadelphia at Washington	1:00
181.	San Francisco at Chicago	12:00

Monday, November 28

| 182. | Cincinnati at Miami | 9:00 |

**Thursday, December 1
(Fourteenth Weekend)**

| 183. | Los Angeles Raiders at San Diego | 6:00 |

Sunday, December 4

184.	Atlanta at Washington	1:00
185.	Buffalo at Kansas City	12:00
186.	Chicago at Green Bay	12:00
187.	Cincinnati at Pittsburgh	1:00
188.	Cleveland at Denver	2:00
189.	Dallas at Seattle	1:00
190.	Los Angeles Rams at Philadelphia	1:00
191.	Miami at Houston	12:00
192.	New Orleans at New England	1:00
193.	New York Jets at Baltimore	4:00
194.	St. Louis at New York Giants	1:00
195.	Tampa Bay at San Francisco	1:00

Monday, December 5

| 196. | Minnesota at Detroit | 9:00 |

Saturday, December 19 (Fifteenth Weekend)

| 197. | Atlanta at Miami | 4:00 |
| 198. | Pittsburgh at New York Jets | 12:30 |

Sunday, December 11

199.	Baltimore at Denver	2:00
200.	Chicago at Minnesota	12:00
201.	Cleveland at Houston	12:00
202.	Detroit at Cincinnati	1:00
203.	Kansas City at San Diego	1:00
204.	New England at Los Angeles Rams	1:00
205.	New Orleans at Philadelphia	1:00
206.	St. Louis at Los Angeles Raiders	1:00
207.	San Francisco at Buffalo	1:00
208.	Seattle at New York Giants	1:00
209.	Washington at Dallas	3:00

Monday, December 12

| 210. | Green Bay at Tampa Bay | 9:00 |

Friday, December 16 (Sixteenth Weekend)

| 211. | New York Jets at Miami | 9:00 |

Saturday, December 17

| 212. | Cincinnati at Minnesota | 3:00 |
| 213. | New York Giants at Washington | 12:30 |

Sunday, December 18

214.	Buffalo at Atlanta	1:00
215.	Denver at Kansas City	12:00
216.	Green Bay at Chicago	12:00
217.	Houston at Baltimore	2:00
218.	Los Angeles Rams at New Orleans	12:00
219.	New England at Seattle	1:00
220.	Philadelphia at St. Louis	12:00
221.	Pittsburgh at Cleveland	1:00
222.	San Diego at Los Angeles Raiders	1:00
221.	Tampa Bay at Detroit	4:00

Monday, December 19

| 224. | Dallas at San Francisco | 6:00 |

Post-Season Games

Saturday, 24 December 1983	AFC First Round Playoff
Monday, 26 December 1983	NFC First Round Playoff
Saturday, 31 December 1983	AFC and NFC Divisional Playoffs
Sunday, 1 January 1984	AFC and NFC Divisional Playoffs
Sunday, 8 January 1984	AFC and NFC Championship Games
Sunday, 22 January 1984	Super Bowl XVIII at Tampa Stadium, Tampa, Florida
Sunday, 29 January 1984	AFC-NFC Pro Bowl at Honolulu, Hawaii